CAR SAVVY*
An Annual
1991

Published by
Edmund Publications Corporation
515 Hempstead Turnpike
West Hempstead, N.Y. 11552

Library of Congress Catalog Card Number: 79-55705
Standard Book Number: 87759-361-2

Edmund books are available at special quantity discounts when purchased in bulk by corporations, credit unions, organizations and special interest groups. Custom covers and/or special copy on available pages may also be done to fit particular needs. For further information, quantity rates, and advertising rates write to: Edmund Publications Corp. at 515 Hempstead Turnpike, West Hempstead, N.Y. 11552 or call 516-292-0044.

Compiled and Written by
Edmund's Editorial Staff

Note: All information published herein is gathered from sources which are considered reliable by the editors. However, under no circumstances is the reader to assume that this information is official or final. The publisher does not assume responsibility for errors of omission or interpretation.

**formerly published as Autopedia*

Table Of Contents

Subscribe to Edmund Car Guides

Get a complete picture of the 1991 automotive market

CHOICE OF SUBSCRIPTION OPTIONS

1 Subscription to **USED CAR PRICE books only** (published quarterly).
(Total of 4 books, mailed within a 1 year period)
Domestic: $16.85 plus $3.00 postage (bulk rate) and handling $19.85
Other Countries: $16.85 plus $10.00 (via air mail) $26.85

2 Subscription to **NEW CAR PRICE books only**, *includes*
three NEW (American), two (New) IMPORT** editions.
(Total of 5 books, mailed within a 1 year period)
Domestic: $21.00 plus $3.00 postage (bulk rate) and handling $24.00
Other Countries: $21.00 plus $12.50 (via air mail) $33.50

3 Subscription to the **complete automotive market** of **NEW VEHICLES**
includes three NEW (American); two (New) IMPORT;** three (New)
VAN, PICKUP, SPORT UTILITY; and one (New) ECONOMY CAR.
(Total of 9 books mailed within a 1 year period)
Domestic: $37.85 plus $5.15 postage (bulk rate) and handling $43.00
Other Countries: $37.85 plus $22.50 (via air mail) $60.35

4 Subscription to **NEW and USED CAR PRICE books**, *includes*
three NEW (American), four USED, two (New) IMPORT.**
(Total of 9 books mailed within a 1 year period)
Domestic: $37.85 plus $5.15 postage (bulk rate) and handling $43.00
Other Countries: $37.85 plus $22.50 (via air mail) $60.35

5 **COMBINATION SUBSCRIPTION**, *includes* Edmund's full line—
three NEW (American); four USED; two (New) IMPORT;**
three (New) VAN, PICKUP, SPORT UTILITY; one ECONOMY CAR;
plus complimentary copy of CAR SAVVY.
(Total of 14 books mailed within a 1 year period)
Domestic: $54.00 plus $7.00 postage (bulk rate) and handling $61.00
Other Countries: $54.00 plus $35.00 (via air mail) $89.00

SCHEDULED RELEASE DATES FOR 1991

VOL. 25	Release Date	Cover Date
# 1 - USED CAR PRICES (Winter Edition)	Jan. 1	April '91
* - VAN, PICKUP, SPORT UTILITY BUYER'S GUIDE	Feb. 1	June '91
# 2 - NEW (American) CAR PRICES (First Rev.)	Feb. 1	June '91
# 3 - (New) IMPORT CAR PRICES	Mar. 1	July '91
* - ECONOMY CAR PRICE BUYING GUIDE	Mar. 1	Summer '91
# 4 - USED CAR PRICES (Spring Edition)	Apr. 1	July '91
* - VAN, PICKUP, SPORT UTILITY BUYER'S GUIDE	June 1	Dec. '91
# 5 - NEW (American) CAR PRICES (Final Rev.)	June 1	Dec. '91
# 6 - USED CAR PRICES (Summer Edition)	July 1	Oct. '91
# 7 - (New) IMPORT CAR PRICES	July 1	Dec. '91
# 8 - USED CAR PRICES (Fall Edition)	Oct. 1	Jan. '92
# 9 - (1992) NEW (American) CAR PRICES	Dec. 1	Feb. '92
* - CAR SAVVY	Dec. 1	1992
* - (1992) VAN, PICKUP, SPORT UTILITY BUYER'S GUIDE	Dec. 1	Feb. '92

No number necessary.   **USE COUPON ON PAGE 4 FOR ORDERING**

Formerly published as Foreign Car Prices.

Mail This Coupon Now! With your Check, Money Order, MasterCard or VISA

## Chapter 1

How This Book Can Help You

Hundreds of satisfied customers have written to **Edmund's** over the years to tell us that **Car Savvy*** has helped them buy a new car, assisted them in dealing with complaints against mechanics, or has helped them out of a tight spot while stranded on a lonely highway. From J.L. of Carbondale, Illinois, "**Car Savvy** was the best gift I ever gave my daughter when she first began to drive." In fact, **Car Savvy** is so informative, some driver education course instructors use it as a text in their classes.

Beginning with Chapters 2 and 3, we outline some precautionary procedures to consider when buying a new or used car. For instance, most people simply decide they need a new car without considering the relative costs of maintaining their present car versus the higher costs of a new one. **Car Savvy** helps you look at prices and budgets in a realistic manner. Detailed information on how to negotiate a deal on a new car is presented in Chapter 2. In Chapter 3 we provide you with figures that tell you how expensive it can be to own and maintain a car. How to inspect a used automobile is detailed in Chapter 4—most people just kick the tires.

Read the latest results of the Federal Government's crash test results in Chapter 5. The detailed information provided on head injury you could suffer from a 35 mile per hour crash may help you decide what car will be safest for you and your passengers.

With car thefts on the rise, many readers will find the information in Chapter 6 to be of great importance. Expensive auto alarms are not always the answer. Read about some "tricks of the trade" in this chapter.

Purchasing new tires for your car is one of the most important safety precautions you can take. But, how are tires rated? Solve the mystery of all those numbers on tires by reading Chapter 7.

To save yourself headaches and dollars, a reading of Chapter 8 is recommended. It details some simple steps to prevent costly problems in your car. Chapter 9 describes some tried-and-true methods for keeping your car's inside and outside clean.

Chapter 10 is, in part, done with the permission of the New York State Consumer Protection Board. What they have provided is a step-by-step procedure for returning a new or used car if you are dissatisfied with its performance. The emphasis is on documentation of each step you take, so keep that copying machine warm.

Before you insure that new or used car, read Chapter 11. The nitty gritty of how much insurance to buy and where to get it at the best price can be found here.

Everyone wants to save money on gasoline bills. In Chapter 12 we list forty-six ways to cut down the cost of fuel consumption. Many hints require no expenditure and little effort. In Chapter 13 we provide a basic description of how your car works—great stuff for the beginner or uninformed.

Chapter 14 describes how to identify and avoid unscrupulous mechanics, while Chapter 15 lists some handy tools and safety items everyone should have in their car. A reader from Pontiac, Michigan wrote to tell us that after stocking his car with the things we list, he was able to safely get his car started in a blinding winter storm.

If you are unfortunate enough to have your car break down on the roadside, pull out your **Car Savvy** and read Chapter 16. You might be able to get your car started without help from an expensive roadside repair service.

Everyone has experienced those special driving situations that call for extra safety. Adverse road and traffic conditions including extra emphasis on winter driving is described in Chapter 17. Chapter 18 tells you how to handle the road under the most unexpected and perilous situations.

Many satisfied consumers have let us know that they have saved some tax dollars by organizing and documenting their car-related expenses as detailed in Chapter 19. Also most valuable has been the accident report form in Chapter 20 which has helped them get all of the information at the accident scene, even though they were very anxious and understandably nervous. Their attorneys were most grateful.

Now that you have learned it all, put yourself to the test. Chapter 21 gives you some sample questions and quizzes on information you may need to know to pass your written driver's examination.

Not every chapter in **Car Savvy** is necessarily indispensible to everyone. However, judging from reader responses, each finds at least six or seven chapters that make reading the book fun, informative and worthwhile dollar-wise.

So buy a copy for each glovebox, and give copies to your friends. If you have any suggestions or comments about **Car Savvy**, let us hear from you.

The Editors

*formerly published with the title *Autopedia*

## Chapter 2

Buying A New Car

In the near future, the way we buy a car may see some drastic changes. Already, some dealerships are experimenting with computerized information systems that allow a prospective customer to shop for the car of his choice after regular business hours. All the customer has to do is select the model and make. The computer then supplies the options available, special features and price information. As we move toward the year 2000, special options might include choosing between cable or regular TV or between solar or gasoline power as an energy source. In Japan, a buyer can decide if the dealer should install (for $1700) a facsimile machine for the busy executive on the move.

In America, women are making more new car purchases. In fact, two of every five sales are made to women. Cognizant of this trend, Detroit will begin to feature seats that will not snag fragile materials, flooring that will not scuff shoes, and special seat adjustments for expectant mothers. Some makers are testing their door handles and interior accessories to make sure they can be utilized with long fingernails.

Plans are being developed to allow consumers to shop for a car in much the same way they would shop for a pair of pants at their local shopping mall. Competing companies would rent space and display their cars under one roof. This one-stop car shopping center has already begun construction in Houston. But until the future arrives, most consumers still must shop around to make their best deal; and that deal still is made with a salesman, not a computer.

Whether or not you let a computer or a salesman help you with your purchase, one thing is certain in purchasing a car in 1991—prices are up. Estimates range from 6 to 10%. Beyond the purchase price, the cost of maintaining that vehicle has risen a whopping 13%—insurance up $89, registration up $15, depreciation up $250, financing up $75, and gas and oil up 8%.

Before you consider purchasing a new car, perhaps you should ask "Should I keep my old car and repair it?" With the recent escalation of new car prices, many used car owners have been asking themselves this question. In part, the answer will depend upon your current financial status, and, of course, the condition of your used car.

Even though the Department of Transportation has rated the average used car life at ten years or 100,000 miles, most Americans keep their car for an average of only seven years. This represents about a two year increase from the early 1970's. Many owners have found that the cost of replacing parts on an older automobile is less expensive than new ownership. The Hertz Corporation found that owners who drive a car for ten years save $1,726 a year versus owners who trade annually. But the fact remains that not all cars kept for ten years will realize this savings due to certain types of driving and driver habits, and we Americans just get plain tired of the ol' clunker.

The purchase of an automobile represents a major financial investment. Much care and considerable thought should go into car selection. The following guide reviews the important elements in a new car purchase: (a) selecting the right car, (b) disposing of your present car, (c) picking the right dealer, and (d) financing methods.

Select the right size for you: The key is to buy as much car as you actually need—no more. The size of the car will depend on how you intend to use it, the size of your family, the extent of your budget, the degree of comfort and luxury desired, or any combination of these.

For simplicity we have prepared a chart outlining these influencing factors. While not intended to be all-inclusive, the chart presents a general form which you can utilize to help you select a car size best suited to your special requirements. For instance it might be interesting to you that the government's 1984 study revealed that four-year costs for purchasing and maintaining a large car were $14,908; for a mid-sized about $13,400; for a compact $11,156 and for a subcompact, $9,458.

Other general considerations may include: *Safety*—are seatbelts adequate?; did the car pass the 1979-90 crash tests? (see Chapter 5); are the headrests adjustable?; is the dashboard padded and well lit?; is visibilty good while driving?; *Maintenance*—is there an expensive preventive maintenance schedule?; are parts easy to get?; are tire changing tools easy to find and use?; *Extras*—how many included are useful?; what is the quality of the standard tires?; *Costs*—consider the base price, dealer preparation, trade-in allowance, optional equipment, taxes and registration, financing method (discussed in this chapter), fuel and maintenance costs and insurance costs.

Understanding new terms: For years, car sizes were pretty standard. A full-size car had a certain dimension, a compact and sub-compact had a certain size specification; however, full-size cars in 1991 are not the same as full-size cars from 1975. You will find that full-size ranges vary as do their prices. Below are definitions of all the different car terms with estimated price ranges.

Mini-compact: Priced lower than most sub-compacts ($5000-$9000), these cars are sure to interest the car buying public. Cars in this category include the Daihatsu Charade Hatchback, Ford Festiva, Geo Metro, Subaru Justy, Suzuki Swift and Yugo GV and Cabrio.

Sub-compact: These cars are becoming increasingly popular because of their mileage ratings. At one time, the sub-compact models were the least expensive to purchase. Now the base sticker prices of these models could be as high as a full-size car. The base sticker price of sub-compact cars begin at around $6,500 and go as high as $20,000 plus, especially foreign models. When you consider that some standard cars run from $15,000 to $25,000, you realize that gas mileage and demand have pushed up the price of sub-compact cars. Following is a list of sub-compacts:

Acura - Integra

Audi - Coupe Quattro, 80, 90

Isuzu - Impulse

Infiniti - M30

BMW - M3, 325 Series
Chevrolet - Camaro, Sprint
Chrysler - Le Baron Convertible
Daihatsu - Charade Sedan
Dodge - Colt, Daytona, Omni
Eagle - Talon
Ford - Mustang
Geo - Prizm, Storm
Honda - Civic
Hyundai - Excel, Precis

Mitsubishi - Eclipse, Mirage
Nissan - Pulsar NX, Sentra
Plymouth - Colt, Horizon, Laser
Pontiac - Firebird, Sunbird Convertible
Saab - 900 Convertible
Toyota - Celica, Corolla, Supra, Tercel
Volkswagen - Corrado, Fox

Compacts: Even though most of the foreign cars come under the classification of sub-compacts, there are many imports that can be labeled compacts. Compact cars normally have a longer wheelbase and body and start at around $7,000. Unlike compact cars produced in the 1970's, the compact class generally does not have the value it once did. However, with gasoline plentiful, many of these gas savers have been overstocked on dealer lots, and may once again be a good buy. Following are the compact class cars:

Acura - Legend
BMW - 525i, 535i
Buick - Skylark
Chevrolet - Beretta, Cavalier
Chrysler - LeBaron
Dodge - Shadow
Eagle - Summit
Ford - Escort, Probe, Tempo
Honda - Accord
Jaguar - XJ6, XJ-S
Lexus - ES250
Mazda - 323, Protege
Mercury - Topaz

Mitsubishi - Galant, Sigma
Nissan - Stanza
Oldsmobile - Cutlass Calais
Peugeot - 405
Plymouth - Sundance
Pontiac - Grand Am, Le Mans, Sunbird
Saab - 900 Sedan & Hatchback
Subaru - Legacy, Loyale
Toyota - Camry, Cressida
Volkswagen - Golf, GTi, Jetta
Volvo - 240, 780

Mid-size: This class is rapidly becoming one where you can get real value for your money. If you have a family, the intermediate class will give you enough room and good enough gas mileage to make it a feasible alternative. The sticker prices of these models also have come down. With the engineers going to work on these cars to make them more fuel efficient, they are becoming a logical choice for the driver who needs a larger than compact car. Prices for these models begin at $10,000. The cars in this class are:

Audi - Quattro V8, 100, 200
BMW - 735i, 735iL, 750iL
Buick - Century, Regal, Riviera
Cadillac - Eldorado, Seville
Chevrolet - Corsica, Lumina
Chrysler - New Yorker
Dodge - Dynasty, Spirit
Ford - Taurus, Thunderbird
Hyundai - Sonata

Lincoln - Mark VII
Mazda - 626, MX-6, 929
Mercury - Cougar, Sable
Nissan - Maxima
Oldsmobile - Cutlass Ciera, Cutlass Supreme, Trofeo, Toronado
Plymouth - Acclaim
Pontiac - Grand Prix, 6000

Infiniti - Q45
Lexus - LS400

Volkswagen - Passat
Volvo - 740, 760

Large-size (standards): The standard size car dimensions haven't changed much, and their price tags are still pretty high. Bargain hunters may not find much to pick from here, but if you're willing to spend between $15,000 and $25,000, one of these cars can be yours. Mileage ratings in this grouping vary widely, so check estimates and price before you buy. Because gasoline is not such a worry, dealers who once had to unload these cars are not giving such heavy discounts as interest in them has renewed. These models are listed below:

Buick - Electra, Park Avenue, Le Sabre
Cadillac - Brougham, Fleetwood Series, De Ville Series
Chevrolet - Caprice
Chrysler - New Yorker Fifth Avenue
Dodge - Monaco
Eagle - Premier

Ford - LTD Crown Victoria
Lincoln - Continental, Town Car
Mercury - Grand Marquis
Oldsmobile - Eighty-Eight, Ninety-Eight, Touring Sedan
Pontiac - Bonneville
Saab - 9000

Luxury: These luxury models are just as the name implies, luxurious. No expense has been spared to make these cars as good as they can be. If you're willing to spend $20,000 and up, one of these can be yours:

Acura - Legend
Audi - all models
Buick - Electra, Reatta, Riviera
BMW - all models
Cadillac - all models
Chevrolet - Corvette
Chrysler - Imperial, New Yorker Fifth Avenue
Infiniti - all models
Jaguar - all models
Lexus - all models
Lincoln - all models

Mazda - RX-7 GXL, Turbo and Convertible
Mercedes-Benz - all models
Nissan - 300ZX
Oldsmobile - Ninety-Eight, Toronado, Trofeo, Touring Sedan
Peugeot - 505
Pontiac - Bonneville
Porsche - all models
Saab - all models
Toyota - Cressida, Supra
Volvo - all models

Select the body type that fits your needs: Various body types affect cost. In selecting the type you want, consideration should be given to safety, appearance, and your specific needs.

Two door sedan: Its advantages are lower cost and a rigidly constructed roof which offers reasonable protection in turnover accidents. It is particularly suited to families with small children as it permits them no access to doors from the rear seats. Its shortcomings lie in the difficulty of entering and exiting the rear, a problem even more pronounced in smaller cars. Another disadvantage is the wider door which creates some difficulties in tight parking situations.

Four door sedan: This body type offers the most room and convenience for entering and leaving. It is sturdily constructed and offers good protection. The doors are smaller than the two door model, making it easier to get out in tight parking situations; however the number of doors makes it more susceptible to drafts and squeaks. This body type is ideal for family trips.

Hardtop, two & four door: Stylish, airy and better looking in the judgment of most designers, the hardtop is the most popular body type. It offers unobstructed side views with the windows down. Although its initial cost is higher than the sedan models, it has a better resale value. It is less rigidly constructed than the sedan.

Three door hatchback: The hatchback is as long or longer than a compact car yet its "third" door is a hatch in the back which pops up for easy access to an open trunk. In most hatchback designs, the second seat folds down for greater luggage space. The loading area of a hatchback is often double the room in a conventional trunk.

Hatchback designs started with the smaller imports, but now the domestic designers use it. Also, hatchbacks are becoming more popular with families desiring the room of a station wagon without buying its large size. The hatchback design also simplifies the loading and unloading of groceries, and for people with families requiring constant dashing to and from the food store, the "hatch" has become a necessity. Some people object to the hatch because of its "see-through" design, allowing thieves to inspect their prey first.

These hatchbacks normally come with compact cars that have excellent gas mileage ratings. With the price of gasoline at an average of $1.25 a gallon, the hatchback provides roominess in a very economical vehicle.

If your're still not sure about what size car to get, take the quiz on the following page and let the total figure be your guide.

Foreign cars: Foreign cars now make up about 33% of the domestic car market. Currently, the Japanese are selling 2.6 million cars every year in the U.S. market. With the increased cost of gasoline, the foreign car has become very popular. Even American designers rate them highly. In a survey of American design engineers, 60% rated the Japanese designs as excellent followed by German designs and Swedish designs. Only 6.2% thought highly of American design.

The price tag on many foreign cars is up due to import quotas and exchange rates. Many cost as much as $2,500 or more than their American counterparts. Also more expensive are replacement parts due to increased demand and importing costs. Another concern about foreign cars used to be that they were smaller than their American counterparts and would not stand up well under the stress of an accident. With the total car market downgrading the sizes of automobiles, this is becoming less of a factor. If you wish to buy a foreign car, buy a more popular model; otherwise you may have trouble getting parts and experienced mechanics to fix it. Also remember that present voluntary restrictions on imports limit the buyer's ability to negotiate the price, in contrast to most American models.

Choose the options you actually need: Optional equipment can add as much as $2,500 or more to the cost of your car and is offered for safety, driving ease or to enhance motoring pleasure. However, some

What Size Car To Buy? Rate Your Priorities.

Rate the statements from one to five, according to your agreement or disagreement. When you have finished, add all your scores together and compare your total score with the range of scores listed below. It will give you a good indication of the car size(s) that you should consider.

(1) Indicates no agreement with the statement
(2) Indicates little agreement with the statement
(3) Indicates some agreement with the statement
(4) Indicates much agreement with the statement
(5) Indicates total agreement with the statement

______ 1. I want my car to have the longest list of available options.

______ 2. I frequently need towing power.

______ 3. Gasoline prices have no effect on the size of the car I buy.

______ 4. I need a car that is very quiet at highway speeds.

______ 5. In my car, a very smooth ride is very important.

______ 6. I always use my car to entertain.

______ 7. I drive many more highway miles than city miles.

______ 8. My family needs a car with a lot of room.

______ 9. I always need to carry large packages in my trunk.

______ 10. The cost of maintenance is not important to my car buying decision.

______ 11. I want the highest level of luxury in my car.

______ 12. I don't feel comfortable in a car with a small interior.

______ 13. I frequently travel with more than four passengers.

______ 14. I would rather have a car with a large interior than one which has top fuel economy.

______ 15. Passing power and towing ability are more important to me than great fuel economy.

______ 16. A large rear seat is more important to me than ease of parking.

______ 17. Six-passenger room is very important to me.

______ 18. Eight-cylinder performance is more important to me than low driving costs.

______ 19. I want room to stretch out in the car that I drive.

______ 20. The level of luxury and room in my car has to make me look very successful.

______ 21. I feel more comfortable in a car that weighs a lot.

______ 22. My new car will be the primary family car, not a second car.

______ 23. Room and luxury are more important to me than the price I pay for my new car.

______ 24. Having many options is more important to me than paying the lowest price.

______ 25. Excellent power and performance are very important to me.

______ **TOTAL SCORE**

25-40 Subcompact   35-65 Compact   60-85 Mid-Size   80-100 Full-Size

Where Your Score Puts You

There is a five-point overlap between the sizes in each category. This reflects the recent model downsizing and the similarity of features and uses between different model sizes. Model differences, engine and drivetrain choices, and price are some of the factors that will affect your size needs.

SOURCE: The Ford Corporation, "Car Buying Made Easier"

options seem to serve no practical purpose. Check with the list below before ordering your optional equipment.

1. The car you buy will have those options necessary for safe and efficient operation.
2. Go over the list of optional equipment before you negotiate with the salesman. Decide at your leisure what additional equipment is really necessary for comfort, safety and appearance.
3. Once you have made out the list and are satisfied with it, stick to it. Don't let high pressure sales techniques sway you toward new gimmicks which may be nice but not necessary for you.
4. Remember, smaller cars do not need the power systems found in larger cars. The engines that come with your car have ample power unless you intend special use, such as towing trailers or carrying many heavy loads. A three-speed manual transmission is recommended for best acceleration. As for tires, those that come standard on the car you buy will be sufficient to carry a full rated load at normal inflation pressure.
5. When you have determined the size and type car that can best satisfy your needs, consider other important factors such as number of cylinders and type of transmission. Then use miles per gallon estimates and the fuel cost charts to help you decide which model to buy (see chart on page 15). For those preferring the metric system, 3.785 liters equals one gallon. The m.p.g. ratings are estimates, NOT guaranteed fuel economy claims. They are published to help you compare the relative m.p.g. of each model in a vehicle class.

How much should I pay? Most people select a car and then attempt to fit the monthly expenses of owning it into their budget. The proper way is to first decide how much per month you can pay for a car, including gas, maintenance, insurance, and the monthly payment given your present income. If you are stretching your budget to unreasonable limits, you should either select another car or save additional cash to put down in an effort to keep the monthly payments within your budget range. Don't decide on the car of your dreams and let it sway you into an unreasonable financial bind. After you have decided how much you can spend on your new car, purchase a copy of **Edmund's New Car Prices** and/or **Edmund's Import Car Prices**. This guide can be ordered on the form found on page 4, and will provide you with an accurate list of wholesale and retail prices for the models and their options.

Consulting with these guides and using the tables on the following pages can help you narrow down the decision on which model to buy, and will enable you to bargain with the dealer more effectively. An informed buyer armed with accurate wholesale price figures might save $500 or more on the purchase of a new car. If you can't get satisfaction on a price from one dealer, move to another. Competition for new car sales has never been keener.

Consider resale: Most economists would agree that the purchase of a new automobile is not an investment in one's future because of loss due to depreciation. However, some cars depreciate more than others—some, like a used 1987 Dodge Caravan actually went up in price the

AUTOS' AVERAGE RESALE VALUES

Sports cars and utility vehicles generally hold their values better over 7 years than other cars or light trucks. How the values compare, based on average reported resale values:

Domestic Cars
Percentage of original value retained

Category	1st yr	3rd yr	5th yr	7th yr
Sub-compact	89	64	58	50
Compact	82	61	50	40
Mid-size	82	64	51	41
Large-size	82	65	51	38
Luxury	81	66	58	46
Sports	84	81	74	68
Small wagon	83	62	54	ND
Mid-size wagon	86	68	55	41
Large-size wagon	84	67	51	43
Utility vehicle	94	84	78	74
Pickup	90	69	66	ND

Foreign Cars

Category	1st yr	3rd yr	5th yr	7th yr
Sub-compact	90	72	57	44
Compact	90	74	59	51
Mid-size	81	68	50	32
Luxury	81	68	55	41
Sports	88	76	73	61
Small wagon	90	74	59	51
Mid-size wagon	92	82	71	ND
Utility vehicle	88	77	54	ND
Minivan	95	94	ND	ND
Pickup	82	64	50	ND

ND = Not enough data

following model year. You can avoid heavy depreciation losses by checking the car's resale history in **Consumer Reports**, or by comparing used car prices of similar models with their original retail prices. Use **Edmund's Used Car Prices** to learn these figures. Cars that have a good repair history (require few repairs and have had no recalls) often hold their price for longer periods. Try to avoid purchasing a car if you know that model will be discontinued in favor of a newer, more efficient design. Choosing options such as power steering, brakes and air conditioning also can help a car retain its value. Conversely, options such as exterior trim packages or special interior options add little value to used cars, and may cost you a lot initially.

Annual fuel costs: Fuel costs are changing rapidly and vary considerably by area. The chart on page 15 enables you to estimate annual fuel costs using fuel prices in your area. These costs are based on 15,000 miles driven per year.

What to do with your present car? You have three options: trade it in as a down payment on the car you buy, sell it outright in a direct sale, or keep it as a second car.

ANNUAL FUEL COSTS CHART
Based on 15,000 Miles Per Year

Est. MPG	*Dollars Per Gallon*						
	1.55	1.45	1.35	1.25	1.15	1.05	.95
50	465	435	405	375	345	315	285
49	474	444	413	382	352	332	291
48	484	452	421	390	359	329	297
47	495	463	431	399	367	335	303
46	505	472	439	407	375	343	310
45	516	483	450	416	383	351	317
44	528	494	460	426	392	359	324
43	542	507	472	437	401	368	331
42	553	518	482	446	411	378	339
41	567	531	494	458	421	389	348
40	581	544	506	469	431	399	356
39	595	557	518	480	442	410	365
38	611	572	533	493	454	422	375
37	628	587	547	506	466	434	385
36	646	605	563	521	479	447	395
35	665	622	579	536	493	462	407
34	684	639	595	551	507	476	419
33	704	659	614	568	523	490	432
32	725	679	632	585	539	506	445
31	751	703	654	606	556	523	460
30	774	724	674	624	575	542	475
29	802	750	699	647	595	562	491
28	830	776	723	669	616	583	509
27	860	805	749	694	639	608	528
26	895	837	780	722	663	632	548
25	930	870	810	750	690	660	570
24	970	907	844	782	719	690	594
23	1011	946	881	816	750	720	620
22	1058	990	921	853	784	754	648
21	1107	1035	964	892	821	782	679
20	1162	1088	1012	938	862	822	713
19	1223	1144	1065	986	908	866	750
18	1293	1209	1126	1042	958	906	792
17	1367	1279	1191	1102	1015	956	838
16	1453	1359	1266	1172	1078	1016	891
15	1551	1451	1351	1251	1150	1096	950
14	1660	1553	1446	1339	1232	1176	1018
13	1788	1673	1557	1442	1327	1270	1096
12	1937	1812	1687	1562	1438	1390	1187
11	2113	1977	1841	1704	1568	1510	1295
10	2325	2175	2025	1875	1725	1660	1425
9	2583	2416	2250	2083	1917	1850	1583

Keep it: If you have future needs for a second car in the family whether for commuting or increased family demands, it would be more economical for you to keep your present car than trade it and then purchase a car of similar vintage in the future (assuming it is in good mechanical condition). However, a key to your decision should be the need for the car weighed against the added expense and upkeep a second car entails.

Sell it: If your present car is comparatively new (less than 4 years old) and in good mechanical and physical condition, you stand a good chance of getting more money on a retail sale than trading it in to a dealer who will give you only wholesale price. However, you must weigh the advantages against the time you will spend showing your car, and the expense of advertising. A good guide which can assist you in establishing a price for your car is **Edmund's Used Car Prices**. Order forms are on page 4.

Trade it: If you're thinking in terms of a trade in, take your car to a number of dealers and have it appraised, not as a trade in, but as a direct sale. Use the best offer and apply that offer in negotiating for the trade. It is a good idea to take your used car to an agency where a dealer doesn't have a lot of the same type of car you want to sell or trade, especially if that dealer handles the same model as yours as does a new car dealer. People come to him looking for specific used models, and if you have one to sell or trade, chances are he will give you top dollar because he knows he can move it quickly.

If you are trading in your car for a new car, get a wholesale cash offer from the dealer, not an allowance off your new car price. Compare this offer with the wholesale value of your car found in **Edmund's Used Car Prices**. If it doesn't compare favorably, seek out another dealer. Remember, if your used car is very clean, a popular model, and less than 4 years old, you should get top dollar for it.

Car preparation: Whether trading or selling, present your car honestly. Extensive repair work is usually spotted and is eyed suspiciously. Wash and polish the car, clean the upholstery and mats. Find a car wash that does detail work for car dealerships. They do a thorough cleaning for about $75-$100. In our experience, this pays. Buy matching paint and touch up small scratches and rust spots. Replace broken lenses. Give the car as good an appearance as you can. Remember, appraisers deduct for cleaning and retouching a car.

How do you select a dealer? If you, like most people, are at a loss in determining what dealer to do business with, there are several guiding points you may wish to consider:

Reputation: One guide, but not an infallible one in determining business standing, is the length of time a dealer has been at his location—the longer the better. A second, even better method of determining dealer ethics is to talk to customers waiting in the service department of the dealership. You may also consider calling the Better Business Bureau to find out whether many complaints have been lodged against the dealer.

Model variety: Does the dealer have a large selection of models? If not, you may have to wait a month or more for your choice. If the dealer stocks many of the car make and model you want, he may be able to give you a better price break.

Location: Is the dealer centrally located to your business or home? You might get a better deal twenty miles away, but is the extra travel worth it? Remember, your new car will require servicing and maintenance and you may be required to leave it in the service department for more than a day.

Facilities: How extensive are the dealer's facilities for service and maintenance? You certainly would want well-trained mechanics using the most modern tools and equipment working on your car.

Service: This is something you cannot readily assess in advance. However, if service is not up to your expectations, feel free to discuss your problems with the service manager. If this fails to satisfy you, consult the Regional Office Customer Service Department of the manufacturer. You will generally find sympathy for your problem there.

Contracts: Have a firm commitment from the salesman in the form of a sales contract before you offer money or sign anything. Read the contract before you sign.

Advertising: Beware of misleading advertisements by some dealers as inducements to do business with them. Be highly suspicious of dealers who offer better deals because of high volume sales. Such dealerships, usually large, have proportionately higher overheads.

Test drive: A good dealer allows unlimited test drives. Always test drive the car before you commit yourself to buy. The car may look good and may fill all your driving requirements, but unless you feel comfortable and fully at ease behind the wheel, there is no point in buying it. When driving, try to put the car through as wide a variety of tests as possible: hills, curves, parking, backing up, stop and go traffic, and the open road for acceleration. Choose a rough street to determine how the car handles bumps. Listen for unusual noises and vibrations. Close the window and listen to the engine sounds. Satisfy yourself before you buy.

What about financing? The Truth-in-Lending Act requires that banks, finance companies, credit unions and all lending and credit institutions provide certain information to you, the borrower. When negotiating a loan, insist on knowing the dollar value of the interest rates being charged and the actual annual percentage rates you will be paying. Compare the figures given you by the auto dealer with figures from your own bank. If you have sufficient cash reserves, it may be advantageous to negotiate a pass-book loan, borrowing against the amount you have on deposit. If you are a member of a credit union, you would do well to inquire there before having the dealer arrange the financing. If you own your home, consider a home equity loan to pay for your car. The interest paid on a home equity loan is the only type that is still fully tax-deductible. Remember, the longer the term of the loan, the more you pay. By providing the highest down payment you can afford, and arranging the highest installments you can reasonably meet, you will have made a substantial savings in interest payments.

Paying cash: To gain full use of your future income and free yourself from the headaches of monthly remittances, all cash payment can be made to purchase your car. Paying cash has certain benefits and detriments.

Buying on credit: One type of credit plan available is the single payment plan. These loans usually carry a somewhat lower interest rate, but require a single, prearranged payment on a yearly basis. People who can expect large lump sums of money through bonuses or salaries may find this plan convenient.

The installment loan is by far more popular. This type of loan allows the borrower to repay the amount in equal monthly payments. The lending institution will hold the title of the car until the payments have been completed. If for some reason you cannot meet your payments, get in touch with your creditor. Emergency arrangements can be made.

Some dealers offer installment loans through the car agency. The dealer contracts with a lender for a discount rate and writes the loan to you at a higher rate. The difference is usually what the market will bear. Many times these loans are in line with any lending institution and, because the dealer completes the forms, obtaining them may be easier for you.

Because credit costs you money, think very carefully about how large you want your monthly payments to be and over what period of time. Also consider taking out a home equity loan if you can, as the interest paid on this source of cash is tax deductible, whereas a regular car loan is not.

If you can, make a large down payment and higher payments over a shorter period of time. This will help save money. Refer to the table below to figure your monthly payment. To use the table, find the percentage rate of the proposed loan on the top line and the number of years you are borrowing for on the left side. Then find the dollar amount in the table which corresponds to those points. For example, if you're borrowing money for 3 years at 11%, the dollar payment per $1,000 borrowed is $32.74. Suppose you are borrowing $4,250. To calculate your monthly payment, multiply the number of thousands you're borrowing by $32.74; 4.25 × $32.74 = $139.145. Thus, your monthly payment will be $139.15.

years	8%	9%	10%	11%	12%	13%	14%	15%	16%
1	$86.99	$87.46	$87.92	$88.39	$88.85	$89.32	$89.79	$90.26	$90.74
2	45.23	45.69	46.15	46.61	47.08	47.55	48.02	48.49	48.97
3	31.34	31.80	32.27	32.74	33.22	33.70	34.18	34.67	35.16
4	24.42	24.89	25.37	25.85	26.34	26.83	27.33	27.84	28.35
5	20.28	20.76	21.25	21.75	22.25	22.76	23.27	23.79	24.32

Warranties: There are many different types of warranties emerging on the car-buying scene. Where the one-year, 12,000 mile warranty was once standard, it is slowly becoming a thing of the past. All of the major automobile manufacturers are now offering extended coverage warranties, meaning that they are offering warranties beyond the one-year,

12,000 miles, either as part of the sales package or for a slight yearly charge. Some car makers are offering a five-year, 50,000 mile warranty. On the following page is a warranty comparison chart detailing the standard coverages offered by each car company. Extended warranty information is available from the manufacturers. It is important that before buying your new car, you investigate any additional warranty information that the dealer may have available. It could be a very good investment of time. If you choose to purchase extended warranty coverage on the car or on a specific system, be sure to follow all directives in the maintenance schedule. If you miss an inspection, for instance, the warranty may be invalidated, rendering your original expenditure worthless.

When the time comes to make a deal: You now are ready to purchase your new car. You have selected the type your budget can withstand, and you know the exact wholesale price of your trade-in. You have selected a likely dealer. You have put yourself in an advantageous position, something most dealers don't count on. Let them know up front you are prepared and that if they can't give you the deal you want, someone else can.

When should you shop?: Believe it or not, some of the best deals on new cars can be had depending on the time of the month, the time of day, or the weather! New car agencies are anxious to fill monthly quotas, and the pressure rises to fill them at month's end; therefore, they may make rock-bottom deals. Shopping at closing time may help lower your price. Dealers are tired, and rather than subjecting you to an extensive bargaining process, are quick to get to the bottom line and get home. Not many people shop for new cars when the weather is inclement. Dealers are anxious to make a sale on slow days and this may work to your advantage. If you pay attention to monthly sales figures, such as those published in **Automotive News**, you can shop for your new car when inventories are high which means the dealer is more likely to pass on savings to you in order to reduce his inventory.

What about the price?: If you have consulted **Edmund's New Car Prices** or **Edmund's Import Car Prices**, you should know what the dealer's cost of your automobile is. Your goal should be to pay no more than 2% over this cost, not the 10 to 12% the dealer wants you to pay. Remember, the price of a car has built-in payoffs for dealerships and salesmen, so don't think they aren't making a buck when you pay 2% over their wholesale cost.

Don't let the dealer talk you into fancy extras, especially at prices 10% above their cost. Pay only the cost to the dealer for specialty add-ons like their service contract, paint sealers, glazing, or special tires. Take only what you really want.

It is probably not a good idea to discuss the fact you have a trade-in. Get the dealer's best cash price first and then dicker over your trade-in. Again, get a wholesale price, not an allowance on your trade. Remember, you have the advantage in knowing the difference by using **Edmund's Used Car Prices**, and because you have already shopped around for the

1990 WARRANTY COVERAGE COMPARISON

	Basic Protection #years/#miles*	Extra Drivetrain/ Major Component #years/#miles*	Corrosion Coverage #years/#miles*
DOMESTIC			
BUICK	3/50,000	3/50,000	6/100,000
CADILLAC	4/50,000	4/50,000	6/100,000
CADILLAC Allante	1/12,000	7/100,000	7/100,000
CHEVROLET	3/50,000	3/50,000	6/100,000
CHRYSLER MOTORS	1/12,000	7/70,000	7/100,000
CHRYSLER Captive Imports	3/36,000	3/50,000	5/Unlimited
CHRYSLER New Yorker/ New Yorker Landau/Imperial/ Maserati	5/50,000	7/70,000	7/100,000
EAGLE Summit	3/36,000	7/70,000	7/100,000
FORD	1/12,000	6/60,000	6/100,000
LINCOLN/MERKUR	1/12,000	6/60,000	6/100,000
MERCURY	1/12,000	6/60,000	6/100,000
OLDSMOBILE	3/50,000	3/50,000	6/100,000
PONTIAC	3/50,000	3/50,000	6/100,000
FOREIGN			
ACURA	3/36,000	3/36,000	3/Unlimited
ALFA ROMEO	3/36,000	3/36,000	6/60,000
ASTON MARTIN	2/24,000	—	—
AUDI	3/50,000	3/50,000	6/Unlimited
BMW	3/36,000	3/36,000	6/Unlimited
DAIHATSU	3/36,000	—	3/Unlimited
FERRARI	2/Unlimited	—	—
HONDA	3/36,000	3/36,000	5/Unlimited
HYUNDAI	3/36,000	3/36,000	3/Unlimited
INFINITI	4/60,000	4/60,000	7/Unlimited
ISUZU	3/36,000	3/36,000	5/Unlimited
LEXUS	4/50,000	6/70,000	6/Unlimited
JAGUAR	3/36,000	3/36,000	6/60,000
LOTUS	2/Unlimited	2/Unlimited	8/Unlimited
MASERATI	2/24,000	2/24,000	—
MAZDA	3/50,000	3/50,000	5/Unlimited
MERCEDES-BENZ	4/50,000	4/50,000	4/50,000
MITSUBISHI	3/36,000	3/50,000	5/Unlimited
MITSUBISHI Precis	3/36,000	3/36,000	3/Unlimited
MITSUBISHI Galant/Mirage/ Eclipse	3/36,000	3/50,000	7/100,000
NISSAN	3/36,000	3/36,000	5/Unlimited
PEUGEOT	3/36,000	5/50,000	3/36,000
PORSCHE	2/Unlimited	2/Unlimited	10/Unlimited
RANGE ROVER	3/36,000	3/36,000	6/Unlimited
ROLLS-ROYCE	3/Unlimited	3/Unlimited	—
SAAB	3/36,000	3/36,000	6/Unlimited
SUBARU	3/36,000	3/36,000	6/60,000
SUZUKI	2/24,000	2/24,000	3/Unlimited
TOYOTA	3/36,000	5/60,000	5/Unlimited
VOLKSWAGEN	2/24,000	5/50,000	6/Unlimited
VOLVO	1/Unlimited	3/Unlimited	8/Unlimited
YUGO	1/12,000	4/40,000	36/Unlimited

*whichever comes first   — not available at presstime

best dealer purchase price, you therefore know exactly what the wholesale price should be.

Sealing the deal: After you have test driven the car and have agreed on a price, sign the buyer's order form only after the manager has signed first. This will eliminate any further haggling by the salesman. After the buyer's order is signed, put down a small deposit, say $100. When you go to pick your car up, don't forget to inspect it thoroughly before signing the buyer's acceptance. Look especially for body and chrome scratches and dents. Best inspection is done during the daytime in bright sunlight.

Edmund's
STEP-BY-STEP COSTING FORM

MAKE ________________________________   EXTERIOR COLOR ________________________

MODEL _______________________________   INTERIOR COLOR ________________________

BODY STYLE __________________________   TOP COLOR (IF APPL.) ___________________

ITEMS—COMPLETE DESCRIPTION	DEALER COST	LIST PRICE	BEST DEAL
Basic Model Price Only			
Optional Equipment			
1.			
2.			
3.			
4.			
5.			
6.			
7.			
8.			
9.			
10.			
11.			
12.			
13.			
14.			
15.			
16.			
17.			
18.			
19.			
20.			
Dealer Advertising Amount			
Dealer Preparation Amount			
Initial Gas & Oil			
Freight Amount (to your area)			
TOTAL COST*			

***Excluding Local Sales Tax, Registration & Inspection Fees**

## Chapter 3

Costs Of Owning An Automobile

The cost of owning and operating a motor vehicle is of major significance, as Americans experience increasing demands on their incomes. It costs more than $15,000 to purchase a 1991 model year large-size car. If it is driven 120,000 miles over a period of twelve years, the total cost to the owner will be about $36,741. During that time it will cost about $8,217 (excluding taxes) for some 7,059 gallons of gasoline, about $6,181 for maintenance and repair work, $5,933 to insure the vehicle, $1,129 for parking and tolls, $2,572 in taxes, and $12,000 in depreciation. Containment of these costs is important in planning a budget for purchasing and maintaining your car.

Types of costs: Most owners think of costs only in terms of outlays for gasoline, oil, tires and tolls. A more careful examination shows that some costs occur whether or not the vehicle is driven, while others are directly related to the amount of travel. The travel-related group is generally referred to as operating costs and the other group as ownership costs. Analysts often differ on the costs that should be included in each category. Some of the more common ones are included in the following table:

SUBURBAN-BASED OPERATION
Total Costs: Cents Per Mile

SIZE	ORIGINAL VEHICLE COST DEPRECIATED	MAINTENANCE ACCESSORIES PARTS & TIRES	GAS & OIL (EXCLUDING TAXES)	PARKING & TOLLS	INSURANCE	STATE & FEDERAL TAXES	TOTAL COST
LARGE — WITH STANDARD EQUIPMENT, WEIGHT MORE THAN 3,500 LBS. EMPTY	9.6	6.0	7.0	0.9	4.9	2.2	30.6
INTERMEDIATE — WEIGHT LESS THAN 3,500 LBS. EMPTY	8.6	5.2	5.7	0.9	5.6	1.8	27.8
COMPACT — WEIGHT LESS THAN 3,000 LBS. EMPTY	7.3	4.6	4.6	0.9	4.3	1.6	23.3
SUBCOMPACT — WEIGHT LESS THAN 2,500 LBS. EMPTY	5.9	5.1	4.4	0.9	5.0	1.4	22.7
PASSENGER VAN — WEIGHT LESS THAN 5,000 LBS. EMPTY	10.7	6.9	9.1	0.9	8.9	2.7	39.2

Ownership costs: These include depreciation, insurance, registration and titling fees, scheduled maintenance, and any taxes applied to these items. No matter how little a vehicle is driven, some portion of each of these items is incurred.

Depreciation is the loss in value of the vehicle during its lifetime due to passage of time, its mechanical and physical condition, and the number of miles it is driven.

National vehicle dealer groups issue vehicle value books for different regions of the country, usually on a quarterly basis. These values are determined by a survey of vehicle selling prices by make and model year in each geographic area. The values are based on normal travel, so lower or higher odometer readings will be reflected as higher or lower remaining vehicle values. The depreciation costs in the chart are an average for the nation, and are based on information from such a publication.

Depreciation is the single greatest cost of owning and operating most passenger vehicles during a twelve year life span. In the majority of cases the age of the vehicle is the most important factor in determining resale or trade-in value. Such factors as mileage, brand popularity, body style, size, and color are also considered. For large cars and vans, by far the largest dollar depreciation occurs in the first few years. For smaller cars, the depreciation is spread more evenly over the years. Since newer vehicles are assumed to be driven more miles than older vehicles, the depreciation cost on a per-mile basis is held down the first few years. For example, consider depreciation for a large-size car. If the car were bought new for $11,554 and sold or traded at the end of the first year after being driven 14,500 miles, the depreciation would be about $2,879 or 19.8 cents per mile. At the end of the second year, total depreciation would be about $4,655 or 16.5 cents per mile. As a vehicle gets older, the depreciation rate decreases, but the outlay for maintenance and repair rises. As time passes it becomes increasingly difficult and expensive to keep a car in satisfactory operating condition.

Insurance costs are determined by the amount and type of coverage selected, the purpose for which the vehicle is used, and the location in which it is operated. Automobiles are continuously exposed to the possibility of damage, whether on the highway or parked. The large numbers of vehicles on the roads and streets and in parking lots make each vehicle highly susceptible to accident involvement. While the improved bumper design required on most cars protects against damage in collisions at very low speeds, the cost of repairing even minor damage has increased considerably and is reflected in insurance rates.

The uninsured deductible portion of accident costs is included in the maintenance and repair costs. A spokesperson for the insurance industry ventured the opinion that the average motorist will be involved in an accident twice during an eight year period, and one of these will probably be his fault. If the owner carries collision insurance for the first five years of the vehicle's life, his out-of-pocket cost during this period will be the deductible amount (usually $200). That amount can be considered the minimum he will pay for accidents during the life of the vehicle if he continues this coverage. After collision insurance is discontinued, the owner will have to pay the entire cost of any accidents for which he is responsible.

Registration and titling or sales taxes are payments to the state in which the vehicle is registered. The registration fee customarily is due each year, and the titling or sales tax is due only once—when the vehicle is purchased. The cost of the registration fee is applied to the year in which it is charged, and the titling tax is applied in the first year of ownership.

Scheduled maintenance includes the services shown in the owner's manual. Generally, the suggested maintenance intervals are expressed in miles driven or period of time owned. The services include maintenance of the emissions control and cooling systems, oil changes, safety checks, tune-ups, and lubrication (see Chapter 8). When the owner's manual recommends that an item (e.g. brakes) be checked for wear, the cost of the labor to make such an inspection is considered scheduled maintenance. If a repair is found to be necessary, the cost of the replacement parts and the labor to install them are included in nonscheduled repairs. Nonscheduled repairs and maintenance are part of the operating costs (see Chapter 8).

Accessory costs cover the value of any add-on feature for a car or van which has no effect on its mechanical operations. These items customarily include extra wheels for snow tires, protective floor mats, seat covers, and miscellaneous items. Accessories, as defined in this analysis, do not include optional equipment such as air conditioning, power steering, or automatic transmissions that are included in the purchase price of the vehicle. The cost of miscellaneous accessories is assigned in equal increments to each year. All other accessory costs are spread over the benefit period based on vehicle's usage.

Finance charges: Most vehicle buyers either pay interest on money they borrow to buy their vehicles, or they forgo interest they would have earned if they elect to use savings or other investments to pay for the vehicles outright.

Lending institutions and vehicle dealerships have various financing plans available. They may differ regarding the portion of the vehicle cost they are willing to finance, the rate of interest charged, and the length of the loan term. Interest charged should be considered in the cost of owning a vehicle. The lender will provide the total interest charges, which may be divided by the accumulated miles of travel for the length of the loan.

The computation of interest lost on savings is more difficult. The cash payment for the purchase of a vehicle, the type of savings plan, the current rate of interest, and the period of time for monthly deposits to equal the cash payment, will vary greatly among purchasers.

Savings institutions will provide the amount of interest that could be earned by the deposit of an amount equal to the cash payment for the selected period of time and the amount of interest that can be earned if equal monthly amounts are paid into the savings account for the same period. The difference between these two interest amounts is the interest lost by paying cash for the purchase of a vehicle.

If $9,000 is needed to purchase a vehicle and three years (36 months) is selected as the period of time needed to save this amount, the monthly payment into savings would be $250 ($9,000 divided by 36). The difference in interest earned by these payments and the interest earned on $9,000 on deposit for three years is the interest lost by paying cash. At 6% interest, $9,000 on deposit for three years would earn $1,760.54. This would be lost if the money were withdrawn from savings to pay cash for a car. To replace the $9,000 in savings over three years, the purchaser would have to deposit $250 each month. These deposits would earn $878.70 in interest. The difference between these two interest amounts ($1,760.54 − $878.70 = $881.84) would be the interest cost of paying for the automobile purchase from savings.

Alternative methods of financing a new vehicle purchase can make important cost differences. Merits of different plans should be weighed carefully before a particular plan is selected.

Operating costs: Operating costs include repairs and maintenance, gasoline, oil, tires, parking, tolls, and the taxes applied to these items. These costs are each a function of vehicle usage.

Gasoline is a major cost item for vehicles of all sizes. The difference in gasoline costs alone between the 1991 large-size car and the subcompact over the lives of the vehicles is $3,044 (excluding taxes). Gasoline will cost $1,038 more for the large car than for the subcompact. The difference between the large and compact car is striking, when considering the large car provides only about 15% more interior space for the approximately 50% larger fuel costs (see chart at the end of this chapter).

Gasoline costs about $1.20 per gallon, including state and federal taxes, for unleaded gasoline. This represents typical full-service costs. Self-service costs are usually about $0.10 per gallon lower; therefore, the vehicle owner can realize substantial savings in the purchase of fuel by selecting self service. Using a credit card usually costs more.

Oil costs for a new or relatively new vehicle are mainly dependent on the car manufacturer's instructions for oil changes. The oil change interval is 7,500 miles for most cars; 3,000 for the perfectionist. The subcompact has a four quart capacity; larger cars use five quarts.

Tires receive 480,000 miles of wear when an automobile is driven 120,000 miles. The number of replacement tires is based on a life expectancy of 35,000 to 40,000 miles for radial tires and 30,000 miles for bias belted tires.

Parking and tolls include metered curb parking, fees charged in parking lots, and toll charges for using private or public highways, tunnels, and bridges.

Taxes on gasoline and oil are the primary component of operating cost taxes. These taxes are paid on a per-gallon basis. The federal gasoline tax is $0.11 per gallon.

Unscheduled repairs and maintenance include the amount you will spend on normal items that need replacing during your car's life. These include replacement of brake lining, spark plugs, wiper blades, light bulbs, fan belts, and shock absorbers. Unscheduled repairs might include replacement of items that might normally last the lifetime of your car with proper maintenance like rings, pistons, and the transmission. The average labor rate one can use to figure cost is $30.00/hr.

GASOLINE COST PER MILE AT VARIOUS PRICES

Gasoline Price Per Gallon*	Large Car	Intermediate Car	VEHICLE Compact Car	Subcompact Car	Passenger Van
1.00	5.00	4.55	4.00	3.85	5.88
1.01	5.05	4.59	4.04	3.88	5.94
1.02	5.10	4.63	4.08	3.92	6.00
1.03	5.15	4.68	4.12	3.96	6.06
1.04	5.20	4.73	4.16	4.00	6.12
1.05	5.25	4.77	4.20	4.04	6.18
1.06	5.30	4.82	4.24	4.08	6.24
1.07	5.35	4.86	4.28	4.12	6.29
1.08	5.40	4.91	4.32	4.15	6.35
1.09	5.45	4.95	4.36	4.19	6.41
1.10	5.50	5.00	4.40	4.23	6.47
1.11	5.55	5.05	4.44	4.27	6.53
1.12	5.60	5.09	4.48	4.31	6.59
1.13	5.65	5.14	4.52	4.35	6.65
1.14	5.70	5.18	4.56	4.38	6.71
1.15	5.75	5.23	4.60	4.42	6.76
1.16	5.80	5.27	4.64	4.46	6.82
1.17	5.85	5.32	4.68	4.50	6.88
1.18	5.90	5.36	4.72	4.54	6.94
1.19	5.95	5.41	4.76	4.58	7.00
1.20	6.00	5.45	4.80	4.62	7.06
1.21	6.05	5.50	4.84	4.65	7.12
1.22	6.10	5.55	4.88	4.69	7.18
1.23	6.15	5.59	4.92	4.73	7.24
1.24	6.20	5.64	4.96	4.77	7.29
1.25	6.25	5.68	5.00	4.81	7.35
1.26	6.30	5.73	5.04	4.85	7.41
1.27	6.35	5.77	5.08	4.88	7.47
1.28	6.40	5.82	5.12	4.92	7.53
1.29	6.45	5.86	5.16	4.96	7.59
1.30	6.50	5.91	5.20	5.00	7.65
1.31	6.55	5.95	5.24	5.04	7.71
1.32	6.60	6.00	5.28	5.08	7.76
1.33	6.65	6.05	5.32	5.12	7.82
1.34	6.70	6.09	5.36	5.15	7.88
1.35	6.75	6.14	5.40	5.19	7.94
1.36	6.80	6.18	5.44	5.23	8.00
1.37	6.85	6.23	5.48	5.27	8.06
1.38	6.90	6.27	5.52	5.31	8.12
1.39	6.95	6.32	5.56	5.35	8.18
1.40	7.00	6.36	5.60	5.38	8.24
1.41	7.05	6.41	5.64	5.42	8.29
1.42	7.10	6.45	5.68	5.46	8.35
1.43	7.15	6.50	5.72	5.50	8.41
1.44	7.20	6.55	5.76	5.54	8.47
1.45	7.25	6.59	5.80	5.58	8.53
1.46	7.30	6.64	5.84	5.62	8.59
1.47	7.35	6.68	5.88	5.65	8.65
1.48	7.40	6.73	5.92	5.69	8.71
1.49	7.45	6.77	5.96	5.73	8.76
1.50	7.50	6.82	6.00	5.77	8.82

Gasoline Price Per Gallon is listed in cents, ie. 6.97 = 6.97 cents.

## Chapter 4

Buying The Right Used Car

According to a Hertz Corporation study, motorists in the U.S. buy an estimated 18,805,000 used cars. The average age of the car is about 4.0 years. They are driven 45,439 miles and their average cost is $6,406.

The most important rule in buying a good used car, having determined your requirements for vehicle size, economy, performance, and equipment, is to inspect it as thoroughly as you would a house. When possible, have the vehicle run through a diagnostic center or inspected by a competent mechanic to determine its overall general condition.

Service requirements: When shopping for a good used car, *be cautious and suspicious*. Remember, the previous owner had some reason for getting rid of it. The reason may have been that he wanted a new car, or it may have been that the car had gone 200,000 miles and required major, costly repairs to make it both safe and dependable.

Remember that you seldom get more than you pay for when purchasing a used car, and often can get less than you paid for if you're not careful. If you think you're getting a good used car at a "dirt cheap" price, you may be buying somebody's expensive troubles instead.

Before you decide to buy a specific used car, think about the general condition, your specific need for it (running around town versus highway driving), the warranty offered, overall mileage, and availability of parts and service (foreign versus domestic). Remember that all cars require service at regular intervals, and the older the car, the greater the chance it will require major repairs.

What to buy: Generally, your best buy in a used car is one that is only two or three years old. Look for a year and model you like, and when you find one, check the odometer to see how far it has been driven. If cars only a few years old have been given reasonable care by their previous owners, they still have a lot of driving life left in them. Because of their mechanical condition, they also should be safer than older vehicles. However, such cars are still fairly expensive and may cost more than you can afford.

Some authorities recommend the deluxe model of the make you have chosen since the original cost may be associated with the onwer's financial ability to keep it well maintained. Also, sticking with a more luxurious used car makes sense when you consider the large difference in price between a Cadillac and a Chevrolet when new, but a much smaller differential when used.

Many used car buyers check with the major rental companies, especially in October and November when they rejuvenate their fleets, for used cars that have been refurbished and come with a warranty. Keep in mind though that rental cars have been used by many drivers, some of whom have likely not treated them with the same care they might have used with their own car.

If you find several cars within your price range, consider the one with the least mileage on the odometer and the best general overall condition. Unless you are specifically in the market for one, stay away from rare or sporty cars. Owners of rare cars will tell you it's hard to find parts and mechanics to keep them running. Sports models typically receive what the industry refers to as "hard driven miles." That is, their owners drive them in such a way as to put excessive wear on engine parts. Also, it is best to avoid used cars that feature power options as they tend to fail easily. From time to time **Consumer Reports** publishes information on those used cars which spend more time in the shop than on the road. Such knowledge, of course, is useful when you are making your decision on which used car to buy.

Used car warranties: With a used car you may not get a warranty, especially if you buy it from a private party or from an organization that has no facilities to service the cars it sells (e.g., a repossessed car purchased from a finance company). Even when provided, warranties differ from one dealer to another. You may get a complete warranty for parts and labor for periods up to thirty days, or a ninety day warranty on parts only with the buyer paying for the labor, or a fifty-fifty warranty for a certain period, with the buyer paying half the cost for parts and labor. The major rental car companies usually have specific warranties on used cars that are accompanied by excellent service records.

Make sure you understand the warranty before you purchase the car, and make it work for you. If you suspect something is wrong with your used car and it's still under warranty, don't wait. Take it back right away. Do this over and over until you're sure the dealer has corrected your problem. If possible, obtain a written description of any work done during the warranty period so that you will have a record if the same problem occurs after the warranty expires (see Chapter 10 on how to return your car).

Odometer information: On April 29, 1989, the Congressional mandate establishing the Truth in Mileage Act went into effect. The spirit of the law requires that the odometer mileage at the time of vehicle transfer must appear on the title documents as well as on appropriate forms for all transfer of ownership transactions. Failure to complete this statement by the buyer and the seller can void the transaction. This law was put into effect to help protect the used car purchaser from buying a car with incorrect mileage information on the odometer. In this manner, the mileage of every used car may be monitored by each state's motor vehicle division; discrepancies can be noted and the transaction voided. As an extra means of protection it is a good idea to obtain the name and address of the previous owner from the dealer so that you might verify the car's mileage history. An example of an Odometer Disclosure Statement is on the following page.

Examine the car: Examine the outside of the car thoroughly. Look for rust, dents, and evidence that portions of the car have rusted out and been repaired using body putty. Be especially careful in examining areas around the bottom of doors and the rear fenders.

Look under the car. Check for breaks in the frame or signs that the frame has been welded. Look for weakened or loosened bolts and fittings. Look for excessive rusting of the frame. All of these conditions can signal weaknesses in the vehicle's structure. Also, check the condition of the muffler, tailpipe, and exhaust pipe. Rub your finger inside the tailpipe. If your finger gets oily, it could be a sign that the car is burning excess oil. Look for signs of oil or transmission fluid leakage on the ground or pavement under the car. The transmission oil should not be brown or smell burnt. Look for signs of fluid leaking from shock absorbers. Check the condition of the tires, including inside scratches. Look for signs of brake fluid leaking on the inside of the tires. While under the car, check for fresh undercoating that may be hiding signs of rust.

Walk around the car and check the condition of the window glass. Check the condition of the lenses in all vehicle lights—front, back, and side. Test all the lights to make sure they are functioning (headlights, tail lights, flashers, backup lights, brake lights, turn signals, running lights in fenders).

Push down on the corners of the car, front and back, to check the shock absorbers. If the car bounces up and down several times, the shocks are worn. Stand back some distance from the car and see if it is level. If one corner is lower than another, one of the springs may be weak or broken. While standing at a distance, look for evidence that the car has been in an accident (ripples in the fender, dents, or paint that doesn't match). Look for evidence the car has been in a flood: smell of mildew, silt or sand under the carpets may indicate that the car was recently tilted in a flooded area.

Open the trunk and check the spare tire. If it is worn unevenly or is cupped, something may be wrong with the front end and a front tire was put in the trunk as a spare to hide the problem. Make sure the car has a jack and that it is in good condition. Check the trunk wiring to make sure it hasn't been spliced extensively, a sign of electrical problems. Check all the tires on the car. Front tires with wear only on the inside indicates poor wheel alignment or front end problems. Heavy wear on the rear tires could mean "rubber burning" by a dragster.

Lift the hood of the car and check the condition of the belts and hoses. Check the battery to see if it is cracked. Pull out the oil dipstick to see how dirty the oil is. A check of the mileage on the odometer, and a comparison with mileage indicated on lubrication stickers (affixed to doorposts or sometimes at some location under the hood) will give you an indication as to when the car had its last oil change and lubrication, and whether the previous owner neglected such necessary services. Ask for his receipts. *(Note: if the previous owner changed his oil and lubricated the car himself, you won't find such evidence.)*

Be wary of a steam cleaned engine. At least a dirty engine may show leaks. Turn the key; does the car start up right away? Check for blue smoke from the exhaust which may mean worn piston rings — a costly job. If the car knocks at all, leave the lot and forget about that car.

Get inside the car. Examine the upholstery, safety belts, and carpeting. If the car has seat covers, look under them. Badly worn carpeting or upholstery may be a sign of heavy vehicle usage. Turn on the ignition and check the lights, including the warning lights on the dashboard. Take a friend along, and have him check the various lights from the outside as you turn them on from the inside. Also check the brake pedal for free play. If a car's steering wheel can be turned more than a couple of inches in either direction before moving the front wheel, the car may need an alignment. Such loose steering is usually accompanied by excessive drift or wandering while on the road when trying to keep the car in a straight line.

Take the car for a test drive over various types of roads. Be alert to any vibrations in the steering that may be a sign of front-end trouble. If the car has a manual transmission, be alert to excessive play, grabbing, or rattling of the clutch. Be alert to any vibrations or unusual noises from the engine, transmission, rear end, or wheels that may signal trouble. Push the gearshift through its various positions and see how the car reacts. Check the acceleration and brakes, and look for indications of overheating. Let the engine idle and be alert to noises or vibrations that may indicate a badly tuned engine or one with bad valves. Be alert for any unusual odors inside the car—these should tell you that not all is well.

While test driving the car, pay attention to how the transmission shifts; if the automatic transmission doesn't shift smoothly or if there is hesitation when it shifts, the transmission may need repair work. When it is safe to do so, step on the gas and look into the rearview mirror for smoke from the exhaust; if you see a lot of white or bluish smoke, the engine may be bad and need an expensive overhaul. White smoke when the engine is cold is normal; when the engine is warm it could mean a cracked block or blown head gasket. Black smoke means a tune-up is needed. Check the car's power up a hill; if it has little power, it may need an expensive valve job or an overhaul. Turn on the heater, air conditioner, radio and windshield wipers to make sure all these systems work.

If possible, before you buy the car have it checked mechanically by a diagnostic center or by your mechanic. Check with the National Highway and Traffic Safety Administration to make sure you are not buying a car that was recalled. If you are, it should have a sticker under the hood signifying that the recall work was done. Finally, run it through a car wash to see if it leaks.

Safety recalls: One way to help eliminate a potential used car might be to reject it for safety purposes. From time to time the National Highway & Traffic Safety Information publishes data on which cars have been recalled and the reason for recall. When purchasing a used car that was recalled, make sure the owner can produce evidence that the defect has been corrected. Some recent major recalls are listed below. To find out the latest recall information, or to report a safety problem in your car, call the National Highway Transportation Safety Administration at 202-366-0123.

SAFETY RECALLS

AUTOMOBILE	MODEL YEAR	NUMBER RECALLED	POSSIBLE PROBLEM
Alfa Romeo Milano	1987-1988	6,000	Bad headlight switch might cause sudden headlight failure.
Audi Quattro	1984-1989	35,000	Faulty fuel injection seals may allow fuel to drip and cause engine compartment fire.
Audi 4000 Coupe Volkswagen Quantum	1985-1986	25,000	Faulty idle stabilizer could cause unsatisfactory driveability
Audi 5000	1978-1986	81,000	Faulty idle stabilizer could cause unwanted acceleration
Audi 5000S	1978-1986	251,102	Sudden acceleration
Audi 5000S	1985-1986	80,710	Engine compartment fire due to escaping fuel
BMW Passenger Cars	1986-1987	97,300	Faulty brake light
BMW 735	1988	8,187	Driver/passenger seatbacks may not support occupants in severe impact resulting in serious injury
Buick Electra Oldsmobile 88, 98 Pontiac Bonneville	1987	35,057	Faulty accelerator cable movement could cause accelerator to remain engaged after release resulting in a possible accident

AUTOMOBILE	MODEL YEAR	NUMBER RECALLED	POSSIBLE PROBLEM
Buick Regal Somerset Oldsmobile Calais Pontiac Grand Am	1985	135,623	Loss of accelerator control due to faulty throttle spring
Buick Regal	1988	8,328	Left front brake hose could wear through resulting in a loss of brake power
Buick Regal Pontiac Grand Prix	1988	12,457	Defective hood latch may fly up, obscure forward vision, and cause an accident
Buick Riviera	1986-1987	65,136	Abrasion of power steering pump hose could result in a fluid leak and under hood fire
Buick Riviera Reatta Oldsmobile Toronado	1989	10,535	Brake line could wear through resulting in loss of braking capability
Buick Skyhawk Cadillac Cimarron Chevrolet Cavilier Oldsmobile Firenza	1985	87,174	Engine compartment fire due to loose air cleaner cover
Cadillac Eldorado Seville	1986	37,481	Floor mat could interfere with accelerator pedal, causing possible crash

Chevrolet Cars (all models)
Chevrolet and GMC Trucks
  and Vans (1985-1986)
Buick Estate Wagon
Cadillac Cimarron
  De Ville
  Eldorado
  Fleetwood Limousine
Pontiac Cars (all models)
	1986
	1987
		162,894	Loss of headlights due to faulty switch

Chevrolet Cavalier	1987	65,594	Frozen accelerator cable, causing loss of control and possible crash
Chevrolet Chevette Pontiac T100	1983-1986	370,831	Excessive wear of automatic transmission shift lever button may allow accidental shifting of gears.
Chevrolet Corvette	1986	18,223	Damage to brake cylinder due to severe or unusual conditions
Chevrolet Spectrum Isuzu I-Mark	1985-1986	108,268	Engine compartment fire due to leaky fuel pump
Chevrolet Truck C30 GMC C35	1984-1986	86,152	Greater than acceptable fuel spillage during and after collision could result in fire

Chrysler Fifth Avenue
  Laser
  LeBaron GTS
  LeBaron 4-door
  Town & Country
Dodge Aries 4-door
  Charger
  Daytona
  Diplomat
  Lancer
  Omni
Plymouth Gran Fury
	1986	32,149	Battery case rupture

AUTOMOBILE	MODEL YEAR	NUMBER RECALLED	POSSIBLE PROBLEM
Horizon Reliant 4-door Turismo			
Dodge Dakota	1987	34,000	Speed control cables may disengage and cause throttle to stay partially open when accelerator is released
Ford Aerostar	1986	38,947	Inadequate structural welds could permit rear suspension to separate from the underbody
Ford Aerostar Bronco II Ranger	1986	90,000	Incorrectly routed wiring for the lumbar seat system may become abrased resulting in a short circuit and possible fire
Ford Aerostar	1986-1988	60,000	Vehicles with trailer tow packages may experience short in trailer tail-light assembly which could result in a fire
Ford Aerostar	1990	30,000	Master brake cylinder could fail causing reduced breaking effectiveness that could result in a crash
Ford Ranger	1987	13,430	Improperly installed seat belt
Ford Crown Victoria Lincoln Town Car Mercury Grand Marquis	1987	29,600	Break in steering link, causing diminished steering control
Ford Taurus (Wagon) Mercury Sable (Wagon	1986-1987	28,000	Under high road salt conditions, electrolytic buildup at rear window, causing the glass to fracture during motion or when parked
Honda Civic	1986	17,338	Breakup of left drive shaft
Honda Prelude	1988	66,239	Power steering supply hose might leak onto exhaust manifold, causing smoke and possible underhood fire
Jeep Comanche	1986	41,073	Faulty parking brake assembly
Lincoln Continental Mark VII	1986	38,000	Loss of rear brake function and front brake power assist due to faulty brake system
Lincoln Continental Mark VII	1986	16,000	Improper wiring of brake fluid sensors permitting inaccurate fluid level reading
Lincoln Continental	1988	26,000	Nylon shield wiring harness could melt onto exhaust manifold possibly resulting in an underhood fire
Mazda 626	1986	36,671	Defective throttle
Nissan Maxima	1985-1986	33,000	Loose windshield due to insufficient adhesive
Nissan Stanza	1986	27,000	Fuel tank filler damage in rear-end collision
Oldsmobile Calais	1985-1986	206,651	Unexpected hood release due to faulty latch
Oldsmobile Delta 88	1986	38,309	Loss of vehicle control due to inadequately tightened ball joint stud on control arm

AUTOMOBILE	MODEL YEAR	NUMBER RECALLED	POSSIBLE PROBLEM
Pontiac Fiero	1985-1988	244,000	Unreasonable risk of connecting rod failure and engine compartment fire
Pontiac Grand Prix	1985-1986	20,096	Power door lock may separate, exposing electrical terminal; contact of electrical terminal with steel remote mirror cable could cause short that causes cable to overheat and could result in fire
Pontiac LeMans	1988	72,616	Defective fuel filler neck welding may allow fuel to leak, and after a collision could cause a fire
Pontiac LeMans	1988	85,063	Seatbelt buckles might release unexpectedly increasing risk of injury in an accident
Pontiac 6000 Buick Century Oldsmobile Ciera Chevrolet Celebrity	1988	27,639	Fuel feed hose could leak and result in an engine compartment fire which may spread to passenger compartment
Porsche 944 944 Turbo	1986	17,717	Engine compartment fire due to kinked fuel hose
Porsche 928	1985-1987	6,905	Catalytic converter heat shield could overheat igniting nearby components
Renault Alliance Encore	1985-1987	240,000	Heater core rupture causing possible leakage of hot coolant and steam near driver's legs
Saab 900S 900 Turbo	1986-1987	15,446	Fuel hose rupture, resulting in leakage and fire
Saab 9000	1988	14,000	Throttle kickdown cable could allow chafing causing brake fluid leakage resulting in an accident
Saab 900	1987-1988	70,000	Wiring harness may short causing smoke or fire in passenger compartment
Subaru	1987	57,000	Faulty preheat tubes could result in in engine compartment fire
Subaru Justy	1988-1989	15,000	Insufficient lubrication of 4WD extension housing bearing may result in rear wheel lockup
Toyota Camry	1988	11,486	Car jack may be unable to support vehicle, lower itself unexpectedly, and result in personal injury
Toyota Vans	1986-1988	110,217	Possible water contamination of steering bevel gear assembly may lead to erratic steering
Volkswagen Fox	1987-1989	104,000	Grease on steering shaft and improperly torqued steering wheel nut could result in loosening or separation of steering wheel
Volkswagen Golf and GTI	1985	77,000	Leaky fuel tank
Volkswagen Golf and GTI	1986	23,000	Leaky fuel tank
Volkwagen Golf and GTI	1987	10,000	Improperly torqued front left lug nuts could allow wheel to loosen and eventually separate

AUTOMOBILE	MODEL YEAR	NUMBER RECALLED	POSSIBLE PROBLEM

Volkwagen Jetta
  Golf
  Scirocco
  Cabriolet
	1985-
	1987
		278,520	Fuel filter could restrict fuel supply and cause stalling

Volkswagen Vanagon
  Camper
  Syncro
	1986-
	1987
		15,500	Unusual conditions could restrict fuel flow and cause stalling

Volvo 240 Series	1985- 1986	89,587	Displacement of engine throttle cable in front-end collision, causing cars to lurch forward
Volvo 740	1986- 1988	38,000	Driveshaft could contact the fuel tank and score and scrape outer surfaces of the tank at the point of contact resulting in a fire
Volvo 760 Series	1985- 1987	106,602	Engine wiring harness could chafe against air conditioning pipe and result in short circuit and electrical system malfunction
Yugo GV	1986	12,512	Improper installation of seat belt retractors

Quick Checklist for Used Car Buyers

1. Decide on the make and model you want ... it helps to do a little honest research. There are many publications that rate used cars. **Consumer Reports,** published by Consumers Union, is one of the best and most readily available.
2. Buy only from reputable dealers. One important test of a dealer's reputation is to call the local Better Business Bureau ... if he has a record of complaints, they will tell you. **Car Savvy** recommends dealing with a new car dealer operating a used car lot. They have a reputation to maintain and also have full service facilities.
3. The following tests are a must:

    The Exterior: Look for collision damage. If the car has been in an obvious bad accident, there is probably damage to the frame, and bolts and fittings have been weakened and loosened. This car will prove to be costly in the future, but more importantly, it could be dangerous. Also look for rust. A rusted out car has little value.

    The Interior: Check for wear. Does the mileage on the odometer equal interior wear? Check the driver's seat for wear. If there is heavy wear in the interior, but low mileage on the odometer, there is the possibility that the "clock has been turned back."

    Suspension: Stand back and simply look. If the car is sitting low, it may have a worn out suspension system. Is it level, or is there a sag at either end? This could mean badly worn springs and shocks.

    Tires: Front tires with wear only on the inside or only on the outside indicates poor wheel alignment, or it could be worse: front end problems. Heavy wear on rear tires could mean "rubberburning" by a dragster.

Engine: Be wary of the steam cleaned engine. At least a dirty engine can show you what may be leaking. Turn the key. Does it start right up? Any blue smoke from the exhaust? If so, this could mean worn piston rings, a costly job. Any knocking at all? If so, leave the lot and forget about that car.

Test Drive: Never buy a car without test driving: not just a spin around the block, but put the car through its paces. This is your chance to test for noises, acceleration, brakes, clutch and transmission, as well as overheating.

Finally: For an average of $75.00 you can utilize the services of an "Auto Diagnostic Center" or a reputable mechanic. These diagnosticians can tell you what is wrong with the car and can provide estimates on repairs.

Used Car Buying Work Sheet

ITEM	Car "A"	Car "B"	Car "C"	Car "D"
BODY:	$	$	$	$
RUST				
DENT				
CHROME				
PAINT				
GLASS				
MOTOR:				
VALVES				
PISTONS				
RINGS				
TRANSMISSION:				
ADJUST				
OVERHAUL				
TIRES:				
RETREAD				
WORN				
BRAKES:				
ADJUST				
REPLACE				
ELECTRICAL:				
BATTERY				
WIRING				
GENERATOR				
REGULATOR				
PLUGS & POINTS				
TUNE UP:				
MISCELLANEOUS				
COOLING SYSTEM:				
HOSE				
RADIATOR				
WATER PUMP				
EXHAUST:				
MUFFLER				
FRONT EXHAUST				
TAIL PIPE				
LIGHTS:				
HEAD				
TAIL				
DIRECTIONAL				
WIPER:				
BLADES				
MOTOR				
TOTAL REPAIR COST	$	$	$	$
ASKING PRICE OF CAR				
+ or − = NET PRICE				

## Chapter 5

The Federal Crash Report: Will You Survive?

The Federal Government has been known to start crash programs which are aimed at curing the ills of the nation right before an election, but this government crash program is somewhat different; they're crashing cars and it's for your safety.

Some time ago, the National Highway Traffic Safety Administration (NHTSA) started to crash test cars to see the damage that would be caused by such a crash. When these tests were first released, they received a tremendous amount of coverage on television newscasts throughout the country. The public outcry should have impressed upon automobile makers that people were interested in buying safe cars. Even though many measures have been taken by both domestic and foreign manufacturers to make cars safer, the results of the tests by the Highway Traffic Safety Administration show that there are many cars that are unsafe when crashed at 35 miles per hour into a stationary object.

How are the cars selected? The National Highway Traffic Safety Administration tests about twenty cars every year that it buys off the lot, just as you would. The tests cannot begin until after a new model year has started, so test results on new cars generally begin to be available in the late winter of each year.

The NHTSA chooses the cars it will test so that useful information will be given to as many consumers as possible. Therefore, a popular model is more likely to be chosen, because information on that model would be of interest to many consumers. For the same reason, very expensive cars are not tested as often. If a car that NHTSA has already tested remains essentially the same for the new model year, it will probably not be tested again, but a car that undergoes substantial changes in the new model year is likely to be retested. In using any crash test data, you should always check the model year that was tested and whether the NHTSA believes that the test results should be used to evaluate other model years.

Conditions of the test: All of the crash vehicles are thoroughly inspected for defects or abnormalities which might cause the test results to be different than what would actually happen under normal conditions. There are measuring devices placed inside and around the automobile to measure the crash force upon impact into a barrier, and the length of time the various parts of the body would be exposed to the impact.

It has been concluded by the National Highway Traffic Safety Administration that most highway fatalities occur because of head injuries. Even though other injuries in an automobile accident can cause death, the norm in the NHTSA tests is head injuries.

Many factors that do not seem to be taken into consideration in the federal crash tests. One is the overall health of the individual involved in the crash. An individual who is in exceptional physical condition would be affected differently than a person who is not in good shape. A child's or woman's injuries would be different than those of a normal sized adult male. If there is anything loose in the car at the time of impact, additional serious injuries could result. Despite drawbacks to the tests, the editors of **Car Savvy** conclude that the test results do have merit as all of the crashes are done in exactly the same way with similar controls.

Since the inception of this crash test program, the list of cars tested has grown and the data gathered has become more specific, and therefore, more significant. The tests are conducted under a number of varying conditions with two dummies representing average adult males in the front seat wired to electrical meters to measure the force of the impact. The results that follow were done under two basic conditions, either cars were crashed head-on into a fixed barrier at 35 m.p.h., or some cars were rear impacted into the fixed barrier at 35 m.p.h. to check for fuel leakage. Some cars were also crashed at a 30 degree frontal angle into a barrier at 35 m.p.h. which is five miles faster than the prescribed speed to meet the standard and about 35% more violent than a 30 m.p.h. crash.

According to the NHTSA, a 35 mile per hour frontal collision into a fixed barrier is equivalent to a head-on collision between two identical vehicles, moving toward each other at a closing speed of 70 m.p.h., or each moving at 35 m.p.h. The test is also equivalent to a car moving at 70 m.p.h. striking an identical parked car.

Federal Motor Vehicle Safety Standard No. 208, "Occupant Crash Protection," requires that all passenger cars manufactured after September 1, 1989 be equipped with automatic crash protection. Car manufacturers have met this requirement by installing automatic safety belts or air bags. Testing under this standard is conducted at 30 m.p.h.

In the New Car Assessment Program, testing is conducted at 35 m.p.h. using all available safety equipment, both the automatic crash protection and any manual safety belts in the vehicle. The test results demonstrate the relative crash protection provided to front-seat occupants by these automatic and manual safety systems. The test results do not apply to unbelted occupants.

Measurements were taken from the test dummies in three major areas: first, head injury criteria (HIC), a measurement of how the car helps resist head injury. The upper limit of safety for this measure is set at 1000. Secondly, a chest resultant acceleration level was measured as a function of gravity. The upper limit of safety here was 60 g's. The lower the reported numbers are for the head and chest, the lower the potential is for injury in a 35 m.p.h. frontal crash. Head injury numbers below 750 indicate that head injury is unlikely. Between 750 and 1,250, head injury is possible. Above 1,250, head injury is likely. Chest injury numbers above 60 indicate that chest injury is likely. Test data that measure the potential for upper leg injury are also available and can be obtained by contacting the agency. And finally, femur load, a measure of safety for the lower part of the body was measured in pounds and the upper limit of safety was 2,250 pounds for both driver and passenger.

Loads above this threshold indicate that upper leg injury is likely.

Additional safety measurements in selected models have been compiled on the cars themselves, also in three categories. Category 212 required that a certain percentage of the windshield remain attached. Category 219 required that no vehicle parts from outside the occupant compartment may intrude into a defined zone in front of the windshield. Category 301 measured the amount of leakage from the fuel system after the crash and following a 360 degree rotation.

According to NHTSA, the test results provide comparative data for consumers to use in their vehicle purchasing decisions. Comparisons are meaningful only when made between vehicles of the same type (passenger cars, vans, etc.) and within an approximate weight range of 500 pounds.

The following information was updated from the Department of Transportation's latest report. We have included statistics for car model years from 1981-1990.

EXPLANATORY NOTES

Doors: HB = Hatchback, Liftback, Notchback   MPV = Multipurpose Vehicle   PU = Pickup Truck   W = Station Wagon   **Test Mode:** F = Frontal—Cars were crashed head-on into a fixed barrier at 35mph; O = Oblique—Modified frontal test. Cars were crashed into a fixed barrier at a 30 degree angle at 35 mph; R = Rear—Cars were rear-impacted by a 4,000 pound moving barrier at 35 mph to check for fuel leakage   **Head Injury Criteria (HIC):** The HIC limit is 1,000   **Chest Resultant Acceleration:** The limit for chest acceleration is 60 g's   **Femur Loads:** The femur load limit is 2,250 pounds   **Y** = Yes   **N** = No   * = In order to obtain additional dummy data, limits specified in FMVSS 219 were not measured   **NT** = Not tested   **NA, ND** = No data (instrumentation problem; data not available).   **Note:** where there is no information listed, there was either NA, ND or it was NT.

Make	Model		Model Year		Test Speed (mph)	Test Weight (lbs.)	HIC No. d/p	Chest Resultant Acceleration (g's) d/p	Femur Loads (Pounds) Driver L/R	Passenger L/R	212	219	301 F‡	R‡
Acura	Integra	2HB	1987	F	35.0	2780	599/597	35/34	791/387	262/354	NT	NT	NT	NT
Acura	Integra	4	1990	F	35.0	2915	585/637	ND/42	NA	NA	NA	NA	NA	NA
Acura	Legend LS	4	1988	F	35.0	3710	435/618	50/41	926/730	708/772	NT	NT	NT	NT
American Motors	Jeep Comanche	PU	1986	F	35.2	3555	1147/1636	50/ND	505/837	751/249	Y	Y	Y	
American Motors	Jeep Comanche	PU	1987	F	35.0	3554	1052/2700	62/48	925/923	319/761	NA	NA	NA	
American Motors	Jeep Cherokee	0	1984	F	35.3	3645	850/1548	44/43	333/292	491/125	Y	*	Y	
American Motors	Jeep CJ7	0	1984	F	35.1	3180	460/440	46/49	1730/860	520/750	NA	NA	Y	
American Motors	Jeep Wrangler	MPV	1987	F	35.0	3620	758/1229	44/40	1100/758	1015/783	NA	NA	NA	
American Motors	Spirit	2HB	1981	F	35.0	3190	702/652	43/33	ND/1300	280/560	Y	Y	Y	
American Motors	Spirit	2HB	1981	R	35.4	3213								N
Audi	80	4	1989	F	35.0	3320	600/515	49/39	168/324	1871/245	NA	NA	NA	NA
Audi	100	4	1989	F	35.0	3790	185/710	35/31	998/571	894/757	NA	NA	NA	NA
Audi	5000	4	1981	F	34.7	3361	Invalid	43/52	480/712	628/394	Y	Y	Y	NT
Audi	5000	4	1985	F	35.0	3397	2105/557	39/31	362/357	292/326	Y	Y	Y	
BMW	318i	2	1985	F	35.0	2944	1539/547	41/39	64/296	597/185	N	Y	Y	
Buick	Century	4	1982	F*	35.0	3273	478/395	33/21	774/1052	918/595	Y	Y	Y	
Buick	Century	4W	1984	F*	35.0	3590	518/440	31/28	635/270	580/500	Y	*	Y	
Buick	Century	2	1986		35.1	3360	647/928	37/49	945/740	670/720	Y	Y	Y	
Buick	Century	4	1986	F	35.2	3250	699/672	40/37	740/240	690/490	Y	Y	Y	
Buick	Le Sabre	4	1983	F*	35.3	4120	882/1084	42/47	675/650	600/544	Y	Y	Y	
Buick	Le Sabre	2	1986	F	35.5	3650	908/752	39/40	879/1181	583/368	Y	Y	Y	
Buick	Park Avenue	4	1985	F	34.9	3850	1550/662	50/37	1145/820	710/400	Y	*	Y	
Buick	Park Avenue	4	1988	F	35.0	3855	1467/794	54/37	712/479	1366/686	NT	NT	NT	NT
Buick	Regal	2	1984	F*	34.8	3700	781/1074	40/35	1500/790	450/525	Y	*	Y	
Buick	Regal	2	1988	F	35.0	3710	880/535	50/33	996/686	642/526	NT	NT	NT	NT
Buick	Somerset Regal	2	1985	F	34.5	3210	1140/595	34/35	815/400	585/315	Y	Y	Y	
Buick	Riviera	2	1986	F	35.0	3690	826/650	45/45	944/570	1419/498	NA	NA	NA	NA
Buick	Skyhawk	4	1986	F	35.0	2999	784/602	42/31	79/658	1112/487	NA	NA	NA	NA
Buick	Skylark	4	1986	F	35.0	3150	823/453	36/27	1019/740	526/533	NA	NA	NA	NA
Buick	Skylark	4	1987	F	35.0	3120	405/328	70/40	1085/1737	1435/555	NA	NA	NA	NA
Cadillac	Cimarron	4	1986	F	35.0	2999	784/602	42/31	79/658	1112/487	NA	NA	NA	NA
Cadillac	De Ville	4	1985	F*	34.9	3850	1550/662	50/37	1145/820	710/480	Y	*	Y	
Cadillac	De Ville	4	1988	F	35.0	3855	1467/794	54/37	712/479	1366/686	NA	NA	NA	NA
Cadillac	Eldorado	2	1986	F	35.0	3690	826/650	45/45	944/570	1419/498	NA	NA	NA	NA
Chevrolet	Astro	Van	1985	F	34.8	4090	2202/1597	70/61	1845/940	1160/725	Y	Y	Y	

Chevrolet	Astro	Van	1988	F	35.0	4415	1603/1424	72/63	1572/1695	700/576	NT	NT	NT	NT
Chevrolet	Astro	Van	1989	F	35.0	4630	1849/1838	64/64	2737/1901	1043/365	NA	NA	NA	NA
Chevrolet	Beretta	2	1988	F	35.0	3350	864/559	50/42	1692/1731	1052/796	NT	NT	NT	NT
Chevrolet	C-10	PU	1984	F	35.2	4830	534/514	37/39	2026/353	543/290	Y	*	Y	
Chevrolet	C-1500	PU	1988	F	35.0	4308	892/374	47/46	942/1207	622/306	NT	NT	NT	NT
Chevrolet	G-20	Van	1987	F	35.0	5456	1387/1719	67/43	1298/1507	ND/ND	NA	NA	NA	
Chevrolet	G-20	Van	1988	F	35.0	4872	3665/1452	97/56	1330/2447	963/259	NT	NT	NT	NT
Chevrolet	Camaro	2	1982	F	35.4	3428	563/577	39/32	901/1004	258/358	Y	Y	Y	
Chevrolet	Camaro	2	1983	F*	35.2	3330	408/376	34/32	900/480	100/125	Y	Y	Y	
Chevrolet	Camaro	2HB	1987	F	35.0	3524	733/660	39/39	736/961	353/144	NA	NA	NA	
Chevrolet	Caprice	4	1983	F	35.3	4120	882/1084	42/47	675/650	600/544	Y	Y	Y	
Chevrolet	Caprice	4	1989	F	35.0	4220	1328/1365	64/42	406/260	493/495	NA	NA	NA	NA
Chevrolet	Cavalier	2HB	1982	F	35.0	2830	708/821	42/37	1834/1654	1523/1673	Y	Y	Y	
Chevrolet	Cavalier	2	1982	R	35.4	2865								Y
Chevrolet	Cavalier (conv.)	2	1984	F	35.0	3110	884/401	43/29	780/850	380/440	Y	*	Y	
Chevrolet	Cavalier	4	1986	F	35.0	2999	784/602	42/31	79/658	1112/487	NA	NA	NA	NA
Chevrolet	Celebrity	4	1982	F	35.0	3273	478/395	33/21	774/1052	918/595	Y	Y	Y	
Chevrolet	Celebrity	4W	1984	F	35.0	3590	518/440	31/28	635/270	580/500	Y	*	Y	
Chevrolet	Celebrity	2	1986	F	35.0	3360	647/928	37/49	945/740	670/720	NA	NA	NA	NA
Chevrolet	Celebrity	4	1986	F	35.0	3250	699/672	40/37	740/240	690/490	NA	NA	NA	NA
Chevrolet	Chevette	4HB	1982	F	34.8	2827	1020/715	48/40	1007/1653	449/346	Y	Y	Y	
Chevrolet	Chevette	4HB	1984	F*	35.3	2746	1886/1306	42/57	2512/298	311/663	Y	*	Y	
Chevrolet	Corsica	4	1988	F	35.0	3230	772/752	44/40	1293/614	737/845	NT	NT	NT	NT
Chevrolet	Corvette	2	1984	F	34.7	3680	784/525	40/32	730/560	670/650	Y	*	Y	
Chevrolet	Impala	4	1982	F	35.2	4110	1170/ND	40/41	940/ND	575/375	Y	Y	Y	
Chevrolet	Impala	4	1983	F*	35.3	4120	882/1084	42/47	675/650	600/544	Y	Y	Y	
Chevrolet	Lumina	4	1990	F	35.0	3632	1200/ND	58/ND	NA	NA	NA	NA	NA	NA
Chevrolet	Monte Carlo	2	1984	F*	34.8	3700	781/1074	40/35	1500/790	450/525	Y	*	Y	
Chevrolet	Nova	4	1986	F	35.2	2580	552/562	44/41	2176/745	630/547	Y	Y	Y	
Chevrolet	S-10 Blazer	MPV	1985	F	35.0	3900	1036/1320	62/43	1040/1000	425/155	Y	Y	Y	
Chevrolet	S-10 Blazer	MPV	1989	F	35.0	4096	834/2482	62/48	ND/ND	ND/ND	NA	NA	NA	NA
Chevrolet	Spectrum	2	1985	F	34.8	2346	1559/960	51/56	223/402	476/345	Y	Y	Y	
Chevrolet	Sprint	2HB	1985	F	35.1	2042	1787/1799	52/39	434/674	832/1419	Y	Y	Y	
Chevrolet	Suburban	MPV	1987	F	35.0	6110	1477/1176	50/42	1911/101	257/358	NA	NA	NA	NA
Chrysler	E Class	4	1983	F*	35.2	3100	947/1010	46/48	1180/510	650/580	Y	Y	Y	
Chrysler	Imperial	2	1981	F	35.3	4562	976/590	47/32	742/371	750/564	Y	Y	Y	
Chrysler	Imperial	2	1981	R	35.1	4567								Y
Chrysler	Laser	2HB	1984	F*	35.4	3000	507/566	37/40	740/860	950/530	Y	*	Y	
Chrysler	Fifth Ave.	4	1989	F	35.0	4340	786/682	43/43	1132/766	667/575	NA	NA	NA	NA
Chrysler	Le Baron	2	1982	F*	35.0	3044	520/756	44/41	1080/880	1011/914	Y	Y	Y	
Chrysler	Le Baron	2	1987	F	35.0	3320	791/1698	62/82	1008/1863	1776/853	NA	NA	NA	NA

Make	Model		Year											
Chrysler	Le Baron (conv.)	2	1982	F	35.4	3000	2644/697	39/43	335/110	485/440	NT	NT	Y	
Chrysler	Le Baron GTS	4HB	1985	F*	34.7	3250	2187/445	38/30	835/840	530/610	Y	Y	Y	
Chrysler	New Yorker	4	1983	F*	35.2	3110	947/1010	46/48	1180/510	650/580	Y	Y	Y	
Chrysler	New Yorker	4	1985	F*	35.1	3170	685/760	51/35	800/1150	990/700	Y	Y	Y	
Chrysler	New Yorker	4	1988	F	35.0	3650	1362/424	55/43	730/1580	1102/454	NT	NT	NT	NT
Daihatsu	Charade	2HB	1988	F	35.0	2218	768/642	43/37	574/1188	598/388	NT	NT	NT	NT
Datsun	(See Nissan)													
Datsun	200 SX	2HB	1984	F	34.7	2880	1992/582	44/32	1070/510	20/460	Y	*	Y	
Datsun	810	4	1981	R	34.9	3420								N
Dodge	400	2	1982	F	35.0	3044	520/756	44/41	1080/880	1011/914	Y	Y	Y	
Dodge	600	4	1983	F	35.2	3110	947/1010	46/48	1180/510	650/580	Y	Y	Y	
Dodge	600	4	1985	F*	35.1	3170	685/760	51/35	800/1150	990/700	Y	Y	Y	
Dodge	600ES	4	1983	F*	35.2	3110	947/1010	46/48	1180/510	650/580	Y	Y	Y	
Dodge	Aries	2	1981	F*	34.8	2910	605/1731	52/59	1000/540	720/800	Y	Y	Y	
Dodge	Aries	2	1981	R	35.2	2800								Y
Dodge	Aries	4W	1983	F*	35.1	2910	656/1221	52/52	1300/1100	1560/820	Y	*	Y	
Dodge	Aries	4	1985	F*	35.0	3060	831/843	54/44	1085/925	840/595	N	Y	Y	
Dodge	B-150	Van	1986	F	35.0	4535	983/868	68/44	518/3496	375/319	NA	NA	NA	NA
Dodge	Caravan	Van	1984	F	35.1	3791	973/1200	44/42	457/864	546/304	Y	*	Y	
Dodge	Caravan	Van	1987	F	35.0	3660	903/501	43/47	776/1595	453/275	NA	NA	NA	NA
Dodge	Colt	4HB	1982	F	34.9	2488	932/1730	72/44	517/782	506/276	Y	Y	Y	
Dodge	Colt	4HB	1985	F	34.8	2615	787/741	42/32	480/460	1090/370	Y	Y	Y	
Dodge	Colt	4W	1988	F	35.0	2852	1354/816	53/38	844/402	461/1601	NT	NT	NT	NT
Dodge	Colt	4	1989	F	35.0	2790	960/772	ND/42	827/1367	1218/1078	NA	NA	NA	NA
Dodge	Colt Vista	4W	1984	F*	35.4	2980	1530/1004	71/45	2950/450	640/830	Y	*	Y	
Dodge	Colt Vista	4W	1986	F	35.0	2980	810/1356	45/36	5048/1297	858/517	NA	NA	NA	NA
Dodge	Conquest	2HB	1984	F*	35.3	3170	1118/1035	57/43	410/360	180/320	Y	*	Y	
Dodge	D-150	PU	1988	F	35.0	4178	685/466	40/35	1481/396	361/276	NT	NT	NT	NT
Dodge	Dakota	PU	1987	F	35.0	3640	985/754	44/41	324/213	442/460	NA	NA	NA	
Dodge	Daytona	2HB	1984	F	35.4	3000	507/566	37/40	740/860	950/530	Y	*	Y	
Dodge	Daytona	2HB	1989	F	35.0	3320	399/297	39/32	729/795	908/457	NA	NA	NA	NA
Dodge	Dynasty	4	1988	F	35.0	3650	1362/424	55/43	730/1580	1102/454	NA	NA	NA	NA
Dodge	Lancer	4HB	1985	F	34.7	3250	2187/445	38/30	835/840	530/610	Y	Y	Y	
Dodge	Omni	4HB	1982	F	35.2	2670	639/1703	58/43	460/825	600/1450	Y	Y	Y	
Dodge	Shadow	2HB	1987	F	35.0	3000	1488/653	49/36	1003/748	529/486	NA	NA	NA	NA
Dodge	Shadow	4HB	1987	F	35.0	3050	873/ND	52/41	717/832	467/540	NA	NA	NA	NA
Dodge	Spirit	4	1989	F	35.0	3290	1421/537	47/45	672/1295	772/707	NA	NA	NA	NA
Eagle	Medallion	4	1989	F	35.0	3160	745/589	41/39	1721/1738	1574/1670	NA	NA	NA	NA
Eagle	Premier	4	1989	F	35.0	3560	877/868	46/44	742/1011	765/685	NA	NA	NA	NA
Eagle	Summit	4	1989	F	35.0	2790	960/772	ND/42	827/1367	1218/1078	NA	NA	NA	NA
Ford	Aerostar	Van	1987	F	35.0	3618	1568/1070	49/54	286/518	590/446	NA	NA	NA	

Ford	Bronco II 4x4	MPV	1983	F	35.4	3845	789/1038	49/50	270/380	440/340	Y	Y	Y	
Ford	Crown Victoria	4	1984	F*	35.4	4313	1094/1019	58/39	507/385	534/272	N	*	Y	
Ford	E-150 Club	Van	1985	F	35.0	5237	1986/1198	55/50	1193/2139	1806/1065tNA	NA	NA	NA	
Ford	E-150 Club	MPV	1985	F	34.9	5237	1986/1198	55/50	1193/2139	1806/1065	Y	Y	Y	
Ford	Escort	2HB	1981	F	35.2	2590	618/1011	50/40	640/740	480/280	Y	Y	Y	
Ford	Escort	2HB	1981	R*	34.7	2450							Y	
Ford	Escort	2HB	1981	O	35.2	2368	243/603	32/38	672/934	469/763	NT	NT	Y	
Ford	Escort	4HB	1982	F	34.5	2584	950/1070	47/39	1150/1050	1518/1530	Y	Y	Y	
Ford	Escort	2HB	1987	F	35.0	2740	551/418	42/40	1146/1053	465/619	NA	NA	NA	
Ford	Exp	2HB	1981	F	35.0	2542	745/NA	49/53	857/19	320/189	Y	Y	Y	
Ford	Exp	2	1983	F	35.0	2600	1744/796	46/41	1790/420	330/320	Y	Y	Y	
Ford	Exp	2	1983	F	35.2	2590	1744/796	46/41	1790/420	330/320	Y	*	Y	
Ford	F-150	PU	1984	F	35.2	4076	1362/1443	48/52	408/1155	569/458	Y	*	Y	
Ford	F-150	PU	1988	F	35.0	4385	1074/587	56 38	1024/1090	644/295	NT	NT	NT	NT
Ford	Festiva	2	1988	F	35.0	2190	1014/822	52/43	976/876	747/251	NT	NT	NT	NT
Ford	Granada	4	1982	F	34.6	3430	860/1050	ND/52	980/800	460/340	Y	Y	Y	
Ford	LTD	4	1982	F	35.5	4130	960/808	50/43	360/640	350/180	Y	Y	Y	
Ford	LTD	4	1983	F	35.2	3563	609/957	69/54	168/058	110/158	Y	*	Y	
Ford	LTD	4W	1984	F	34.6	3680	646/647	58/67	ND/ND	1850/590	Y	*	Y	
Ford	LTD Crown Vic	4	1984	F*	35.4	4313	1094/1019	58/39	507/385	534/272	N	*	Y	
Ford	Mustang Conv.	2	1984	F	34.8	3560	894/1112	55/38	830/1180	960/1400	N	*	Y	
Ford	Mustang Conv.	2	1990	F	35.0	3865	651/438	42/50	NA	NA	NA	NA	NA	NA
Ford	Mustang LX	2HB	1987	F	35.0	3343	479/301	42/34	580/1589	921/290	NA	NA	NA	
Ford	Probe*	2HB	1989	F	35.0	3060	970/496	46/35	691/870	579/187tNA	NA	NA	NA	
Ford	Ranger	PU	1987	F	35.0	3361	977/551	52/47	739/526	344/701tNA	NA	NA	NA	
Ford	Ranger 4x4	PU	1990	F	35.0	4131	1270/736	61/52	NA	NA	NA	NA	NA	NA
Ford	Taurus	4	1986	F	35.0	3460	1209/695	53/37	824/1485	566/502	Y	Y	Y	
Ford	Taurus	4	1988	F	35.0	3660	707/359	38/47	NT/775	455/438	NT	NT	NT	NT
Ford	Taurus	4	1990	F	35.0	3620	735/609	46/40	NA	NA	NA	NA	NA	NA
Ford	Tempo	4	1984	F	35.0	3080	2955/1104	63/45	750/480	675/370	Y	*	Y	
Ford	Tempo	4	1985	F	34.8	2990	1207/932	52/40	870/580	440/310	Y	Y	Y	
Ford	Tempo	4	1988	F	35.0	3080	721/470	47/50	1113/1773	1037/702	NT	NT	NT	NT
Ford	Tempo GL	2	1985	F	35.1	2996	1551/1449	63/46	2798/542	736/391	Y	Y	Y	
Ford	T-Bird	2	1983	F	35.2	3580	626/795	70/43	625/1200	895/590	Y	Y	Y	
Ford	T-Bird	2	1984	F*	34.9	3560	652/577	55/37	850/1330	1180/945	Y	*	Y	
Ford	T-Bird	2	1989	F	35.0	4110	541/496	44/40	1224/1138	1264/776	NA	NA	NA	NA
Geo	Metro	2	1989	F	35.0	2060	951/1177	ND/33	789/671	458/571	PT			
Geo	Metro	4	1989	F	35.0	2110	1075/840	56/46	805/244	465/1002	NA	NA	NA	NA
Geo	Prizm	4	1989	F	35.0	2810	994/546	49/45	1101/894	451/681	NA	NA	NA	NA
Geo	Prizm	4	1990	F	35.0	2790	1030/1141	47/53	NA	NA	NA	NA	NA	NA
Geo	Tracker	MPV	1989	F	35.0	2930	1345/1763	64/70	1595/1860	2856/2259	F	NA	NA	NA	NA

GMC	C-1500	PU	1984	F*	35.2	4830	534/514	37/39	2026/353	543/290	Y	*	Y	
GMC	C-1500	PU	1988	F	35.0	4308	892/374	47/46	942/1207	622/306	NA	NA	NA	NA
GMC	G-25	Van	1987	F	35.0	5456	1387/1719	67/43	1298/1507	ND/ND	NA	NA	NA	NA
GMC	G-25	Van	1988	F	35.0	4872	3665/1452	97/56	1330/2447	963/259	NA	NA	NA	NA
GMC	Safari	Van	1985	F	35.0	4090	2202/1597	70/61	1845/940	1160/725	NA	NA	NA	NA
GMC	Safari	Van	1988	F	35.0	4415	1603/1424	72/63	1572/1695	700/576	NA	NA	NA	NA
GMC	Safari	Van	1989	F	35.0	4630	1849/1838	64/64	2737/1901	1043/365	NA	NA	NA	NA
GMC	Suburban	MPV	1987	F	35.0	6110	1477/1176	50/42	1911/101	257/358	NA	NA	NA	NA
GMC	S-15	PU	1987	F	35.0	3228	985/522	58/34	1441/1476	1108/699	NA	NA	NA	NA
GMC	S-15 Jimmy	MPV	1985	F*	35.0	3900	1036/1320	62/43	1040/1000	425/155	Y	Y	Y	
GMC	S-15 Jimmy	MPV	1989	F	35.0	4096	834/2482	62/48	ND/ND	ND/ND	NA	NA	NA	NA
GMC	Safari	Van	1985	F*	34.8	4090	2202/1597	70/61	1845/940	1160/725	Y	Y	Y	
Honda	Accord	4	1982	F	34.8	2635	500/403	43/29	1078/1308	1145/754	Y	N	Y	
Honda	Accord DX	4	1986	F	35.0	3062	909/712	ND/33	228/112	ND/ND	Y	Y	Y	
Honda	Accord	2HB	1987	F	35.0	2920	769/382	46/36	863/695	1244/558	NA	NA	NA	NA
Honda	Civic	2HB	1981	F	35.1	2160	607/492	41/35	200/500	1100/540	N	Y	Y	
Honda	Civic	4HB	1981	F	35.0	2456	985/1391	53/43	462/1386	1194/797	Y	Y	Y	
Honda	Civic	4	1981	R	35.0	2386							Y	
Honda	Civic	4W	1984	F	34.9	2510	586/544	43/32	1600/530	1155/820	Y	*	Y	
Honda	Civic	2	1984	F	35.4	2311	563/846	37/43	1067/602	1566/1275	Y	*	Y	
Honda	Civic	2HB	1988	F	35.0	2542	787/533	37/38	767/816	471/184	NT	NT	NT	NT
Honda	Civic CRX	2	1984	F	35.1	2310	571/959	34/34	2850/1975	1970/1880	Y	*	Y	
Honda	Civic CRX	2HB	1989	F	35.0	2303	750/520	39/37	361/903	791/375	NA	NA	NA	NA
Honda	Civic DX	2HB	1988	F	35.0	2542	787/533	37/38	767/816	471/184	NA	NA	NA	NA
Honda	Prelude	2	1984	F	34.7	2780	659/475	43/31	600/510	690/980	Y	*	Y	
Honda	Prelude	2	1990	F	35.0	3062	1279/854	59/48	NA	NA	NA	NA	NA	NA
Hyundai	Excel	2HB	1987	F	35.0	2610	716/1003	55/43	790/345	1360/775	NA	NA	NA	
Hyundai	Excel	4	1986	F	35.0	2710	999/2662	73/55	2248/785	1597/520	NA	NA	NA	NA
Hyundai	Excel	4	1987	F	35.0	2660	757/345	54/46	2408/1794	1187/1006	NA	NA	NA	NA
Hundai	Excel	2HB	1990	F	35.0	2660	696/419	41/39	NA	NA	NA	NA	NA	NA
Hyundai	Sonata	4	1989	F	35.0	3330	1196/937	54/53	869/603	1717/293	NA	NA	NA	NA
Isuzu	I-Mark Deluxe	2	1981	R	35.5	2626								N
Isuzu	I-Mark	4	1985	F	34.8	2850	1514/1543	38/47	535/365	398/385	Y	Y	Y	
Isuzu	I-Mark	4	1986	F	34.9	2380	2172/1146	43/43	486/176	275/260	Y	Y	Y	
Isuzu	I-Mark	4	1987	F	35.0	2570	1809/1042	53/51	351/747	365/225	NA	NA	NA	NA
Isuzu	Impulse	2HB	1984	F	34.6	3230	1769/2454	46/49	850/1530	470/ND	Y	*	Y	
Isuzu	Spacecab	PU	1987	F	35.0	3349	1764/1067	65/58	274/279	483/480	NA	NA	NA	
Isuzu	Spacecab	PU	1988	F	35.0	3747	1873/723	59/55	325/412	397/172	NT	NT	NT	NT
Isuzu	Trooper II 4x4	MPV	1985	F	35.0	3606	916/2189	58/ND	745/1901	133/357	Y	Y	Y	
Isuzu	Trooper II 4x4	MPV	1989	F	35.0	4310	1269/1520	73/59	932/804	322/262	NA	NA	NA	NA
Jeep	Cherokee 4x4	MPV	1989	F	35.0	3912	968/1796	69/43	401/1486	540/337	NA	NA	NA	NA

Make	Model	Body	Year	Drive		Weight								
Jeep	Comanche	PU	1987	F	35.0	3554	1052/2700	62/48	925/923	319/761	NA	NA	NA	NA
Jeep	Wrangler 4x4	MPV	1987	F	35.0	3620	758/1229	44/40	1100/758	1015/783	NA	NA	NA	NA
Lexus	ES250	4	1990	F	35.0	3770	992/630	55/47	NA	NA	NA	NA	NA	NA
Lincoln	Continental	4	1982	F	34.7	4158	757/728	46/37	723/1136	1393/612	Y	Y	Y	
Lincoln	Continental	4	1989	F	35.0	4240	863/492	48/ND	314/1326	1247/1090	NA	NA	NA	NA
Lincoln	Town Car	4	1984	F*	35.4	4313	1094/1019	58/39	507/385	534/272	N	*	Y	
Mazda	323 LX	2	1986	F	35.2	2510	802/894	66/47	425/440	200/325	Y	Y	Y	
Mazda	626	4	1982	F	35.3	2900	969/1693	47/50	575/1215	550/250	Y	Y	Y	
Mazda	626	4	1983	F	35.3	2900	1196/1087	45/56	450/350	260/360	Y	*	Y	
Mazda	626	4	1987	F	35.0	3040	846/801	52/46	820/1300	1487/1255	NA	NA	NA	NA
Mazda	929	4	1988	F	35.0	3920	273/859	51/49	1093/774	450/450	NT	NT	NT	NT
Mazda	B-2000	PU	1986	F	35.0	3080	1434/1647	65/58	620/97	628/311	Y	Y	Y	
Mazda	GLC	4HB	1981	O	35.3	2427	555/516	48/35	313/507	284/146	NT	NT	Y	
Mazda	GLC	4HB	1981	R	35.2	2412								Y
Mazda	Miata Conv.	2	1990	F	35.0	2570	920/531	59/42	NA	NA	NA	NA	NA	NA
Mazda	RX-7	2	1985	F	35.3	2873	921/1345	40/42	369/476	604/809	Y	*	Y	
Mazda	RX-7	2	1988	F	35.0	3320	921/614	39/48	186/1135	268/650	NT	NT	NT	NT
Mercedes Benz	190E	4	1990	F	35.0	3492	800/833	60/58	NA	NA	NA	NA	NA	NA
Mercedes Benz	300SD	4	1984	F	34.7	4270	890/734	63/44	1410/1150	295/490	Y	*	Y	
Mercury	Cougar	2	1983	F*	35.2	3580	626/795	70/43	625/1200	895/590	Y	Y	Y	
Mercury	Cougar	2	1984	F	34.9	3560	652/577	55/37	850/1330	1180/945	Y	*	N	
Mercury	Cougar	2	1989	F	35.0	4110	541/496	44/40	1224/1138	1264/776	NA	NA	NA	NA
Mercury	Grand Marquis	4	1984	F	35.4	4313	1094/1019	58/39	507/385	534/272	N	*	Y	
Mercury	Lynx	2HB	1981	F*	35.2	2590	618/1011	50/40	640/740	480/280	Y	Y	Y	
Mercury	Lynx	2HB	1981	R	34.7	2450								Y
Mercury	Lynx	4HB	1982	F*	34.5	2584	950/1070	47/39	1150/1050	1518/1530	Y	Y	Y	
Mercury	Lynx	2HB	1987	F	35.0	2740	551/418	42/40	1146/1053	465/619	NA	NA	NA	NA
Mercury	Marquis	4	1983	F*	35.2	3563	609/957	69/54	168/58	110/158	Y	Y	Y	
Mercury	Marquis	4W	1984	F*	34.6	3680	646/647	58/67	ND/ND	1850/590	Y	*	Y	
Mercury	Merkur	2HB	1985	F	35.0	3452	1009/1450	55/52	446/736	670/953	NA	NA	NA	NA
Mercury	Sable	4	1986	F	35.1	3570	1237/680	48/44	1039/1780	671/465	Y	Y	Y	
Mercury	Sable	4	1988	F	35.0	3720	712/410	51/35	NA/1512	862/913	NT	NT	NT	NT
Mercury	Topaz	4	1984	F*	35.0	3080	2955/1104	63/45	750/480	675/370	Y	*	Y	
Mercury	Topaz	2	1985	F*	35.1	2996	1551/1449	63/46	2798/542	736/391	Y	Y	Y	
Mercury	Topaz	4	1985	F*	34.8	2990	1207/932	52/40	870/580	440/310	Y	Y	Y	
Mercury	Topaz	4	1987	F	35.0	3180	743/626	64/40	585/1277	957/455	NA	NA	NA	
Mercury	Topaz	4	1988	F	35.0	3080	721/470	47/50	1113/1773	1037/702	NA	NA	NA	NA
Mercury	Tracer	4HB	1989	F	35.0	2690	940/425	48/38	2073/733	658/851	NA	NA	NA	NA
Mitsubishi	Cordia	2	1986	F	35.0	2827	576/997	48/35	306/1967	730/511	NA	NA	NA	NA
Mitsubishi	Eclipse	2HB	1990	F	35.0	2977	772/612	44/40	NA	NA	NA	NA	NA	NA
Mitsubishi	Galant	4	1985	F	35.0	3360	747/986	52/42	910/960	480/440	Y	Y	Y	

Make	Model		Year												
Mitsubishi	Galant	4	1989	F	35.0	3260	971/998	50/40	1613/1229	584/526	NA	NA	NA	NA	
Mitsubishi	Mighty Max	PU	1983	F	35.2	3094	1475/1934	68/71	240/170	320/200	Y	Y	Y		
Mitsubishi	Mirage	4	1989	F	35.0	2790	960/772	ND/42	827/1367	1218/1078	NA	NA	NA	NA	
Mitsubishi	Montero	MPV	1983	F	34.9	3873	1641/1415	54/48	350/127	391/353	Y	Y	Y		
Mitsubishi	Montero	4x4	1988	F	35.0	3926	1320/488	45/50	1303/1001	329/302	NT	NT	NT	NT	
Mitsubishi	Starion	2HB	1987	F	35.0	3450	952/377	48/46	1260/1752	1369/1323	NA	NA	NA		
Mitsubishi	Tredia	4	1984	F	34.7	2740	1314/1521	87/57	1475/350	610/450	Y	*	Y		
Mitsubishi	Van	Van	1989	F	35.0	4066	805/713	49/51	1568/1607	1427/791	NA	NA	NA	NA	
Nissan	(See Datsun)														
Nissan	200SX	4	1987	F	35.0	3218	1226/664	53/37	1390/740	103/89	NA	NA	NA	NA	
Nissan	240SX	2HB	1989	F	35.0	3120	407/525	41/44	1234/656	687/854	NA	NA	NA	NA	
Nissan	300ZX	2	1984	F	35.0	3370	789/1038	45/39	1140/2085	720/1775	Y	*	Y		
Nissan	Axxess	4HB	1990	F	35.0	3433	1051/654	46/46	NA	NA	NA	NA	NA	NA	
Nissan	Maxima	4	1985	F	34.9	3760	1014/1500	63/38	1155/945	720/430	N	Y	Y		
Nissan	Maxima	4	1988	F	35.0	3690	907/861	64/49	1422/1500	885/1049	NA	NA	NA	NA	
Nissan	Maxima	4	1989	F	35.0	3650	808/736	51/44	611/664	1409/1043	NA	NA	NA	NA	
Nissan	Maxima SE	4	1988	F	35.0	3690	907/861	69/49	1422/1500	885/1049	NT	NT	NT	NT	
Nissan	NL Lev	PU	1988	F	35.0	3259	1528/1242	67/53	242/609	655/198	NT	NT	NT	NT	
Nissan	Pickup	PU	1987	F	35.0	3360	1465/1244	57/45	252/531	420/617	NA	NA	NA	NA	
Nissan	Pickup	PU	1988	F	35.0	3259	1528/1242	67/53	242/609	655/198	NA	NA	NA	NA	
Nissan	Pickup	PU	1989	F	35.0	3330	742/965	46/35	794/ND	621/332	NA	NA	NA	NA	
Nissan	Pulsar	4HB	1983	F	35.4	2460	1139/1134	54/39	230/490	270/1100	Y	*	Y		
Nissan	Pulsar NX	2HB	1988	F	35.0	2840	1134/430	40/31	NT/122	226/1742	NT	NT	NT	NT	
Nissan	Sentra	4	1982	F	35.2	2455	549/865	43/46	499/103	1111/251	N	Y	N		
Nissan	Sentra	4	1987	F	35.0	2701	2034/799	61/ND	803/615	304/415	NA	NA	NA	NA	
Nissan	Sentra	4W	1988	F	35.0	2675	1047/526	53/42	880/686	1030/853	NT	NT	NT	NT	
Nissan	Stanza	4HB	1982	F	34.6	2686	974/879	55/39	377/449	704/1289	Y	Y	Y		
Nissan	Stanza	4	1984	F	35.2	2814	1459/2216	58/53	197/714	706/536	Y	*	Y		
Nissan	Stanza	4	1990	F	35.0	3270	1105/629	59/47	NA	NA	NA	NA	NA	NA	
Nissan	Van XE	Van	1988	F	35.0	4190	949/597	54/36	1326/1708	661/1331	NT	NT	NT	NT	
Oldsmobile	98 Regency	4	1985	F*	34.9	3850	1550/662	50/37	1145/820	710/400	Y	*	Y		
Oldsmobile	98 Regency	4	1988	F	35.0	3855	1467/794	54/37	712/479	1366/686	NA	NA	NA	NA	
Oldsmobile	Calais	2	1985	F*	34.5	3210	1140/595	34/35	815/400	585/315	Y	Y	Y		
Oldsmobile	Calais	2	1986	F	35.0	3150	823/453	36/27	1019/740	526/533	NA	NA	NA	NA	
Oldsmobile	Calais	2	1987	F	35.0	2990	846/601	44/41	879/1848	497/529	NA	NA	NA	NA	
Oldsmobile	Calais	4	1987	F	35.0	3120	405/328	70/40	1085/1737	1435/555	NA	NA	NA	NA	
Oldsmobile	Cutlass Ciera	4	1982	F*	35.0	3273	478/395	33/21	774/1052	918/595	Y	Y	Y		
Oldsmobile	Cutlass Ciera	4W	1984	F*	35.0	3590	518/440	31/28	635/270	580/500	Y	*	Y		
Oldsmobile	Cutlass Ciera	2	1986	F	35.0	3360	647/928	37/49	945/740	670/720	NA	NA	NA	NA	
Oldsmobile	Cutlass Ciera	4	1986	F	35.0	3250	699/672	40/37	740/240	690/490	NA	NA	NA	NA	
Oldsmobile	Cutlass Sup	2	1984	F	34.8	3700	781/1074	40/35	1500/790	450/525	Y	*	Y		

Oldsmobile	Cutlass Sup	2	1988	F	35.0	3710	880/535	50/33	996/686	642/526	NA	NA	NA	NA
Oldsmobile	Delta 88	4	1983	F*	35.3	4120	882/1084	42/47	675/650	600/544	Y	Y	Y	
Oldsmobile	Delta 88	4	1986	F	35.4	3710	688/681	50/33	476/978	731/364	Y	Y	Y	
Oldsmobile	Delta 88	2	1986	F	35.0	3650	908/752	39/40	879/1181	583/368	NA	NA	NA	NA
Oldsmobile	Delta 88	4	1988	F	35.0	3950	710/539	51/38	1350/2119	520/593	NT	NT	NT	NT
Oldsmobile	Firenza	4	1986	F	35.0	2999	784/602	42/31	79/658	1112/487	NA	NA	NA	NA
Oldsmobile	Toronado	2	1986	F	35.3	3690	826/650	45/45	944/570	1419/498	Y	Y	Y	
Peugeot	505	4	1987	F	35.0	3360	1831/1786	60/50	300/546	535/176	NA	NA	NA	NA
Peugeot	505	4	1988	F	35.0	3500	1701/1457	60/45	1657/930	751/328	NA	NA	NA	NA
Peugeot	505 G1S	4	1988	F	35.0	3500	1701/1457	60/45	1657/930	751/328	NT	NT	NT	NT
Peugeot	5056	4	1989	F	35.0	3510	1983/2192	64/77	966/839	1024/554	NA	NA	NA	NA
Peugeot	5055	4	1983	F	35.1	3617	819/1157	52/49	ND/ND	ND/319	Y	*	Y	
Plymouth	Acclaim	4	1989	F	35.0	3270	663/810	46/50	1201/1552	840/873	NA	NA	NA	NA
Plymouth	Caravelle	4	1985	F	35.1	3170	685/760	51/35	800/1150	990/700	Y	Y	Y	
Plymouth	Colt	4HB	1985	F*	34.8	2615	787/741	42/32	480/460	1090/370	Y	Y	Y	
Plymouth	Colt	4	1989	F	35.0	2790	960/772	ND/42	827/1367	1218/1078	NA	NA	NA	NA
Plymouth	Colt Vista	4W	1984	F	35.4	2980	1530/1004	71/45	2950/450	640/830	Y	*	Y	
Plymouth	Colt Vista	4	1986	F	34.7	2980	810/1356	45/36	5048/1297	858/517	Y	Y	Y	
Plymouth	Conquest	2HB	1984	F	35.3	3170	1118/1035	57/43	410/360	180/320	Y	*	Y	
Plymouth	Horizon	4HB	1982	F*	35.2	2670	639/1073	58/43	460/825	600/1450	Y	Y	Y	
Plymouth	Reliant	2	1981	F	34.8	2910	605/1731	52/59	1000/540	720/800	Y	Y	Y	
Plymouth	Reliant	2	1981	R*	35.2	2800								Y
Plymouth	Reliant	4	1981	O	34.9	2798	355/566	31/50	1655/883	886/1429	NT	NT	Y	
Plymouth	Reliant	4W	1983	F	35.1	2910	656/1221	52/52	1300/1100	1560/820	Y	*	Y	
Plymouth	Reliant	4	1985	F	35.0	3060	831/843	54/44	1085/925	840/595	N	Y	Y	
Plymouth	Sapporo	2	1981	R	35.0	3247								N
Plymouth	Sundance	2HB	1987	F	35.0	3000	1488/653	49/36	1003/748	529/486	NA	NA	NA	NA
Plymouth	Sundance	4HB	1987	F	35.0	3050	873/ND	52/41	717/832	467/540	NA	NA	NA	NA
Plymouth	Voyager	Van	1984	F*	35.1	3791	973/1200	44/42	457/864	546/304	Y	*	Y	
Plymouth	Voyager	Van	1987	F	35.0	3660	903/501	43/47	776/1595	453/275	NA	NA	NA	
Pontiac	1000	4HB	1984	F	35.3	2746	1886/1306	42/57	2512/298	311/663	Y	*	Y	
Pontiac	2000 Conv.	2	1984	F*	35.0	3110	884/401	43/29	780/850	380/440	Y	*	Y	
Pontiac	6000	4	1982	F*	35.0	3273	478/395	33/21	774/1052	918/595	Y	Y	Y	
Pontiac	6000	4W	1984	F*	35.0	3590	518/440	31/28	635/270	580/500	Y	*	Y	
Pontiac	6000	4	1986	F	35.0	3250	699/672	40/37	740/240	690/490	NA	NA	NA	NA
Pontiac	6000	2	1986	F	35.0	3360	647/928	37/49	945/740	670/720	NA	NA	NA	NA
Pontiac	Bonneville	4	1988	F	35.0	3950	710/539	51/38	1350/2119	520/593	NA	NA	NA	NA
Pontiac	Fiero	2	1984	F	35.1	3000	309/356	31/30	850/840	740/800	Y	*	Y	
Pontiac	Firebird	2	1982	F*	35.4	3428	563/577	39/32	901/1004	258/358	Y	Y	Y	
Pontiac	Firebird	2	1983	F	35.2	3330	408/376	34/32	900/480	100/125	Y	Y	Y	
Pontiac	Grand Am	2	1985	F*	34.5	3210	1140/595	34/35	815/400	585/315	Y	Y	Y	

49

Make	Model		Year											
Pontiac	Grand Am	4	1986	F	35.0	3150	823/453	36/27	1019/740	526/533	NA	NA	NA	NA
Pontiac	Grand Am	2	1987	F	35.0	2990	846/601	44/41	879/1848	497/529	NA	NA	NA	NA
Pontiac	Grand Am	4	1987	F	35.0	3120	405/328	70/40	1085/1737	1435/555	NA	NA	NA	NA
Pontiac	Grand Prix	2	1984	F*	34.8	3700	781/1074	40/35	1500/790	450/525	Y	*	Y	
Pontiac	Grand Prix	2	1988	F	35.0	3710	880/535	50/33	996/686	642/526	NA	NA	NA	NA
Pontiac	Le Mans	2	1988	F	35.0	2670	819/897	57/44	1263/792	378/389	NT	NT	NT	NT
Pontiac	Parisienne	4	1984	F	34.9	4140	ND/1055	52/48	540/180	495/465	Y	*	Y	
Pontiac	Sunbird	4	1987	F	35.0	2961	603/404	36/37	428/1079	483/211	NA	NA	NA	
Renault	181	4	1981	F	35.2	2750	1150/1659	47/36	360/280	800/700	N	Y	Y	
Renault	181	4	1981	R	35.5	2688								Y
Renault	181	4	1981	O	34.5	2808	731/1001	38/39	269/458	430/543	NT	NT	Y	
Renault	Alliance	4	1984	F	34.8	2460	940/ND	55/42	315/445	1550/225	Y	*	Y	
Renault	Alliance Conv.	2	1985	F	34.9	2810	1519/2678	62/47	175/280	630/1185	Y	Y	Y	
Renault	Encore	4HB	1984	F	34.9	2600	912/1045	63/49	248/810	980/268	Y	*	Y	
Renault	Fuego	2	1982	F	35.0	2902	3768/2484	50/35	493/684	396/1136	N	Y	Y	
Renault	Medallion	4	1988	F	35.0	3100	1656/873	57/38	205/617	411/1193	NT	NT	NT	NT
Renault	Sportwagon	4W	1984	F	35.1	3102	2053/2721	43/52	247/1476	1138/1319	Y	*	Y	
Saab	900	4	1982	F	35.3	3220	734/1166	39/35	990/725	800/1275	Y	Y	Y	
Saab	900S	2HB	1988	F	35.0	3340	718/1250	46/35	1776/1395	4369/1535	NT	NT	NT	NT
Saab	9000	4	1986	F	34.9	3390	773/1443	71/46	484/ND	541/421	Y	Y	Y	
Saab	9000	4	1987	F	35.0	3520	584/440	37/35	120/346	435/638	NA	NA	NA	
Subaru	DL	4	1985	F	35.1	2698	1361/792	57/39	716/276	622/409	Y	*	Y	
Subaru	GL	4	1986	F	35.0	2712	1728/898	51/52	838/376	456/402	NA	NA	NA	NA
Subaru	GL	4	1987	F	35.0	2740	1339/884	58/44	1016/694	485/309	NA	NA	NA	NA
Subaru	Justy DL	2HB	1987	F	35.0	2110	611/547	42/38	529/1256	595/426	NA	NA	NA	NA
Subaru	XT	2	1986	F	35.0	2759	744/646	38/30	978/185	440/568	NA	NA	NA	NA
Suzuki	Samurai 4x4	2	1986	F	35.1	2666	984/865	48/34	1230/110	264/1116	Y	N	Y	
Suzuki	Sidekick	MPV	1989	F	35.0	2930	1345/1763	64/70	1595/1860	2856/2259	NA	NA	NA	NA
Suzuki	Swift	4	1989	F	35.0	2110	1075/840	56/46	805/244	465/1002	NA	NA	NA	NA
Toyota	4-Runner 4x4	MPV	1985	F	35.5	3897	1478/949	64/52	1400/243	570/317	Y	Y	Y	
Toyota	4-Runner 4x4	MPV	1990	F	35.0	4530	1306/1133	48/47	NA	NA	NA	NA	NA	NA
Toyota	Camry	4	1983	F	34.9	2980	809/495	48/40	220/370	395/550	Y	*	Y	
Toyota	Camry	4	1987	F	35.0	3250	871/973	51/46	1380/1200	1160/1167	NA	NA	NA	NA
Toyota	Celica	2	1982	F	34.7	3060	702/530	36/45	456/448	360/359	Y	Y	Y	
Toyota	Celica	2	1986	F	34.9	2950	627/430	42/40	382/721	439/593	Y	Y	Y	
Toyota	Celica	2	1990	F	35.0	2980	834/685	50/37	NA	NA	NA	NA	NA	NA
Toyota	Corolla	4W	1983	F	35.3	2760	767/1367	67/43	1823/700	334/353	Y	Y	Y	
Toyota	Corolla	2	1984	R	35.0	2680	432/602	37/47	1100/450	580/300	Y	*	Y	
Toyota	Corolla	4	1984	F	34.9	2610	630/611	41/42	1320/730	340/395	Y	*	Y	
Toyota	Corolla	4	1989	F	35.0	2810	994/546	49/45	1101/894	451/681	NA	NA	NA	NA
Toyota	Corolla FX	2HB	1988	F	35.0	2750	593/397	42/40	719/1162	300/393	NT	NT	NT	NT

Make	Model		Year											
Toyota	Corona	4	1982	F	34.9	3040	842/828	59/40	1400/1178	888/507	Y	Y	Y	
Toyota	Cressida	4	1981	F	35.1	3417	1980/771	55/50	1710/1982	1644/1807	Y	Y	Y	
Toyota	Cressida	4	1981	R	34.9	3371								Y
Toyota	Cressida	4	1985	F	35.0	3690	883/914	50/58	1725/1820	1355/1820	NA	NA	NA	NA
Toyota	Cressida	4	1989	F	35.0	3940	790/544	51/51	1632/1554	1246/1107	NA	NA	NA	NA
Toyota	MR-2	2	1985	F	35.3	2918	655/515	34/34	238/61	612/327	Y	Y	Y	
Toyota	Pickup	PU	1987	F	35.0	3222	1184/699	57/39	437/500	364/532	NA	NA	NA	NA
Toyota	Pickup	PU	1989	F	35.0	3171	1520/883	47/46	1340/614	1053/493	NA	NA	NA	NA
Toyota	Starlet	2HB	1981	F	35.1	2214	1836/1351	65/48	830/989	652/124	Y	Y	Y	
Toyota	Starlet	2	1981	R	35.4	2221								Y
Toyota	Tercel	4HB	1984	F	35.1	2440	658/492	43/41	245/370	200/160	Y	*	Y	
Toyota	Tercel	2HB	1988	F	35.0	2470	1005/398	40/42	1245/572	367/261	NT	NT	NT	NT
Toyota	Tercel 4x4	4W	1983	F	35.2	2826	839/535	43/42	121/186	274/170	Y	Y	Y	
Toyota	Van	Van	1989	F	35.0	3805	1183/530	59/54	1199/2741	474/847	NA	NA	NA	NA
Toyota	Van Wagon	Van	1984	F	35.4	3616	984/748	50/54	2263/2450	615/1011	Y	*	Y	
Volkswagen	Fox	2	1987	F	35.0	2610	1801/2140	52/52	484/723	924/450	NA	NA	NA	NA
Volkswagen	Fox	2	1988	F	35.0	2700	1114/1425	55/44	344/NT	663/478	NT	NT	NT	NT
Volkswagen	Fox	2	1989	F	35.0	2640	787/818	64/58	139/738	1019/508	NA	NA	NA	NA
Volkswagen	Golf	4HB	1986	F	35.0	2620	896/644	48/46	1695/1482	1511/1660	NA	NA	NA	NA
Volkswagen	Jetta	4	1981	F	34.9	2650	1210/1272	68/52	1276/1191	1559/1286	N	Y	Y	
Volkswagen	Jetta	4	1981	R	35.0	2650								Y
Volkswagen	Jetta	4	1981	O	34.8	2521	161/517	35/31	758/1295	1547/1163	NT	NT	Y	Y
Volkswagen	Jetta	4	1985	F	34.8	2844	898/1008	50/51	362/396	711/516	Y	Y	Y	
Volkswagen	Quantum	4	1982	F	34.6	2954	1353/1194	53/41	180/436	561/413	Y	Y	Y	
Volkswagen	Scirocco	2	1982	F	35.1	2680	1482/683	54/37	330/275	200/175	Y	Y	Y	
Volkswagen	Scirocco	2	1986	F	35.0	2580	887/1070	52/ND	394/481	184/449	Y	Y	Y	
Volkswagen	Vanagon	Van	1985	F	34.9	3780	1905/1060	52/44	2140/1615	2430/1050	NT	NT	Y	
Volkswagen	Vanagon	Van	1988	F	35.0	4120	1320/899	59/48	2930/1963	1911/1014	NT	NT	NT	NT
Volvo	740 GLE	4	1988	F	35.0	3550	519/445	42/42	1143/1793	723/634	NT	NT	NT	NT
Volvo	760 GLE	4	1983	F	35.2	3560	791/778	45/41	1360/286	505/630	Y	Y	Y	
Volvo	DL	2	1982	F	34.9	3354	550/381	45/35	154/1147	892/227	NT	NT	NT	NT
Volvo	DL	4	1985	F	34.7	3400	651/310	36/25	350/1020	590/ND	Y	Y	Y	
Volvo	DL Wagon	4	1985	F	34.6	3590	621/262	33/31	100/1005	630/615	Y	Y	Y	
Yugo	GV	2	1986	F	35.1	2320	1415/1318	59/38	870/86	695/525	N	Y	Y	
Yugo	GV	2	1987	F	35.0	2320	1855/379	45/41	ND/585	701/172	NA	NA	NA	

Please note that where there is no information listed, either the data was not tested (NT) or not available (NA or ND).

## Chapter 6

Keeping Your Car: Preventing Car Theft

For every 46 registered cars in the U.S., one will have a theft associated with it. With car thefts on the upswing, more people should become conscious of how they park their cars and where they leave their keys.

According to the F.B.I. and federal and local governments, more than 1,000,000 cars are stolen in the United States each year. Out of those million cars, statistics show that 800,000 cars were left open, and 400,000 had their keys left in the ignition! Logically, 400,000 car thefts might have been avoided last year alone if motorists would have taken their keys with them.

With such staggering statistics, it would appear that no car is theft proof. However, about 25% of the cars stolen in the United States are stolen by amateurs. Such thefts can be avoided and many thefts perpetrated by professionals can be prevented simply by adding some anti-theft devices and/or by disabling the car yourself. However, these measures still are not fool-proof. According to the F.B.I., 35,000 cars a year are stolen by being towed away!

The Top 20 car theft capitals are listed below. People residing in these high-risk areas need to be particularly cautious.

CAR THEFT CAPITALS

Cities with over 50,000 population that led the nation in car theft rates in 1986 (per 100,000 population)

	THEFT RATE		THEFT RATE
1. Newark, NJ	4,052	11. Pittsburgh, PA	2,283
2. Southfield, MI	3,768	12. National City, CA	2,263
3. Boston, MA	3,409	13. Elizabeth, NJ	2,227
4. Detroit, MI	2,909	14. Fort Worth, TX	2,209
5. Irvington, NJ	2,832	15. Cleveland, OH	2,148
6. West Palm Beach, FL	2,804	16. Miami, FL	2,123
7. Huntington Park, CA	2,565	17. Providence, RI	2,051
8. Camden, NJ	2,438	18. Memphis, TN	1,962
9. Brockton, MA	2,377	19. Houston, TX	1,921
10. East Orange, NJ	2,350	20. Union City, NJ	1,896

Source: FBI Uniform Crime Reports, 1986

Some ways to prevent theft: There are four things you can do to thwart many of the over 250,000 amateur car thefts in the U.S. each year.

Replace fat lock buttons with thin ones: The key to discouraging an auto theft is to deny the thief access to your car. Many cars still come equipped with button-type door locks, while others are furnished with tapered models. If your car is equipped with button-type knobs, replace them immediately as they are easily snared with coat hangers.

Never keep a spare set of keys in the car: Keep the spare set of car keys with you at all times. Even an amateur thief knows that there are only a few places in or about your car where you can hide them.

Keep the windows rolled up tightly: All a thief needs is a slightly opened window, a bent wire hanger, and a car with button door lock knobs, and he's in your car. Keep the windows up and the car locked even when your car is in your own driveway. Most car thefts occur in residential neighborhoods, particularly late at night.

Park your car nose out: This especially holds true when you are parked in a driveway. If anyone is tampering with the hood of your car, he could be spotted by a passerby or by a cruising patrol car. In parking garages or in parking lots, if you park with the nose out, someone who is trying to open your hood or someone tampering underneath the hood can be seen more readily.

Never leave your car running: The F.B.I. attributes many thefts to cars that were left running while the driver dashed into a store to "pick up a quart of milk." Many thieves hang out in front of convenience stores just to steal autos left running while the driver is out of the car.

Change all the locks: One key shouldn't open all the locks in your car. Have a special lock installed for the trunk and one for the front door. You should have three different keys: door lock, trunk, and ignition. This makes it tougher for some thieves who have a series of keys to certain makes and models of cars. In fact, the automobile manufacturers make up more than two dozen keys for each different model car. Dispite your best efforts however, if a thief is equipped, he can probably open you door, start your car, and drive it away.

It has been scientifically proven that a thief with the proper tools and know-how can steal a car in less than three minutes. By making it as time consuming as possible to steal your car, you are improving the odds against it becoming a theft statistic.

Anti-theft devices: There has yet to be an anti-theft device that has been proven beyond a shadow of a doubt to be fail-safe. They can all be beaten. What an anti-theft device gives you is time, time that a crook doesn't have, therefore, it increases your chances of keeping your car.

Plug-Type Kill Switch: This has been proven to be one of the most effective ways to prevent theft. This plug can be detached from the dashboard and carried around comfortably until the driver is ready to start the car. The plug is made up of a series of adapters that plug into little steel shafts. Without this device plugged in, there is absolutely no way to start your car. The typical way that a thief gets your car started is to cross two ignition wires. When he reaches your car and he finds that this plug type anti-theft device exists he will probably walk away. Only one ignition wire exists, the other one is in the plug, safely tucked away in your pocket.

Kill Switch: This has become the most popular way to avoid car theft.

It is a plain switch hidden somewhere in your car. This switch has to be activated before your engine will even turn over.

Alarm System: Alarms on cars are becoming more elaborate. If anyone touches your car's door handle, the alarm will go off. If anyone touches the hood, the trunk, or even jostles your automobile, the alarm will go off. Most alarm systems have a secondary system. If the thief beats the primary system and actually gets into the car, by the time he tries to start the ignition by crossing the two ignition wires, another alarm will go off. Alarms do work, and are priced relative to how intricate they are. Many are offered as options on new cars. A comparison guide to alarm type and cost is presented on the following page.

Fuel Switch: This device is designed to shut off the flow of gasoline into your carburetor. It can be hidden virtually anywhere in your car. Even if a thief gets the car started, it won't stay started for long; it stalls out before he gets anywhere.

The Armored Collar: This is a steel plate that locks around your steering column and over your ignition.

Crook Lock: This is a bar that attaches around your brake pedal and steering wheel, securing both in place. Both the crook lock and armored collar are somewhat cumbersome but they are effective. They can be seen through the window and discourage the amateur thief.

Disabling your own car: There are some people who just don't go for the frills of an anti-theft device. They prefer to disable their own cars. There are several ways that this can be done.

Remove the ignition lead: The coil which starts your car has a wire lead which goes from the coil right into your distributor. It is easy to take off. Take the lead off the coil, follow it down into the distributor and take it off the top of the distributor cap. You can carry the wire with you in your pocket or purse.

Remove the rotor: Inside your distributor cap, there is a small plastic device called the rotor. The rotor is the device that distributes the electrical current to the leads of the distributor which are connected to the spark plugs. The car will not start without the rotor.

Getting your car back after it's stolen: Even after you've accomplished the aforementioned tasks, your car could be stolen. Then the real trouble begins. Even if law enforcement officials eventually find your car, it may not look like your car. Most thieves try to change the complexion of a stolen car. They may paint it a different color, grind off the serial numbers, and remove any identifying marks. There are certain things you can do to identify your car even if it has been changed:

Engrave some unnoticed areas: You can get an engraving tool and put your name or any other identifying mark on some hidden parts of your car. You can engrave your car anywhere; pull up some of the rug and engrave it on the floor or engrave the upper inside portion of your trunk, underneath the rocker panels, or anyplace that is not conspicuous.

Leave a calling card: It seems odd, but leaving a calling card in your car where it will not be noticed is one of the best things to do. You can drop a calling card down the window wells. If the police have trouble identifying a changed car, you can have them remove the door to discover

HOW ALARMS COMPARE

The table shows some of the companies that manufacture, sell and install theft-prevention devices for cars. Additional accessories can be added to most systems at extra cost. The "hood protection" column includes devices that feature either a hood alarm hook-up or hood lock. "Motion sensor" systems react to motion or vibration outside the car. "Interior sensor" systems generally react to sound or "current interrupt," when a door opens or a light goes on in the car.

Active Arming	Passive Arming	Alarm	Hood Protection	Motion/Vibration Sensor	Interior Sensor	Disabling Device	Remote Control	Steering Lock	Paging Device	Homing Device	VIN Etching System	COMPANY	PRICE
												PROFESSIONALLY INSTALLED	
	•				•	•	•		•			AUTO PAGE AP/4600	$377
•	•	•					•					AUTO PAGE RF/09	$499
											•	AUTO SECURITY CO.	$ 40*
•		•		•			•					CLIFFORD CLIFFALARM	$250†
•		•		•		•	•					CLIFFORD IPS	$295†
•	•	•		•	•	•	•					CLIFFORD SUPER III	$499†
•	•	•	•	•		•	•					CLIFFORD ADVANTAGE	$695†
•	•	•		•		•	•					CLIFFORD SYSTEM III	$399
•	•	•		•		•	•					CLIFFORD INTELEGUARD 500**	$600
	•	•	•	•	•				•			CRIMESTOPPER CP-4901	$180
	•	•	•		•	•	•					CRIMESTOPPER CS-8706	$300
	•	•	•	•	•	•						HI-PRO HP-2502	$400-$430
•	•	•	•	•	•	•	•					HI-PRO HP-8710	$450-$475
	•									•		LO-JACK SYSTEM	$595
•	•	•	•	•			•					SECO-LARM ENFORCER 5300	$300*
	•	•	•	•								SECO-LARM CRIMEBUSTER 9	$100
	•	•	•						•			SECO-LARM ENFORCER 5900	$250
•	•	•	•		•	•	•					SENACO S-910	$199
•	•	•	•	•	•	•						SERPICO PO7	$ 80
•	•	•	•	•			•					TECHNE UNGO TL-1600RF	$314
•	•	•	•	•			•					TECHNE UNGO TL-1275	$199
•		•	•		•	•	•					VSE DERRINGER	$339
•	•	•	•		•	•	•					VSE QUANTUM VS-8603	$395
	•					•						VSE SURE STOP	$ 40
												DO-IT-YOURSELF DEVICES	
•								•				ANES AL-300 AUTO-LOK	$ 20
•			•			•						ANES HL-PRO-10 HOODLOCK	$ 49
•	•	•	•		•	•	•					ANES RC-300	$129
											•	AUTOMARK VIN KIT	$ 20
•		•		•			•					AUTO PAGE RF/06S	$140
•								•				THE CLUB	$ 60
•		•	•	•	•		•					SERPICO GR-2	$180

*Price includes installation. †West Coast price; includes installation. **Price includes options not listed here.

55

your calling card.

Marked cars: On April 24, 1986 Congress ruled that certain parts on "high-theft" cars must be marked with an indentification number put on by the manufacturer. Cars affected are the Buick Riviera, Toyota Celica Supra, Cadillac Eldorado, Chevrolet Corvette, Pontiac Firebird, Mazda RX-7, Chevrolet Camaro, Porsche 911, Pontiac Grand Prix and the Oldsmobile Toronado.

Keeping your car safe in a parking lot: Cars often are stolen from parking lots by thieves who are in cahoots with the attendants. Don't tell the attendant how long you will be; it only assists the thief's timing. Write down odometer readings in view of the attendant so your car cannot be moved and parts replaced. Be sure to lock all packages, CB radios, and tapes in the trunk before arriving at the parking lot. Leave only the ignition key with the attendant so that the trunk is inaccessible. Some thieves even have duplicated house keys left on the chain if given the chance. You may not have your car stolen, but when you get home you could be in for an unpleasant surprise. Finally, be sure to keep your claim check. Supposedly, no one can remove your car without it.

## Chapter 7

Buying Replacement Tires: Understanding The Ratings

Have you ever wondered what the letters and numbers mean on the side of a tire, the ones that look like P175/80ZR13? The "P" stands for passenger meaning that it is for use for the typical weights a passenger vehicle would carry. The "175/80" refers to the tread width and height. The higher the numbers, the larger the tire dimensions. The "Z" is a speed rating. Speed ratings are marked either with "H", "V", or "Z". Speed ratings of up to 130 m.p.h. are rated H, up to 149 m.p.h. are rated V, and over 149 m.p.h. are rated Z. The "R" denotes it is a radial tire. If it were a "B", it would be a bias-belted tire. The number "13" stands for the wheel diameter in inches. These numbers usually range from 13 to 17 inches. Remember that it is possible for three tires that have identical sizes printed on the sidewall to vary in width by as much as an inch of tread they put down on the street. This is due to some differences in the mold shape and construction design.

There are four kinds of tires commonly used: bias ply, bias belt, steel belted and glass belted radials.

Bias Ply Tires have two or more layers of material. The cords in each layer run at an angle to the tread.

Bias Belted Tires have an additional layer of material above the angled or biased layer. It follows the circumference of the tire.

Steel Belted Radials have one layer of material running radially around the tire. This layer is covered by another belt of material. Radial tires are longer lasting but reputed to give a less comfortable ride. Some authorities claim the treads tend to flatten more readily on radials.

Glass Belted Tires have fiberglass reinforced belts over a construction of rubber and other materials. They are constructed similarly to steel belted radials but with different components.

Some basic rules should be followed in selecting tires for your car. Never choose a smaller tire than those which came with the car. They should always be replaced with the same size designation, or approved options, as recommended by the automobile or tire manufacturer. Interchangeability of different types is not always possible due to differences in load ratings, tire dimensions, clearances and rim sizes, particularly with older cars. Tires of different size, construction, and stages of wear may affect vehicle handling and stability. For best all-around handling, tires of the same type of construction should be used on all four wheel positions unless designed for special service to improve performance, such as winter or snow tires. In selecting only a pair, the replacement tires should be the same size and construction. They should be put on the rear wheels for better traction, handling, and extra protection against flats. A single new tire should be paired on the rear axle with the tire having the most tread depth of the other three.

Careful attention to proper inflation can increase tire life and assure a safer and more comfortable ride. If tires are unevenly inflated, the car may pull to one side. Tire pressures must follow the recommendations of the manufacturer with respect to type of travel and load. Tire pressure must always be checked when the tires are cool. Tire pressure can drop by as much as 7 pounds in the winter.

Buying a tire to fit your needs: Tire products have improved in quality during the past ten years and consumers can look forward to even more innovations. Soon tires will be mass produced by a casting or injection molding process that will take a 20 inch rim instead of the standard 15 inch, and they will be guaranteed for 100,000 miles.

As described previously, there are several different tire styles to buy. The most popular tires today are steel-belted radials. In fact, the latest statistics indicate that more than 70% of cars rolling off the showroom floor are equipped with steel-belted radials. This does not mean that steel-belted radials are standard equipment on 70% of the new car models, but rather that up to 70% of all new car buyers specifically request that steel-belted radials come with the car. Glass-belted radials are a distant second with only 20% of the new cars sold using them, while 2% of all new cars are being equipped with bias-belted tires.

Eventually most cars will have some sort of belted tire. It has been proven that belted construction stands up better under wear and tear, but their air pressure must be monitored carefully at the manufacturer's recommended intervals to maintain their life.

Steel-belted radials are supposed to be long-lasting, high performance tires which could last up to 50,000 miles. However, as in all consumable items, the quality of tires changes from manufacturer to manufacturer. That's why there has been a tire rating system devised called the Uniform Tire Quality Grading System.

You will be able to discover the tire rating of your new replacement tires by looking at the label affixed to the tread. Unravelling the tire rating maze may be simplified by being familiar with the components of the label.

Traction rating: Television advertisements often demonstrate the effectiveness of a tire by showing it's stopping ability on a water soaked highway. An independent laboratory in Texas working for the Federal Government actually uses a drenched roadway to test traction as this is the best way to learn the stopping ability of a tire. The Texas lab uses two types of surfaces for the testing: asphalt and concrete. Car tires were tested identically on both surfaces.

The test is conducted with a car going 40 M.P.H. around a track. At a certain point the car brakes, and the length it takes for the car to come to a complete stop is then translated into a Traction Rating. The wet pavement gives the car a longer stopping distance upon which to gauge the actual traction of a tire. Each of the tires tested can get an "A" rating if the car stops at below the prescribed distance on both asphalt and concrete surfaces.

If a tire passes on both surfaces, it gets an "A" rating. It it fails on one but passes the other, then the tire will get a "B" rating. Another way for a tire to get a "B" rating for traction is by beating the "B" rated distance on both concrete and asphalt. If the car goes beyond the "B" rating distance on either surface, then it is given a "C" rating. Tires that make the "C" length for stopping on both surfaces will be rated as a "C" for traction. There is no way to tell if a tire failed only one part of the "B" rating to earn it a "C," or if the tire just made the "C" rated distance.

The editors of **Car Savvy** recommend that you buy "A" or "B" rated tires for traction. These will give you better handling and will last longer.

Treadwear rating: Rating a tire's treadwear is difficult. Treadwear is the most common selling tool for the tire manufacturer. The tire center in Texas has used the number 100 as the average number for rating treadwear on tires. A rating of 100 means that a tire will go 30,000 miles, with that distance changing according to a driver's personal driving habits and how well the driver keeps his tires conditioned.

For instance, if you buy a car with a treadwear of 110, you can expect to get approximately 33,000 miles on your tires. In order to figure the ratings and mileage for yourself, you must figure that 110 means 10% over 30,000 or 33,000 miles. If a tire is given a treadwear rating of 90, you can then expect your tire to get 90% of 30,000 or 27,000 miles.

The editors of **Car Savvy** recommend that you buy a tire with at least a 100 treadwear rating. However, this can change according to your driving needs. For example, if you must buy tires but you only anticipate keeping your present car for another 5,000 miles, you would probably be better off buying a tire with a lower treadwear rating. However, if you anticipate selling your car and you feel that better tires will enhance the value of your automobile when you sell it, then you should buy a tire with a better treadwear rating.

Temperature rating: The temperature rating test is the most grueling test of all. In order to get an "A" rating for temperature resistance, a tire must survive a sustained run at 115 m.p.h. in a test room that is heated to almost 100°F. A tire gets a "B" rating if it sustains 100 m.p.h. in a 100°F heated room. All tires are required by law to have a "C" rating which is a run of 85 m.p.h. in a room heated to 100°F.

During the temperature rating test, the tires are overloaded to stretch them to the limit. Very few tires can withstand the punishment of getting an "A" rating, but those that do are exceptional. The majority of the tires tested get a "B" rating. "C" rated tires are the most frequently sold tires today. They make up approximately 50% of the market.

The temperature rating on a tire comes into play during summer driving. Blow-outs can occur during summer driving because of overheating. If a tire is properly inflated, and it is an "A" rated tire for temperature, the chances of sustaining a blow-out because of an overheating condition are minimal.

Steel belted vs. bias ply tires: Several years ago there was a great controversy as to whether steel belted tires were better than bias-ply tires. Even though tests have shown that steel belted radials are more puncture resistant, there are bias-belted tires with identical treadwear, temperature and traction ratings. On the whole, however, steel belted

TIRE DATA

Rim Size __________   Tire Size __________

Brand Name	Serial Number	Speedometer Reading ON	Speedometer Reading OFF	Total Tire miles	Purchase Price
	1				
	2				
	3				
	4				
	5				
	6				
	7				

The figures 1 to 7 identify the individual tires of your car for use in a planned rotation program as illustrated on the following page. Proper tire care pays dividends in safety, comfort and cost. Use of the chart takes the guessing out of tire rotation. Keeping snow tires on their own rims will result in easier installation and, in the long run, less cost.

TIRE AIR PRESSURE

TIRE ROTATION RECORD

NORMAL		WITH LOAD		SNOW TIRES	
Summer	Winter	Summer	Winter	Normal	Load

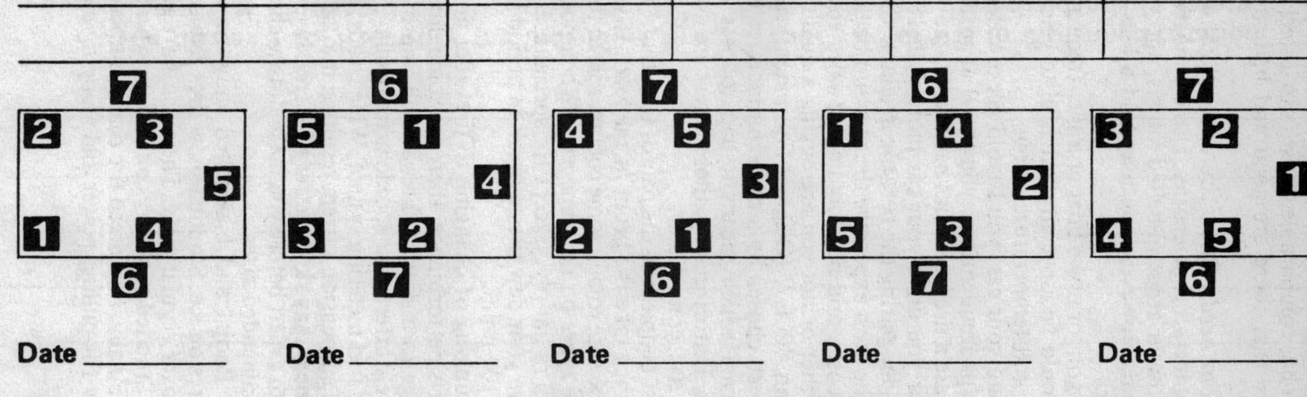

Date __________   Date __________   Date __________   Date __________   Date __________

Miles __________   Miles __________   Miles __________   Miles __________   Miles __________

The numbers shown in the above chart represent tire placement positions. In the first diagram numbers 1 through 4 correspond to the four tires in use, #1 and #2 the left and right front respectively, #3 and #4, the right and left rear. Number 5 represents the spare. The succeeding diagrams follow the movement of the tires in subsequent rotations. Numbers 6 and 7 correspond to snow tires which are placed only in the rear and alternated there. Below the rotation patterns is a convenient space for recording date and mileage at the time of rotation. It is generally recommended that tires be rotated every 10,000 miles. However, heavy use may dictate a shorter span between rotations.

radials cost more. By reviewing the tire ratings, you may be able to purchase a bias-ply tire which has comparable statistics to a steel belted one for less money. Be aware that there are good and bad tires in each category.

Purchasing a tire for your needs: Buy a tire with a high rating in the traction, treadwear and temperature categories. Usually the highest rated tires for traction and treadwear are steel-belted radials, and you can expect to pay more for them. However, you may find a bias ply tire to meet your needs.

If you own a station wagon, or tow a boat or trailer frequently behind your automobile, you should be especially watchful to get a tire with a highly rated treadwear and temperature rating.

If you normally overload your car, you should get a wider or radial tire. If you go on long trips frequently or you travel at sustained high speeds, you should purchase a tire which has been well rated in all three testing categories. Also, if you drive your car more than 18,000 miles per year you should consider getting the best tire available that's affordable. Don't forget that the most expensive tire may not be the best due to import duties, testing costs, and possibly limited sales volume. One easy way to find out whether or not you are buying a quality tire is to ask your dealer if it has an "O.E." (Original Equipment) rating. This means that the tire has been chosen by a car manufacturer to be standard equipment on its cars which means it had to pass *all* of the appropriate rigorous tests. Unfortunately, those letters are not stamped on the tire, so you must ask your dealer.

Replacement tires: Most people find the pair of tires that "drive" the vehicle wear out first as they take the brunt of the load. If you choose to replace only two tires, be sure to buy some comparable to the original. Make sure not to mix tire types on the same axle. When possible have either all bias-belted or all radial-ply. Except for special uses, tire sizes should be equivalent. Give your new tires a break-in period by limiting your highway speed for 100 miles.

Tire size: If you are thinking of changing to tires that are wider or taller to improve your car's performance, there are some things to consider. In general, a change to a shorter sidewall will improve steering response, but may negatively affect your speedometer reading, gear ratio, load-carrying capacity, or fuel metering system. Wide treads, if not used properly, may change the suspension system resulting in road clearance difficulty. At the same time it may slow the car by increasing rolling and wind resistance. Consult an expert before you make drastic changes from the manufacturer's recommended sizes.

Winter traction facts: Radial and bias-belted snow tires offer no advantage over regular tires on ice. Studded snow tires reduce breaking distance on ice by 20% over regular tires. They also have three times the pulling power on ice. Studded snow tires on all four wheels improve cornering speed by 25%. Finally, reinforced tire chains outperform studded tires on ice and snow for pulling power and stopping capabilities.

## Chapter 8

Preventive Maintenance

Most Americans are learning that exercise and eating properly assist in maintaining good health. In effect, we are trying to prevent illness by following a prescribed plan. The same is true for the life of your automobile.

Simple preventive maintenance checks can save hundreds of dollars over the lifetime of your car. Catching potential problems before they erupt into major ones is the mark of a wise car owner. Preventive maintenance may take a little time, but the time spent is well worth it, unless you have unlimited funds to spend on repairs.

Owners of cars that go beyond 100,000 miles all agree that there are three basic preventive maintenance activities even the most marginal weekend mechanic can perform. At the top of the list is regular oil and filter changes, twice as often as the manufacturer's recommendation. Secondly, keep the car clean to avoid dreaded rust damage. Finally, perform the ten minute visual inspection regularly to spot any trouble early.

The Ten Minute Inspection

Inspecting and testing a few key areas of your car on a monthly basis will identify small problems before they become big headaches. The car owner should recognize that certain parts should be replaced regularly because their expected service life has expired. For example, most radial tires begin to wear at 35,000 miles and most shock absorbers last for 20,000 miles. However, some parts fail before they should, and regular inspections can uncover these deficiencies. The inspection should include aspects inside and outside of the car. See the end of this chapter for a quick checklist.

Outside The Car

1. Body scratches: New body scratches are a part of living. Left unattended they may quickly turn to rust and quickly dissolve your car's exterior. Get some touch-up paint from a car dealership and follow the directions for application.

2. Windshield wiper blades: Make sure the blades are free from dirt and are soft and pliable. Hard, cracked blades should be replaced. Wiper blades are easily replaced on most cars, but differ in size so check your owner's manual. Clean blades with soapy water. The cleaning efficiency of a worn or hardened wiper blade can be improved in an emergency by the use of a knife or the striking portion of a matchbook cover. Rub the edges of the blade to scrape away the hard rubber surface to expose softer rubber below. Check wiper blades at least four times a year for pliancy, especially important under adverse driving conditions (see Chapter 17, Special Driving Situations).

3. Lights: You will need help for this one. Have a friend start the car. Make sure headlights, taillights, brakelights, and side lights are working. Test the directional signals. Put the car into reverse to check the back-up lights. Check four times per year.

4. Shock absorbers: Weak shocks may affect the car's steering, stopping, and handling performance. To check for shock absorber efficiency push down hard on one fender and see how much the car bounces. If it bounces easily two or three times after you release it, consider replacement. Most shocks will need replacing every 20,000 miles. Repeat this procedure for all four shocks. Weak shocks may affect the car's steering, stopping, and handling performance.

5. Tires: Inspect carefully for excessive wear. If treadwear indicators (now found on most tires) are showing through, you need new tires. Excessive wear in the center of the tire indicates overinflation, whereas excessive equal wear on outer edges is a sign of underinflation. Uneven wear on only one edge may be a sign of misalignment. Most radial tires need replacing every 35,000 to 40,000 miles. Bias-belted tires need replacing every 30,000 miles. In addition, you should grease the wheel bearings every 15,000-20,000 miles.

6. Leaks: Look under your car for obvious leaks. If a fluid puddle is far forward, it is suggestive of possible trouble in the cooling system. Puddles further back are suggestive of oil leaks, while puddles toward the middle may indicate transmission problems.

Inside The Car

1. Dashboard lights: Make sure the dashboard is lit for safety at night.
2. Horn: Test the horn. It is a most important safety tool.
3. Brakes: Depress the brake pedal. If it goes more than halfway to the floor it may need adjustment or repair. Next, keep pressure on the pedal for ten seconds. If the pedal continues to go down (the "spongy" feeling) you may need work on your master cylinder. Cars equipped with power brakes must perform these tests with the engine on. Finally, set the parking brake and attempt to move forward. If the car moves, the brake may need adjustment. The life of brake pads/lining is 25,000 miles. It is suggested that you have the brakes checked every 10,000 miles. Brake life is usually 25,000 miles.
4. Windshield wipers: Turn them on to make sure they are functional. Getting stuck in rain or snow without functional wipers could send you walking to the closest garage.

Under The Hood

1. Hood release: Check the lubrication and operation of the hood latch. A defective hood latch could send the hood flying up while you are driving. (see Chapter 18, Emergency Driving Situations)
2. Radiator: The radiator is usually the first thing you see directly under the hood latch. Squeeze the connecting hoses to make sure they are pliable. Hard hoses tend to crack and leak. If the hoses and connections are free from defects, but coolant leaks are apparent, have the system pressure tested by your mechanic. Normal life of hoses is 30,000 miles. *With the engine cool*, remove the radiator cap to check fluid levels. Make sure the seal on the cap is not worn, as a tight cap prevents boilovers.

3. Fan belts: Behind the radiator is a series of black belts. Inspect them for cracks or excessive wear. Press down on each belt to check the tension. If you can depress it more than a quarter of an inch, have it adjusted or replaced. Normal replacement is at three years.

4. Battery: If your battery is not maintenance free, it must be checked regularly, especially in hot weather. Make sure you are not smoking during this check as your battery emits volatile hydrogen. Water levels should be slightly above the filter neck. Make sure all connecting cables are not frayed. Most importantly, do not allow corrosion to build up on battery terminals as this is a frequent cause of engines failing to turn over (see Chapter 15). Batteries may need replacing as often as every three years.

5. Power steering and brake fluid levels: The reservoirs for power steering and brake fluids may be found in different locations depending on the make and model of your car. Be sure to clean off the filter caps before checking, as any dirt which drops into the reservoir may cause a malfunction of the system.

6. Oil level: Remove the oil dipstick and wipe it clean. Re-insert the dipstick taking care to push it all the way down. Bring it back out slowly and read the level on the stick. Oil levels should be between the "add" line and "full." Check levels while the engine is off. Change the oil filter at 6,000 miles or at 3,000 miles as recommended by the experts.

7. Carburetor air cleaner: On top of the carburetor is a casing which houses the air cleaner. After removing the top of the casing, inspect the air cleaner. A dirty air cleaner will be very discolored and the vertical baffles will appear warped. Most cars need a new cleaner every 20,000 to 30,000 miles. A clean air cleaner improves gas mileage.

8. Windshield wash levels: The windshield wash reservoir is usually found on one extreme side of the engine and looks like a plastic milk carton. Keeping adequate amounts of fluid in the container is especially important in driving conditions of inclement weather. Most windshield washing fluids now come with antifreeze to avoid freeze-ups in winter.

9. Spark plugs and spark plug wires: If the plugs are loose or the wires are frayed, the car will throttle unevenly. Tighten the plugs and/or change the wires. Spark plug replacement normally is done every 24,000 miles while spark plug wires are changed at 30,000.

10. Transmission oil: The transmission oil should be changed every 24,000 miles together with the filter. The differential oil, a heavier lubricant, also should be changed according to the manufacturer's recommendations, usually every 30,000 miles.

Performing Maintenance Under Warranty

Whenever you buy a new car, and sometimes a used car, there will be an owner's manual in the glove compartment. This owner's manual will give you detailed information on when to bring your car in for servicing, and the parts that probably will need replacing during the course of this servicing. Before the time comes for this type of preventive maintenance, you could buy these parts and bring them into your mechanic or dealer service center. Note that many times a dealer will not let you do this; he will only maintain your car with his own parts. However, if you talk to the service manager, he might allow you to use your own parts, as long as they meet specifications.

While a new car is under warranty, you are obligated to bring it back to the dealership where you bought it, or any other authorized dealership service center. In most of these cases, the dealer insists on supplying the parts for these servicing intervals. However, after the warranty period, the dealer is more likely to allow you to supply your own parts. Use the handy Maintenance Checklist found at the end of this chapter to keep track of all repairs and service done by the dealership during the warranty period.

Performing Additional Maintenance

There are more and more do-it-yourself mechanics who prefer to maintain a car themselves after warranty, rather than bringing the car back to the dealership shop. Others prefer to take their car to a private mechanic for service. In either case, it is important to keep track of all repairs on a repair log as provided in this chapter. Having a description, date, and cost of the repair can help document how long a problem has existed and helps to establish whether or not the repair is still under warranty. Having it signed by the service manager can verify the fact that the work was performed. A log of repairs also is useful when selling the car. If your records are kept accurately, a prospective buyer can easily recognize the fact that the car has been properly maintained, enhancing its resale value.

Buying replacement parts. Many car owners are now buying their own automobile replacement parts. Usually this saves money and saves your mechanic a trip to the same parts store where you are likely to buy your replacement part; however, many car-owning consumers don't know how these parts stores operate and therefore never attempt to buy their own replacement parts.

A repair garage will establish a relationship with a parts outlet. In return, the garage can expect a 30% to 40% discount. The parts outlet does not charge the garage tax because the part is eventually for "resale" to you, the consumer.

For example, a rebuilt carburetor for a 1974 Mustang II may list at $47.50 but, after trade discounts, may cost a garage around $30. The garage in turn may charge you up to $65 for that rebuilt carburetor. If allowed to supply your own parts, you could buy this rebuilt carburetor for $47.50 to save up to $17.50 from the garage's repair bill.

Many garages frown on the idea of consumers buying their own replacement parts, but if you establish a good relationship with a service manager, he probably will allow you to do so. Some of the many parts in your car that can be bought rebuilt include the carburetor, fuel pump, oil pump, radiator, and heater.

Be sure to look for a parts dealer who has reference books on his premises so that you can match your replacement needs with the appropriate parts. Never buy a part on the say-so of a parts merchant that it will surely fit your car, particularly if you are patronizing one who deals on a no-return, no refund basis. It's a good idea to stay away from these dealers anyway; if the part is defective or you need to return it for any other reason, you will have no recourse. Stick with dealers who guarantee their parts.

Where to buy parts: There are several big chains of automobile supply stores, and many associations that become affiliated with independently owned parts outlets. These are normally the best places to buy your own replacement parts. With a large chain or association, you can guarantee yourself a good stock of the parts you need at a reasonable price. These big chains have an excellent return policy in case the new or rebuilt part does not work and they also have a wide selection of rebuilt parts that invariably will save you money.

A good investment for those planning to buy their own parts and possibly to do the repairs themselves is the repair manual that is offered for sale by all car manufacturers. These repair manuals not only tell you the parts to get for your car, but they give you detailed instructions on how to do every type of car repair, both major and minor, thus making them a "must" for the consumer who plans to do his own repairs or to buy his own replacement parts.

Most good service manuals also give you details on how to rebuild parts that don't necessarily have to be bought new. However, this can be a long and involved process, appealing only to the most enthusiastic "Do-It-Yourselfer." If you decide to purchase your rebuilt parts, a service manual usually will give you a list of other parts that can be substituted for the ones specified. For example, if you need a gas filter for a 1989 Plymouth Colt, and your dealer is out of that exact part, the repair manual might specify that a gas filter from a 1989 Mitsubishi Mirage may be used in place of the original part. This situation often occurs in the auto parts business, especially within the same family of cars. Always record the part you replaced on the handy form "Record of Parts Replaced" found at the end of this chapter.

10 MINUTE CHECK-UP TO KEEP YOUR CAR IN GOOD SHAPE

Outside:
1. Scratches ☐ ☐ ☐
2. Wiper blades ☐ ☐ ☐
3. Lights
   a. Head ☐ ☐ ☐
   b. Tail ☐ ☐ ☐
   c. Rear ☐ ☐ ☐
   d. Side ☐ ☐ ☐
   e. Backup ☐ ☐ ☐
   f. Blinkers ☐ ☐ ☐
4. Shocks
   a. Left front ☐ ☐ ☐
   b. Right front ☐ ☐ ☐
   c. Left rear ☐ ☐ ☐
   d. Right rear ☐ ☐ ☐

5. Tires ☐ ☐ ☐
6. Leaks ☐ ☐ ☐

Inside:
1. Dashlights ☐ ☐ ☐
2. Horn ☐ ☐ ☐
3. Brakes
   a. Main ☐ ☐ ☐
   b. Parking ☐ ☐ ☐

Under the Hood:
1. Hood release ☐ ☐ ☐
2. Radiator
   a. Hoses ☐ ☐ ☐
   b. Level ☐ ☐ ☐
   c. Cap ☐ ☐ ☐

3. Fan belts ☐ ☐ ☐
4. Battery
   a. Levels ☐ ☐ ☐
   b. Cables ☐ ☐ ☐
   c. Terminals ☐ ☐ ☐
5. Power steering fluid level ☐ ☐ ☐
6. Brake fluid level ☐ ☐ ☐
7. Oil level ☐ ☐ ☐
8. Air cleaner ☐ ☐ ☐
9. Windshield wash ☐ ☐ ☐

✓ = OK   x = Needs Work

Maintenance Checklist

NAME _______________ SERIAL NO. _______________

ADDRESS _______________ LICENSE _______________

_______________ KEY NOS. _______________

HOME PHONE _______________ DEL. DATE _______________

BUSINESS PHONE _______________

YEAR _______________

MAKE _______________

MODEL _______________

TYPE _______________

SOLD BY _______________ CODE _______________

DATE	REPAIR ORDER NUMBER	MILEAGE	AMOUNT PAID	LUBRICATION						MOTOR CHASSIS AND BODY																		MISC.	
				LUBRICATE	CHANGE OIL	CHANGE OIL FILTER CART.	CLEAN OR REPLACE AIR CLEANER	PACK FRONT WHEELS	TRANSMISSION	TUNE MOTOR	CARBURETOR	CLEAN CARBON GRIND VALVES	IGNITION & ELECTRICAL	CLEAN & REPAIR RADIATOR	AIR CONDITIONER	EMISSION CONTROL	EXHAUST SYSTEM	BALANCE WHEELS	STEERING & FRONT END ALIGN.	ADJ. OR REPAIR CLUTCH	ADJ. OR RELINE BRAKES	BODY WORK	WASH & POLISH	ROTATE TIRES	STATE INSPECTION		

Repair Log

Date	Description of Problem	Repaired By (Signature)	Cost
Date	Description of Problem	Repaired By (Signature)	Cost

RECORD OF PARTS REPLACED

Date	Type of Part (New or Rebuilt)	Place of Purchase	Cost
Date	**Type of Part (New or Rebuilt)**	**Place of Purchase**	**Cost**

## Chapter 9

Keeping Your Car Clean Inside And Out*

A car is the second biggest investment most people ever make. To protect that investment, you've got to take care of the car's body as well as its mechanical parts.

To learn more about car upkeep, we talked with some real experts: the craftsmen at Harrah's Automobile Collection in Reno, Nevada, the largest car museum in the world.

Then we held a car fix-up clinic for some teachers from a local high school. We showed them how to take care of common problems; rust, dents, scratches, upholstery stains and more. The following are some of the things we did, things you can do to keep *your* car in good shape.

Q. What can I do to prevent rust?
A. Plenty. Keep your car as clean and dry as you can. Though some people say today's paints don't need it, a good wax job still helps a lot. Wax often and use chrome polish on the bumpers to keep moisture off the metal.

But remember that the worst rust starts from the *inside*. So when you wash the car, be sure to clean the dirt from underneath too. A dirty undercarriage holds moisture and accelerates rusting, especially if road salt is used in your area.

Undercoating will fight the rust that starts under the body, but of course it can't help other high-moisture areas like the chrome strips around the rear windows.

If you have your car undercoated, don't cover the driveshaft. It could destroy the balance and bring on excessive vibration. And don't cover the exhaust system. That could create objectionable odors.

Q. How do I fix a rust hole?
A. Many fiberglass body repair kits (available in auto parts stores) can be used for patching rust holes. Always be sure to follow the specific directions on the kit you are using.

Q. Can I fix a dent myself to save money?
A. If it's a relatively minor dent, maybe so. Just remember that a little dent can mean a lot of work. You have to decide whether it's worth doing yourself. Here are the steps we used.
1. Carefully determine the extent of damage.
2. To take the dent out, try to get behind it and pop it out with your hand, or tap it out with a mallet or hammer. If you can't, you will probably have to drill holes and use a "dent-puller."
3. Sand the damaged area to bare metal. (Safety eyeglasses should be used here.)
4. Fill with premixed filler.
5. While the filler is still "cheesey," use a "cheese grater" file to form

the general contour. If imperfections remain, reapply filler and file again.

6. Blocksand with No. 80 dry paper. Featheredge the filler and old paint into the metal. If necessary, apply more filler and resand. Then blocksand with No. 220 paper.
7. Wipe surface clean. Apply primer and let dry. Blocksand with wet No. 320 paper. Repeat until all coarser scratches have disappeared and all bare metal has been primed.
8. Handsand lightly with wet No. 400 paper. Clean a large area with solvent to remove wax, then paint. After the paint is thoroughly dry, rub lightly with fine rubbing compound to smooth and polish.
9. If you've used the right tools with enough time and patience, you should see a job well done.

Q. What about a scratch?
A. Usually a scratch or chipped paint can be touched up easily. It won't look perfect, but it will look better and it will help keep rust away. Most dealers have touch-up paint which will match your color. Directions for use are on the paint container. For paint chips on door edges, buy some inexpensive molding at auto supply stores. The molding simply slips over the door edges protecting them from chipping when the door is opened into a wall or adjacent cars.

Q. How can I fix the rip in my vinyl top?
A. The first thing to do is keep the moisture out until you can get to it. If water gets underneath the vinyl, the patch won't hold. Just put a piece of waterproof tape over the rip until you're ready to mend it. There are vinyl repair kits available to do the job. Be sure to follow the instructions that come with the kit.

Stubborn Stains And How To Remove Them

Warning: Never use naphtha or gasoline as a cleaner. They are dangerous to breathe and can be harmful to your skin. And a careless spark could make them harmful to life and property.

Use a cleaner specified for either vinyl or fabric. An all-purpose cleaner (there are some available) can be used for both.

Blood: Use a rag and cold water. Change frequently to clean sections of the rag. Then apply household ammonia cleaner directly to the spot.

Chewing gum: Ice will harden the gum so it can be scraped away. And believe it or not, on most upholstery peanut butter works too. Spread one teaspoonful on. Leave it on about 15 minutes. The oil in the peanut butter helps unstick the gum and makes it come off easily. Then clean with soap and water.

Car sickness: Scrape off the excess and sponge the spot with cloth saturated in cold water, followed by washing with mild soapsuds in warm water.

Grease: Warm water and soapsuds.

Chocolate: Warm water and mild soapsuds followed by light rubbing with cleaning fluid.

Non-chocolate candy: Very hot water followed by light rubbing with a mild soap solution.

Q. Why won't my vinyl top come clean?

A. Maybe you're cleaning it wrong. Wash vinyl tops with mild soapsuds and lukewarm water.

Use a small, soft-bristle brush and scrub the vinyl top in a circular motion. Then remove the first accumulated soilage with a cloth so it won't be ground into the vinyl.

This type of cleaning, with a little commercial mildew remover, will also rid your top of that pesky fungus.

Always follow the cleaning with a vinyl top dressing. A new vinyl top often costs between one and two hundred dollars, so keep yours "looking new."

Q. What kind of soap should I use to wash my car?

A. You should use only soap that's specifically formulated for washing cars. There are many available.

Most laundry soaps are too strong and can dull the finish. It's also best to wash your car in the shade. That way it won't dry prematurely and end up with streaks.

Q. A cigar burned clear through my carpet.

A. Replace it with a piece of carpet from underneath the seat.

Q. How can I make my seat covers last longer?

A. Clean them often. Dirt is upholstery's worst enemy. Left to sit, it acts as an abrasive and causes seat covers to wear out before they should.

Different types of upholstery require different types of cleaning. On vinyl, use only lukewarm water and the suds from a mild detergent. On fabric, use a detergent foam cleaner. Both vinyl and fabric should be vacuumed and wiped with a damp cloth regularly.

Q. Bumper stickers can be tough. How do I get one off?

A. Try soaking it with hot water. Then use a plastic pot scrubber on it. If small pieces of glue remain, use paint thinner to remove them.

* Reprinted with permission of Shell Oil Company.

## Chapter 10

Getting Action With Your Used And New Lemons

The New York State Legislature approved a "lemon law" which took effect in September of 1983. In 1989, Federal legislation, similar in scope, was also enacted. Patterned on legislation from California and Connecticut, the law is an important piece of protection for purchasers of new automobiles. The legislation in New York extends the manufacturer's warranty to two years or 18,000 miles. The responsibility of the owner is to report defects directly to the manufacturer. The manufacturer gets four chances to fix the defect and then the matter goes to the company's arbitration program. Most companies have established their own arbitration panels usually made up of a senior mechanic, company official, independent consumer advocate, the dealer representative, and a member from the public. If this arbitration panel does not settle the issue, the owner has the right to sue for a new automobile or for the refund of the price he paid. If the defective car has over 12,000 miles when replaced, the law allows the manufacturer to deduct a reasonable amount from the purchase price.

Although some of the information contained herein may apply specifically to New York, most states and the Federal legislation is similar but the warranties may have different designations. Buyers' rights in most states are better protected if a car is bought from a recognized dealer rather than from a private seller, although both can be held accountable if the car does not meet certain standards for a specified time period.

Legal Rights Of Used Car Buyers

The most important protection given by law is called the *warranty of serviceability*. Any used car sold by a dealer in most states must contain a Certificate of Adequacy which states that the car is in condition to give satisfactory service on the highway at the time of delivery. The dealer must inspect the car before selling it to make sure it can give satisfactory service. In addition, the following must be in good working order: brakes, steering, lights, directional signals, windshield wipers, defroster, muffler, odometer, horn, mirrors, and, if the car was made after 1963, seat belts. The front wheels must be properly aligned, the tires must have at least 2/32" tread, and you must be able to see through the windshield and other glass windows.

The warranty of serviceability cannot be waived. It applies to all used cars purchased from dealers—even if the contract says you are buying "as is."

Although the warranty of serviceability specifically relates to the car's condition at the time of delivery, you may be protected even if it takes awhile for your lemon to break down. The key point to be proven will be that the car broke down because of a defect that existed at the time of delivery.

There is one limitation to the protection given consumers who purchase used cars from dealers. The warranty of serviceability may not apply to a car sold as "junk." If you sign a Customer's Declaration which states that you do not intend to operate the car on public roads at the time of purchase, that you know the car is unsuitable for operation, and that it needs extensive repairs and must pass inspection before it can be registered, you will not get a Certificate of Adequacy or any guarantee that the car has been inspected.

The warranty of serviceability is by far the most important legal protection for used car buyers in most states, but there are other legal protections, and unlike the warranty of serviceability, these apply whether you bought the car from a dealer or from a private seller.

Advertisements and oral statements: If you bought the car because of an advertisement, the car may have to live up to its claims. In a recent New York case, a car that was advertised as being "in very good condition" turned out to be unsafe and beyond repair. The court held that the ad created an express warranty and awarded the buyer $2,400, the price of the car minus what he was able to sell it for.

Similarly, oral statements and promises made by the seller may be regarded as warranties and the seller will be liable if the statements are not true. (Caution: if you do not have the statements and promises in writing they may be difficult to prove.) In one case in Massachusetts, the seller, by honest error, said that his car was a 1970 Mercedes Benz rather than a 1968. The court awarded the buyer the difference in value of the year as described and its actual year—$1,700.

In order for a warranty to have been created by either an advertisement or an oral statement, you must be able to prove the following:

1. A statement of fact or promise was made by the seller.
2. The natural tendency of that statement would be to induce a buyer to purchase the car.
3. You did, in fact, rely on the statement in purchasing the car.
4. The promise was broken or the fact was untrue.
5. The car is worth less, accordingly.

Fraud: You also may be able to sue the seller on grounds of fraud. To prove fraud, you will have to prove the seller knew of a defect and either tried to hide it from you or failed to disclose important and relevant facts which misled you into thinking the car was in better condition than it was. In the New York case involving the false advertisement, the court also said the seller, who had restored the exterior of a damaged car and then denied to the buyer that the car had ever been in an accident, had committed fraud.

If you have been the victim of either false advertising or a deceptive act or practice by a seller, you may sue for the actual damages you suffered or $50.00, whichever is greater. If the deception was deliberate, a court may increase the award to triple your actual damages (there is a $1000 maximum for the triple damages). If you win your case, the court has the power to order the seller to pay your attorney's fees.

Odometer: You have the right to know how many miles the car you purchase has been driven. Every seller must tell the buyer the cumulative mileage on the odometer (including whether the car has exceeded 99,999 miles) and whether the seller knew the mileage shown to be accurate.

If the seller breaks this law with the intent of defrauding a buyer, the buyer can recover whichever is greater: $1,500 or three times the actual damages suffered. With the new Odometer Disclosure Statement (see Chapter 4), this headache should be eliminated. To prove the intent to defraud, all you need to show is that either (a) there was a change in the odometer reading while the car was in the seller's possession, and the seller did not disclose the change; (b) the statement as to mileage was made recklessly or carelessly; or (c) the seller reasonably should have known the odometer was incorrect but stated the mileage shown was accurate anyway.

The warranty of title: With every sale of a used car, there is an implied warranty that the seller is the rightful owner of the car and has the right to sell the car. The only way this may be excluded is by **specific** language informing the buyer that the seller does not necessarily claim to have the right to sell the car.

In one New York case, an insurance company sold a car which had been stolen. The car was returned to its rightful owner and the buyer sued the insurance company for breach of warranty of title. The court awarded the buyer the sum of the price the buyer paid to purchase the car from the insurance company plus $3,017 the buyer had spent on reconditioning the car.

Minors: If you bought your lemon before your eighteenth birthday, you can probably get out of the contract on the grounds of your youth. (You will have to pay, though, for the time you used the car.) This right exists only until a "reasonable time" after you turn 18. Most law is unclear about exactly how long is reasonable, so you should notify the seller that you intend to rescind the contract either before your eighteenth birthday or as soon as possible after it.

The contract: Be sure you read any contract concerning the sale very carefully. It may give you additional warranty protection (covering extra parts, lasting for a longer time period, or both). Remember, if you bought your car from a dealer, the contract **cannot** exclude or diminish in any way the warranty of serviceability.

Keeping records: Your attempts to resolve used and new car complaints will be a lot easier if you keep good records. You should be able to document each step of the transaction. You might want to set aside a large envelope or shoe box to keep all the papers in one place.

In order to keep your files complete, you should:

1. Save any advertisement that induced you to buy the car.
2. Keep the bill of sale, any contract signed, and notes you took when talking to the seller about the car.
3. Make a copy of every letter you send concerning the car and keep it in your files. Mail the letters by certified mail, receipt requested, so that you will have proof that your letters were received.
4. Keep a list of any communication you have with the seller, whether by letter, phone or in person. Write down the names of the people

you speak to and the dates of the conversation. Keep a record of all verbal promises and statements made by the seller.

5. Keep a list of the car's defects and the date and mileage when they became apparent.

6. Keep a record of any work or maintenance done on the car; save the work orders given you by the mechanic. Also keep a list of general maintenance you perform, such as changing oil. It is crucial that you prove all necessary maintenance was done.

Talking to the seller: Your first step in resolving your complaints should be to talk to the seller. Contact the seller as soon as the problem becomes apparent and see if you can work out a satisfactory solution.

If that proves impossible, you may want to contact a governmental or private agency that handles consumers' automobile complaints.

The Department of Motor Vehicles: If you bought your used car from a dealer, you should call the Department of Motor Vehicles. Trained mechanics from the D.M.V. will investigate your complaint. If they determine that the warranty of serviceability or some other right arising from the sale has been violated, they will recommend to the dealer that the car be repaired at no cost to you. If the car is beyond repair, they will recommend that the dealer take back the car and return your purchase price.

The D.M.V. does not have the authority to force the dealer to follow its recommendations. However, the D.M.V. has the power to conduct a hearing as to a possible suspension or revocation of the dealer's registration and a civil fine. The threat of such a hearing often is enough to convince a dealer to make a satisfactory repair or refund. If the dealer refuses and you sue in court, the D.M.V. will appear as a witness in your behalf.

Legal strategies: If you feel that your complaint has still not been resolved to your satisfaction, there are a variety of strategies you can follow. The one appropriate for you depends on how soon after delivery the car's problems become obvious, how serious the problems are, whether you are willing to let the seller try to correct the problems, and whether you want to keep the car, sell it to a third person, or return it to the seller.

Rejection and revocation of acceptance: One set of options involves returning the car to the seller and obtaining a refund of your purchase price. The major strategies within this set are called "rejection" and "revocation of acceptance." These are serious steps which often wind up in court. You should consult an attorney as to which option is appropriate for your situation.

"Rejecting" the car permits you to cancel the sale. This is only available, however, when you discover at delivery or within a short time after that the car has serious defects which both substantially impair the car's value to you and which violate one of the warranties or rights arising from the sale. Also, a car should only be rejected if the defect is so serious that you are not willing to let the dealer try to repair or replace the defective part.

Like rejection, revocation of acceptance permits you to return the car and cancel your contract if the car has substantial defects that both seriously impair the car's value to you **and** which violate one of the warranties or rights arising from the sale. One difference between the two options is that you can revoke acceptance not only when the defect appears almost immediately after delivery (as with rejection) but also when the defect becomes apparent after you have driven the car awhile (don't forget, for the warranty of serviceability to be violated, the car must have been defective when sold). With revocation, you must notify the seller of the defect within a "reasonable time" after you discover it and give the seller a "reasonable opportunity" to repair the defect. The law is unclear as to the exact scope of "reasonable" but you should notify the seller as soon as possible and give more than one chance to correct the problem.

If the seller is unable to correct the problem, or offers repairs that you think do not satisfactorily correct it, take the car to a reputable mechanic or repair shop for an independent examination. Get a written statement from the mechanic of what the problem is and what solutions would be necessary.

If at this point you want to return the car to the seller and demand that your purchase price be returned, you should contact an attorney. It is very important that all the procedures be followed carefully. An attorney can make sure that you perform the necessary steps correctly.

To both reject a car and revoke acceptance, you will have to return the car and offer the Certificate of Title and keys to the seller. If the seller does not accept them, hold onto them; you have fulfilled your obligation by making the offer. Remove the license plates and return them along with your registration to the D.M.V. but do not remove any of the equipment which came with the car. The car must be returned without any substantial change, other than that caused by the defects and normal wear and tear. Give the seller notice in writing that you are revoking acceptance (or rejecting the car) and list the specific defects. Keep a copy of this notice for your files. You should take photographs that show the car's condition on the day you return it and make a note of the odometer reading. A large increase in mileage on the odometer later will show that the dealer accepts your return of the car and no longer considers you the owner of the car.

Notify your insurance agent in writing that you have rejected the car and returned it to the seller. Do not cancel your insurance until the dispute is resolved, but ask your agent about reducing your coverage to the minimum necessary to protect you while the seller has the car.

If the seller financed the car or arranged the financing for you, you may be able to stop your payments, even if the seller has already sold your contract to a sales finance company or bank. Contact a lawyer before you stop payment to make sure you proceed correctly and that your credit rating is protected. Notify the finance company or bank, if one is involved, in writing, that you are refusing to pay and why, and that the automobile has been rejected and returned to the seller. Eager for your continued payments, the finance company or bank may pressure the seller to resolve your dispute. On the other hand, the seller or finance company may decide to sue you for the balance of the payments. If this happens, your defense is the seller's failure to provide you with a safe and functioning car.

If you financed the car through a bank or credit union loan made directly to you, even if the actual check was issued to the seller, CONTINUE MAKING YOUR PAYMENTS. Such loans are considered separate legal contracts, and your legal duty to pay continues despite your problems with the car.

Suing for damages: The previously discussed options involve returning the car to the seller and fighting in court to get your money back. If you would prefer either to repair and keep the car or sell the car and sue to recover your expenses, there is another action to consider—suing for damages.

As in revocation of acceptance, the first thing to do is bring the car back to the seller for repair. Give the seller a reasonable number of chances to fix the car.

If the seller is unable to correct the problem, or offers repairs that you think do not satisfactorily correct it, take the car to an independent mechanic or repair shop. Get a written statement from the mechanic of what the problem is and what solutions are necessary, and a written estimate of the cost.

You have two options: you can either repair or sell the car. If you have it repaired, tell the mechanic in advance that you want any replaced parts returned to you (this is your right under New York State law whenever you have repairs done on your car other than work by a dealer pursuant to a written warranty). After the mechanic does the repairs, pay the bill and get an itemized receipt. Alternatively, you can sell the car at its fair market value, considering, of course, its defects.

After the car is sold or repaired, ask the seller to reimburse you for your damages. Your damages may include:

1. The difference between the price you paid and the price for which you sold the car,
2. The cost of repairs,
3. The difference in value between the repaired car and a car in the condition you were supposed to receive it, and
4. Any towing charges or payments you made for a rented car or other transportation while your lemon was in the shop.

If the seller refuses, sue. You can use the small claims court if your damages add up to less than $2,000. Small claims court is designed to enable a consumer, without a lawyer, to recover claims quickly and inexpensively.

If your total damages exceed the limits of the small claims court, or if the seller is not within the court's jurisdiction, call your city or county bar association, local consumer agency, or the district office of the Attorney General to find out the name of the court you should use. It is advisable that you consult a lawyer before you sue.

Lawyers: Having an attorney can be very helpful in resolving your used car complaint, especially if you are planning to follow an option which is likely to end in a lawsuit. A lawyer may be able to help you negotiate a satisfactory settlement with the seller without going to court at all. Additionally, an attorney will be able to help you determine your best strategy if legal action is required: whether you should reject or revoke acceptance and return the car to the seller or whether you would have more leverage if you kept the car and sued for damages.

If you do not qualify for Legal Services or Legal Aid, but do not have the money to pay for a lawyer, there are other ways to meet legal fees.

If your car was manufactured after July 4, 1975, and you bought the car from a dealer, you can sue under the federal Magnuson-Moss Act. This law permits the court to order the dealer to pay your costs and attorney's fee if you win the case on the grounds that a warranty provision was violated.

If you've been the victim of false advertising or a deceptive act or practice by a seller, the law permits the court to order the seller to pay your attorney's fee if you win.

Legal Rights Of New Car Buyers

All new cars are sold with written warranties from their manufacturers. Read yours carefully. It gives you specific guarantees for a limited period of time. Additionally, state and federal law provide you with an implied warranty which gives you the right to a safe, efficient, and defect-free automobile. This implied warranty, however, is usually limited by the manufacturer to the duration of the written warranty.

If the new car you purchased turns out to be a lemon—an unsafe, inefficient, or defect-ridden car—there are several strategies you can follow. Which one is appropriate for you depends on how quickly the car's problems become obvious, whether you are willing to let the dealer try to correct them, and whether you want to keep the car.

Talking to the dealer: Your first step in resolving your complaints should be to talk to the dealer. Contact the dealer as soon as the problem becomes apparent and see if you can work out a satisfactory solution. Don't settle for talking to a salesperson. You should try to talk to a person with the authority to resolve your complaints.

If you are not satisfied after talking with the dealer, you may want to contact a private or governmental agency that handles consumers' automobile complaints.

If you are still not satisfied with your car's condition, you may want to consider one of the following three strategies. Strategy One, rejecting the lemon, is available for only a limited time after you get the car. Strategy Two, revoking acceptance, and Strategy Three, suing for damages, are much less restrictive.

All three are drastic. Each can result in your fighting in court—either by suing the dealer or manufacturer for satisfaction of the dispute, or the dealer or financing agency suing you for the payments due. Since you have a lot of money at stake with a new car, we recommend that you seek advice from a lawyer before you start.

Strategy One - Rejecting the Lemon: Some lemons show their true colors right away. In one case that wound up in a New York State

Supreme Court, a 1976 Cadillac burst into flames after 17 miles of driving due to a faulty electrical system. The owner "rejected" the car—gave it back to the dealer, refused the dealer's offer to repair it, and demanded his money back. The dealer refused; the owner sued. The court held that the owner did not have to accept the dealer's offer to repair the car, and ordered the dealer to return the owner's money.

Rejecting your lemon is the first strategy to consider, but it is limited as follows:

1. It can only be done within a short period of time after delivery. (The courts have not defined the exact period of time.)
2. It must be done as soon as the defect becomes obvious.
3. It should only be done if the defect is so serious that you are not willing to let the dealer try to repair or replace the defective part.

When you reject a car, you are saying to the dealer that you did not receive what you ordered and paid for—a safe, efficient, defect-free automobile. If you bought your car based on a description in a manufacturer's booklet or advertisement, and you told the dealer when you ordered the car that you were relying on that description, you can reject the car if it does not match the description.

Once you notify the dealer that you are rejecting the car, the dealer legally has the opportunity to try to resolve your complaint. But you have the right to reject any offer the dealer makes that does not provide you with the safe, efficient, and defect-free new car you purchased.

In extreme cases you do not have to accept the dealer's attempt to repair the car. In one case in New Jersey, a new car stalled repeatedly on its 2.7 mile trip from the dealer's lot to the consumer's home. By the time it reached the home, its maximum speed was 10 miles an hour. The car was towed back to the dealer who determined that the transmission was defective. The court permitted the buyer to reject the car even though the dealer offered to put in a new transmission. The court said that when a consumer's faith in the dependability of a new car is so shaken, the consumer has the right to return the car.

Strategy Two - Revoking Acceptance: If your lemon's problems aren't evident right away, you no longer have the opportunity to reject it and you will have to follow Strategy Two or Strategy Three.

Strategy Two is similar to Strategy One in concept, but it proceeds at a much slower pace. It involves working with the dealer, allowing the dealer a reasonable number of chances to correct the car's defects, contacting the manufacturer's factory service representative, and other steps. Only if all these steps fail can you get rid of the lemon using the procedure called "revocation of acceptance."

Even if your car's defects do become obvious right away, you may prefer to work with the dealer and revoke later if necessary, rather than to reject immediately. This strategy has the following advantages:

1. It gives the dealer a chance to correct the problems, which, if done satisfactorily, is the easiest solution for everyone.
2. It gives you more time to think over your options and find a lawyer. Although you must revoke acceptance within a reasonable time after the defect is discovered, your time to act will be extended if you give the

dealer a chance to correct it.

3. If you eventually revoke acceptance and sue, you can bring suit under state law and under the federal Magnuson-Moss Warranty Act, (a law that allows the court to order the dealer or manufacturer to pay your costs and attorney's fee if you win). If you simply reject a car, it is not clear whether the court can grant you costs and attorney fees.

4. The defect involved in revocation can be anything that "substantially impairs" the car's value to you. Although there is no legal definition of "substantially," courts have allowed revocation for a series of minor defects, as well as major defects such as a faulty engine.

Not every complaint you have with your car is necessarily the basis for revocation. For instance, while poor gas mileage may be an indication that a car is not performing properly, a New York court ruled that the fact that a car does not deliver the E.P.A. mileage estimate, **by itself**, does not permit revocation.

If you decide to follow Strategy Two, the first thing you should do is bring your lemon to the dealer for repair. Give the dealer a list of the car's specific defect(s). Keep a duplicate list for yourself, along with all other records relating to your purchase and repair of the car.

Give the dealer a reasonable number of chances to fix the car's defect(s). If the dealer is unable to correct the problem(s), or offers repairs that you think are not satisfactory, take the car to a reputable mechanic or repair shop for an independent examination. Get a written statement from the mechanic of the problem(s), and what solutions would be satisfactory; for example, whether a part can be repaired or must be replaced, or whether the defect is so serious that the entire car must be replaced.

While you're still trying to work with the dealer, do not allow the independent mechanic to make any repairs on your car. The dealer may claim that these unauthorized repairs void your warranty protection.

If the dealer still will not or cannot correct the problem(s), contact the manufacturer's factory service representative in your area (also called a zone representative). The zone representative can act as a mediator between you and the dealer, and may authorize the dealer to make the needed repair(s) or provide special repair instructions. The name of the factory service representative is sometimes listed in your operator's manual; it also can be obtained from the dealer, your local consumer agency, or the State Consumer Protection Board (see end of chapter).

Some dealers and manufacturers may refer your complaint to an informal dispute settlement system. If the system is not required by your warranty, you don't have to cooperate. If you do, a panel will hear your dispute and make a decision. Neither you nor the dealer has to accept the panel's decision, although the dealer must act in "good faith" in response to it. And if you finally end up in court, the panel's decision, for or against you, will be considered as evidence.

If, after contacting the dealer and the factory representative, your car's defects still are not fixed, you should consider revoking your acceptance. Like rejection, this is a very serious step which can develop into a complex legal proceeding. We recommend you consult an attorney before you act. If you decide to take this step, make sure you can show that:

1. The car's defect "substantially impairs" its value to you.

2. You are revoking within a reasonable time after you discover the defect.

3. Except for the defect that is causing you to revoke, you are returning the car without "substantial change" in its condition.

After confirming that these three conditions are met, notify the dealer in writing that you are revoking acceptance, and follow the rest of the steps outlined under Strategy One: Rejecting the Lemon.

Strategy Three - Suing for Damages: Strategies One and Two basically involve returning your lemon to the dealer's lot and fighting in court to get your money back. If you think the car can be fixed, there is a third strategy to consider—suing for damages.

As in Strategy Two, the first thing to do is bring the lemon back to the dealer for repair. Give the dealer a reasonable number of chances to fix the car.

If the dealer is unable to correct the problem, or offers repairs that you think do not satisfactorily correct it, take the car to an independent mechanic or repair shop. Get a written statement from the mechanic of what the problem is and what solution would be satisfactory, and a written estimate of the cost. Tell the mechanic in advance that you want any replaced part to be returned to you. Then, have the independent mechanic do the repairs. Pay the bill, and get an itemized receipt.

After the car is fixed, ask the dealer to reimburse you for your damages. These include the cost of repairs, the difference in value between a new car and your repaired lemon, and any towing charges or payments you made for a rented car or other transportation while your lemon was in the shop.

Your written warranty from the dealer may state that the manufacturer and dealer are not responsible for incidental and consequential damages. Your argument will be that the limited remedy provided by the written warranty has "failed of its essential purpose" and that you should be placed in as good financial position as if the car had not been defective.

If the dealer refuses to reimburse you, sue. Ask your lawyer whether to sue the car's manufacturer and/or distributor. One court in Minnesota permitted the consumer to sue the distributor of the car because the dealer had gone out of business.

Check the limit for suing in the small claims court (in New York, it's $2000). Use small claims court if you qualify. Otherwise, call your city or county bar association, local consumer agency, or district office of the Attorney General to secure the name of the court you should use.

There is one problem to consider before you sue for damages. If your lemon turns up with other serious defects during the warranty period, the dealer may refuse to correct them claiming that your unauthorized repairs voided your warranty protection. If this happens, you may have to prove in court that the repairs were done properly by a competent mechanic or that the subsequent defect which developed could not have been a result of the independent mechanic's repairs.

Record keeping: It is important that you keep specific and detailed records regarding all attempts to settle your problem. See page 76 for a list of things you should have in order to prove your case against the seller of your new lemon.

After the warranty period: Even if you've driven over the warranty mileage limit or the warranty time period has elapsed, it doesn't mean you are necessarily out of remedies. If the car's defects showed during the warranty period and the dealer did not correct them adequately, you still will have the right to have the defects corrected. In one case in Connecticut, a consumer was permitted to revoke acceptance 14 months after delivery, even though he was only given a 12 month warranty. The court ruled for the consumer because he had been in constant touch with the dealer throughout the warranty period, had relied on the dealer's repeated assurances that the car would be repaired satisfactorily, and discovered after 14 months that the car was still not repaired adequately.

Complaints: When writing to a dealer, try to address your letter to the correct person. The Sales Manager is concerned with sales, the Service Manager is concerned with service. It is probably best also to send a copy to the President and/or Chairman of the Board. Copies also could be sent to the automobile manufacturer or appropriate governmental agency if the matter involves safety or another serious matter.

Below is a list of automobile manufacturers and other organizations that can help with your complaint:

Car Manufacturers

Acura
(see American Honda
Motor Co., Inc.)

**Alfa Romeo Distributors of
North America**
8259 Exchange Drive
P.O. Box 598026
Orlando, FL 32859-8026
407-856-5000

American Honda Motor Co. Inc.
100 W. Alondra Blvd.
Gardena, CA 90247
213-327-8280

American Isuzu Motors Inc.
2300 Pellissier Place
Whittier, CA 90601
213-949-0611

American Suzuki Motor Corp.
3251 E. Imperial Hwy.
Brea, CA 92621-6722
714-996-7040

Audi of America Inc.
888 West Big Beaver Rd.
Troy, MI 48007-3951
313-362-6000

**Austin Rover Cars of
North America**
(see Sterling Motor Cars)

Avanti Motor Corp.
P.O. Box 179
Youngstown, OH 44501
216-744-2821

Bertone
Overseas Motors
32400 Plymouth Road
Livonia, MI 48150
313-427-4840

BMW of North America, Inc.
300 Chestnut Ridge Rd.
Woodcliff Lake, NJ 07675
201-307-4000

Buick Motor Division
General Motors Corp.
902 E. Hamilton Ave.
Flint, MI 48550
313-236-5000

Cadillac Motor Car Division
General Motors Corp.
2860 Clark Street
Detroit, MI 48232
313-554-5067

Chevrolet Motor Division
General Motors Corp.
30007 Van Dyke Ave.
Warren, MI 48090
313-492-8846

Chrysler Corp.
12000 Chrysler Drive
Highland Park, MI 48288-1919
313-956-5741

Daihatsu America Inc.
4422 Corporate Center Dr.
Los Almitos, CA 90720
714-761-7000

Dodge
(see Chrysler Corp.)

Ferrari North America
777 Terrace Ave.
Hasbrouck Heights, N.J. 07604
201-393-4081

Fiat Auto U.S.A. Inc.
777 Terrace Ave.
Hasbrouck Heights, NJ 07604
201-393-4000

Ford Motor Company
The American Road
Dearborn, MI 48121

Ford Division
P.O. Box 43301
300 Renaissance Center
Detroit, MI 48243
313-446-3800

General Motors Corp.
General Motors Bldg.
3044 Grand Blvd.
Detroit, MI 48202

Hyundai Motor America
10550 Talbert Ave.
Fountain Valley, CA 92728
714-965-3508

Infiniti
(see Nissan Motor Corp. in
U.S.A.)

Jaguar Cars Inc.
555 MacArthur Blvd.
Mahwah, NH 07430
201-818-8500

Laforza Automobiles Inc.
3860 Bay Center Place
Hayward, CA 94545
415-732-1600

Lamborghini U.S.A. Inc.
300 E. Long Lake
Suite 280
Bloomfield Hills, MI 48013
313-645-9800

Lexus
(see Toyota Motor Sales,
U.S.A., Inc.)

Lincoln-Mercury Division
Ford Motor Co.
300 Renaissance Center
P.O. Box 43322
Detroit, MI 48243
313-446-4450

Lotus Cars U.S.A., Inc.
1655 Lakes Pkwy
Lawrenceville, GA 30243
404-822-4566

Maserati Automobiles Inc.
1501 Caton Ave.
Baltimore, MD 21227
301-646-6400

Mazda Motor of America, Inc.
7755 Irvine Center Drive
Irvine, CA 92718
714-727-1990

Mercedes-Benz of North America, Inc.
One Mercedes Drive
Montvale, NJ 07645-0350
201-573-0600

Mitsubishi Motor Sales of America, Inc.
6400 West Katella Ave.
Cypress, CA 90630-0064
714-372-6000

Nissan Motor Corp. in U.S.A.
18501 Figueroa St.
Carson, CA 90248
213-532-3111

Oldsmobile Division
General Motors Corp.
920 Townsend St.
Lansing, MI 48921
517-377-5000

Peugeot Motors of America Inc.
One Peugeot Plaza
Lyndhurst, NJ 07071
201-935-8400

Plymouth
(see Chrysler Corp.)

Pontiac Motor Division
General Motors Corp.
1 Pontiac Plaza
Pontiac, MI 48058-3484
313-857-5000

Porsche Cars North America Inc.
100 W. Liberty St.
Reno, NV 89501
702-348-3000

Range Rover of North America Inc.
4390 Parliament Place
P.O. Box 1503
Lanham, MD 20706
301-731-9040

Rolls Royce Motors, Inc.
120 Chubb Ave.
P.O. Box 476
Lyndhurst, NJ 07071
201-460-9600

Saab-Scania of America, Inc.
P.O. Box 697
Saab Drive
Orange, CT 06477
203-795-5671

Saturn Corp.
General Motors Corp.
1400 Stephenson Hwy.
Troy, MI 48007-7025
313-524-5721

Sterling Motor Cars
8300 N.W. 53rd Street
Suite 200
Miami, FL 33166
305-470-1100

Subaru of America, Inc.
P.O. Box 6000
Cherry Hill, N.J. 08034-6000
609-488-8500

Toyota Motor Sales, USA, Inc.
19001 S. Western Ave.
Torrance, CA 90509
213-618-4000

Volkswagen of America Inc.
888 Big Beaver Rd.
P.O. Box 3951
Troy, MI 48099
313-362-6000

Volvo of North America Corp.
Rockleigh, NJ 07647
201-768-7300

Yugo America Inc.
28 Park Way
Upper Saddle River, NJ 07458
201-825-4600

Center For Auto Safety

Complaints About Manufacturers
Center for Auto Safety
1223 DuPont Circle Bldg.
Washington, D.C. 20036
1-800-424-9393

Service Stations

Complaints about service stations in general or in particular can be brought to the attention of the following agency:

National Congress of Petroleum Retailers
2021 K Street N.W.
Washington, D.C. 20006

Consumer Affairs

If the manufacturer has not been of help, write to the *Office of Consumer Affairs* in Washington.

Repair Shop Problems
Director of Consumer Affairs
Office of Consumer Affairs
Office of the President
Washington, D.C. 20506

You may also write to the *Department of Consumer Affairs* in your city or state.

The *Better Business Bureau* in your city or state might also be helpful. Or, you may get some aid from the:
Consumer Federation of America
Suite 1105
1012 14th Street
Washington, D.C. 20005

If you have a problem with a garage affiliated with the American Automobile Association and are a member of the AAA:

American Automobile Association
1000 AAA Dr.
Heathrow, FL 32746-5063
(407) 444-7000

National Automobile Dealers Association
8400 Westpark Dr.
Mclean, Va. 22102
(703) 821-7000

If the problem lies with the tires, call or write to:

Rubber Manufacturer's Association
1400 K St., N.W.
Washington, D.C. 20005
(202) 682-4800

## Chapter 11

The Layman's Guide To Buying Auto Insurance

For most car owners, automobile insurance is a fact of life, yet few consumers are familiar with more than just the basics necessary to register a motor vehicle. Many states have mandatory insurance laws which stipulate that a car will not be registered unless it is insured. Others have some sort of financial responsibility stipulation regarding automobile insurance. For example, some states do not mandate insurance until a driver has been involved in an accident or has received a ticket for a moving violation.

The following list of helpful hints may make your insurance buying decision a wise one—one which will save you money.

Comparison shop: When buying a car, most consumers shop around for the best price. However, very few people go to more than one insurance company before buying insurance even though comparison shopping can be done over the phone. Many states have minimum insurance laws which stipulate the least amount of protection you can buy. If you are contemplating buying the least amount of insurance (which is not recommended), get the minimum coverage specifications from your state motor vehicles department, and check with at least three insurance companies. Buy the one with the best price. If you are planning to purchase additional coverage, comparison shopping may take longer.

Understanding your coverage: There are two basic types of policies. You can buy what is referred to as "single limit" coverage or "split" coverage. The single limit coverage is one amount of insurance. For example, if you have "single limit" coverage for $100,000, the insurance company will pay any combination of personal injury or property damage as long as the amount is not more than $100,000. In most cases this "single limit" coverage only is offered by insurance companies to their better risk drivers; therefore, the cost of this coverage oftentimes is less than split coverage. Before buying this coverage, find out if your insurance company offers it to all its policyholders (not just the better risks), as they then would normally charge more for it.

The split limit may be a better buy for some drivers. The only way to tell is to comparison shop. With this coverage your dollar amounts are split into three categories. For example, you may have coverages of $100,000, $300,000 and $50,000 for a total of $450,000. The $100,000 coverage refers to the amount the insurance company will pay for the medical expenses of one injured person, any loss of earnings, outside claims, or physical and emotional suffering including death. The $300,000 coverage is the amount the company will pay on the same conditions happening to two or more people. The $50,000 coverage represents the amount paid on personal property damage claims.

Generally the lowest coverage that an insurance company will write is a policy calling for $10,000, $20,000 and $5,000. That means that the insurance company will pay $10,000 for injury or death to one person, $20,000 for the injury or death to two or more people and $5,000 for property damage. This minimum coverage is not enough for any consumer who has a bank account, liquid assets, or tangible personal property. Any damages for which you are sued above those limitations would be your responsibility. If you lose a large lawsuit, you may be paying for the rest of your life, and you'll probably have to give up all of your tangible personal property. For a few extra dollars you could get a better insurance policy to protect you, your personal property, and your future earnings.

Personal medical bills: When comparing the cost of premiums, investigate whether the policies have a special stipulation that will pay from $1,000 to $5,000 of your personal medical bills if sustained in an automobile accident. For example, a $100,000, $300,000, $50,000 policy from Insurance Company "A" may cost $475.00 a year, while a policy with the same limits from Company "B" may cost $469.00 a year. You discover they're virtually the same coverage except Company "A" has a $3,000 medical benefits plan while Company "B" does not. If you find that this same medical coverage normally costs $75.00 a year from a health insurance company, then Company "A's" policy is the better buy. Also consider whether this coverage duplicates your regular health insurance policy; if it does, eliminate it from your auto policy. Generally, if an insurance company doesn't state that personal medical coverage is included, it is probably not in the policy, but it is always wise to check.

Umbrella policies: These policies are very inexpensive, from $100-$200 a year additional to a $100,000, $300,000, $50,000 policy with a normal limitation of $1,000,000 meaning that a company will pay any and all damages incurred by you up to $1,000,000. This includes any combination of personal injury, death, damage suits or property damage suits. This is the best coverage that money can buy, and virtually assures you will not be wiped out economically by one accident.

Collision insurance: Every insurance company charges a separate premium for collision insurance. Depending upon the type of car you drive, this insurance can be very expensive.

Almost all collision insurance comes with a deductible, usually in increments of $100, $250, or $500. Meaning if you have $100 deductible, you pay for the first $100 of damage, while the insurance company pays the rest. The same holds true for $250 deductible; you pay the first $250 and the insurance company pays the rest. With repair costs rising, most consumers choose the $250 deductible. Going from the $250 to the $500 deductible saves 35% on the collision portion of your insurance. It is important when picking an insurance company to find out what the procedure is for the company paying off on a collision claim. Will they pay 100% of an agreed estimate or something less? This could mean the difference between buying your insurance from one company or another.

If you have financed your car through a bank or other lending institution, they may require you to buy collision insurance because it is actually they who own the car until you satisfy the loan.

Comprehensive insurance: This type of insurance is also an added extra to your basic insurance. This part of the policy insures you against vandalism, fire, floods, explosions and other types of damage as well as towing costs. Normally this type of insurance covers you from the first dollar lost, but you may be able to get a deductible clause in this part of the policy to lower your cost. This comprehensive insurance also can be very expensive depending upon the type of car and where it is garaged.

Other types of coverage: There are several other types of coverage that are available to the motorist, including two major types: uninsured motorist coverage and wage loss and substitute services coverage. You can buy a policy with an uninsured motorist clause meaning that your insurance company will pay for damages you have sustained in an accident with an uninsured motorist. This is important as there are many drivers who are not insured and who are unable to pay damage claims resulting from an accident.

Substitute services coverage means that if you are injured in an accident and you perform essential services for your family including child or geriatric care, the insurance company will provide you with these services.

There are other types of special addenda that are written into automobile policies. Consult your insurance agent for special coverage packages. This is all part of "shopping around" for insurance. Know what you're covered for and how much it will cost as you compare prices.

What affects insurance rates? There are several factors that insurance companies consider when determining the price the consumer will pay for coverage. There are certain inequities in the way insurance companies determine these rates, but it is unlikely they will change.

Age, sex and marital status: A single man under age 25 normally pays more for insurance than a single woman of the same age. After the twenty-fifth birthday, the premium gap usually shortens between single men and women. Regardless of age, married people normally receive a lower rate than single people of the same age in the under-30 age group.

Residence and occupation: People who live in a city normally pay more for insurance than people living in the suburbs. Also, insurance companies have a list of high risk occupations that will boost your cost. Taxi drivers, bartenders, waiters, cocktail waitresses and restaurateurs are just some of the occupations that will send a premium higher.

Driving record and type of car you drive: Your driving record is one of the leading determining factors of your auto insurance rate. If you have been in an accident and have one or more tickets, you can expect higher rates. If your driving record is clean, there is an excellent chance that your premium will be very low. If you've had a few moving violations, an accident, and drive a sportscar, you can expect to be socked with a very high insurance premium and, perhaps, limited availability of coverage. Sport and luxury cars carry the highest insurance premiums as they are more frequently stolen and the cost of repairs is higher than for an average, everyday sedan. Cars that have higher repair costs and/or more number of claims often carry higher insurance premiums which may be an issue when purchasing a new or used car.

The following table, from the Highway Loss Data Institute, shows the cost for insuring the listed cars. The "Claim Frequency" column rates the auto based on the number of times claims were filed for which the cost of the damage exceeded the deductible. A score of 100 (the average) denotes 11.1 claims per 100 vehicles where the deductible was exceeded. Therefore, the lower the score, the better. Reflected in the scores are each car's relative ability to withstand an accident as well as the respective abilities of the drivers of each auto class.

The "Repair Cost" column shows the cost to repair each listed model and is based on actual claims. The average score of 100 represents a repair cost of $1,921, and also reflects the autos' and drivers' relative strengths.

Model	Claim Frequency	Repair Cost	Model	Claim Frequency	Repair Cost
Small Cars (2-door)			**Mid-Size Cars (cont'd)**		
Toyota Tercel	123	82	Dodge Aries	75	96
Honda Civic	108	103	Plymouth Reliant	82	91
Ford Fiesta	104	114	Mazda 626	80	115
Nissan Sentra	129	91	Chevrolet Corsica	110	85
Ford Escort	131	98	Ford Tempo	87	110
Mercury Tracer	109	118	Honda Accord	108	90
Hyundai Excel	139	96	Renault Medallion	129	97
Mazda 323	114	119	**Mid-Size Wagon/Vans**		
Pontiac Le Mans	146	113	Ford Taurus	75	93
Toyota Celica	153	118	**Mid-Size Sports/Specialty**		
Mazda MX-6	121	166	Lincoln Mark IV	83	113
Small Cars (4-door)			Chevrolet Camaro	128	120
Ford Escort	110	73	Ford Mustang	132	156
Mercury Tracer	88	96	**Large Cars (4-door)**		
Mazda 323	91	102	Chevrolet Caprice	67	65
Honda Civic	132	75	Mercury Grand Marquis	64	69
Toyota Corolla	102	110	Pontiac Bonneville	57	84
Hyundai Excel	118	102	Oldsmobile 98	55	95
Pontiac Le Mans	129	117	Buick LeSabre	76	90
Mid-Size Cars (2-door)			Ford Crown Victoria	80	88
Mercury Cougar	108	89	Buick Electra	79	97
Pontiac Grand Am	97	100	Oldsmobile Delta 88	78	101
Buick Regal	103	101	**Large Wagons/Vans**		
Honda Prelude	113	96	Chevrolet Astro Van	78	40
Oldsmobile Calais	101	108	Plymouth Grand Voyager	63	59
Honda Accord	123	99	Dodge Caravan	66	60
Chevrolet Beretta	118	104	Plymouth Voyager	75	61
Ford Thunderbird	113	121	Dodge Grand Caravan	76	70
Chevrolet Cavalier	113	125	Ford Aerostar	78	84
Mid-Size Cars (4-door)			**Large Sports/Specialty**		
Chevrolet Celebrity	68	79	Cadillac DeVille 4-door	54	104
Ford Taurus	81	76	Lincoln Town Car	77	94
Olds Cutlass Ciera	72	89	Jaguar XJ6	72	183
Toyota Camry	77	91	BMW 735i	89	149

Safe driving classes: Some insurance companies are offering reductions in premium prices if the insured party completes a recognized course in driver safety. Consider investing a few hours to save as much as 10% a year, and have the added benefit of being a safer, more defensive driver.

Additional drivers: Insurance companies consider the number of drivers when setting their rates. For example, if you're a married man with three children who are all eligible to drive the same car, your rates will be much higher than a married man with three children who are not yet eligible to drive the same car. Oftentimes insurance will be cheaper if you buy a second car to split up the number of eligible drivers.

No-fault insurance laws: Many states have adopted no-fault insurance laws which speed up the payment on injuries from your own insurance company and keep a lot of minor personal injury cases out of court. Most no-fault laws have ceilings for injury claims which can be settled under their jurisdiction. For example, a $2500 ceiling means if your personal injury-bills come to under $2500, your insurance company pays automatically.

No-fault insurance laws don't take away an individual's right to sue. They just control the amount for which you can sue and what can be settled with your own insurance company. No-fault laws do not cover the loss of tangible personal property.

Checklist of ways to save on insurance:

1. *Shop around:* A wise consumer who comparison shops between insurance companies can save as much as 25% on an insurance bill.
2. *Inform your insurance company of your marriage and of your twenty-fifth or thirtieth birthday:* You may be entitled to an immediate reduction in your premiums.
3. *Use the collision deductible wisely:* Extend the deductible to $250 or $500 if there is a good savings. Drop your collision insurance on an older car which might not be worth very much.
4. *Do not incur any moving violations:* If you have one on your record, find out from the Department of Motor Vehicles how long it takes for the infraction to be "cleaned" from your record. Check into taking defensive driving classes which may remove points from your license. After your record is cleaned, contact your insurance company; you may be in for a reduction in rates.
5. *Do not buy an expensive and flashy sportscar:* If you do choose to purchase a sportscar, don't get all the optional and excessive equipment; it might keep the cost of your premiums down.
6. *List anti-theft and alarm devices on the insurance application:* They may decrease your rates.
7. *Let your insurance company know of any change in your insurance status:* For example, if you change from a high risk job to a low risk job or move to a more desirable insurance location, inform your insurance company; it may be reflected in lower premiums.
8. *Insure all of your cars with the same company:* This gives you better leverage with your insurance company, and will probably earn you a multiple car and good customer discount.
9. *Avoid listing your children as principal drivers:* Rates are highest for young, single drivers. Buy the cars in your name and list yourself as the primary driver.

10. ***Ask about the discount plans offered by your company:*** For example, you may get a driver education discount or a good driver discount. Also, if you only use your car on the weekends, or only for pleasure driving, you might pay a lower rate. Companies also discount for such things as car-pooling, or advanced driving courses like highway driving and high speed driving.
11. ***Check on discounts for small cars:*** Most companies have small car discounts which could mean savings of up to 40%. Also, some companies give a discount for cars with high fuel economy.
12. ***Don't buy the extras:*** Insurance for rental cars, towing, or club memberships may not be good values. Review your circumstances to decide whether you need these extras and adjust your insurance accordingly.

## Chapter 12

How To Save
$ $ $ On Gasoline

With gasoline prices at an average of $1.20 per gallon, most motorists need to know effective ways to conserve fuel. There are both obvious and subtle ways to save gasoline in your automobile. Both make the amount of money you spend per mile appreciably less. In fact, most motorists can cut their fuel consumption by as much as 42% by observing some basic rules to avoid gas-guzzling.

This chapter includes a list of 46 ways to save gasoline, categorized in three sections—"The Obvious," and "Not-So-Obvious,"and "Changing Your Gas Consuming Lifestyle Comfortably." In the third section are outlined some changes that you, a gas-buying consumer, can make in your car-driving habits which will directly affect your M.P.G.—Money Per Gallon.

The Obvious

1. Keep your car properly tuned at all times: Instead of tuning your car every eight or nine months as most manufacturers suggest, get a major tune-up every six months. The extra money spent is a good investment, especially when you fill up your tank. Clean points and plugs and a correctly timed car can cut gas consumption from 3% to 12%. A well tuned engine also enhances the resale value of your automobile.

2. Cut down your highway driving speed to 55 miles per hour: A car that normally gets 20 miles per gallon on the open highway with a tank capacity of 20 gallons going at an average speed of 65 miles per hour could get 23.5 miles to the gallon by decreasing the average highway driving speed to 55 miles per hour. Staying at 55 miles per hour consistently would give the car in the above example an additional tank range of 70 miles. At an average of $1.20 per gallon, that means $4.20 per tankload savings.

3. Keep your tires properly inflated: According to some experts, (Automobile Club of America, Consumer Reports, Road and Track Magazine, among others), 69% of the drivers on the road today are driving with improperly inflated tires. These experts believe that most cars can save an average of two miles per gallon by keeping the tire pressure within the prescribed manufacturer's specifications. Radial tires save 3-7% over bias tires.

4. Learn to start your car properly: The best way to start a cold car efficiently is to depress the accelerator once before turning the ignition, and then slowly depress the pedal while turning the ignition. Release the accelerator when the engine turns over. *Note: starting a car varies from person to person and from car to car; check the owner's manual.*

5. Avoid fast starts: When accelerating from a stop sign, a red light, or a parking spot, gradually depress the accelerator pedal at an even and continual pace. By slowly accelerating to the speed limit, you can cut your starting gas consumption by 35%. Most drivers lose precious miles per gallon by making fast starts from a stopped, idling position.

6. Accelerate to open highway speeds gradually: Most major highways have long acceleration ramps, but most drivers only use about half of the acceleration lane to get up to 55 miles per hour and beyond. By slowly accelerating on the entrance ramp and using most of the acceleration lane to get up to highway speed, you could save up to 8% of the gas normally used in this facet of driving.

7. Coast to save gas: It is the rare driver who coasts on a downgrade, or who coasts into a red light or a stop sign, yet coasting raises gas economy. If your wheel bearings are properly greased and you are on a 15 degree or greater downgrade, if you take your foot off the accelerator, you will only lose up to 5% of your speed and save up to 17% of gas consumption normally used in this aspect of driving. Coast only when traffic conditions are safe to do so.

8. Turn off your engine if you intend to be stopped longer than three minutes: Most traffic lights throughout the country are timed for 30 seconds, a minute, a minute and 15 seconds, 90 seconds, or two minute intervals; therefore, you shouldn't turn off your engine at traffic lights. However, if you anticipate standing for more than three minutes, you should turn off your engine. It will not cool down completely for at least an hour, so when you restart your car you usually don't need to depress the accelerator pedal before turning the ignition key. Check your owner's manual for recommended instructions for your car.

9. Warm your engine before driving: To properly warm up your car, you should let it idle for at least a minute before starting to drive. The automatic choke should be serviced regularly. *Note: Those cars with semi-automatic chokes should start with the choke pulled out all the way. When the engine turns over, the choke should be pushed in about half-way. Cars equipped with semi-automatic chokes should not be driven until the choke pops in or until the temperature gauge moves slightly.*

10. Keep speed consistent on the highway: If you are anticipating driving on a highway for a long distance, you should keep your speed consistent for optimum gas mileage. Any variation in speed of 5 miles per hour or more can decrease fuel efficiency by almost 2 miles per gallon.

11. Never ride the brake: Some motorists are chronic "Brake Riders." A good driver never applies the brake while traveling unless it is necessary to stop. Motorists who drive with two feet, constantly applying the brake while leaving the other foot on the gas, promote drag on the car, and countless miles to the gallon are lost.

12. Check tire balancing and wheel alignment every 6,000 miles: Wheels which have been knocked out of alignment by potholes and rough roads are a detriment to increased gas mileage. Combine that with tires that aren't balanced and your car will shimmy ever so slightly, robbing a car of an estimated 1-1.5 miles per gallon.

13. Start off slower in cold weather: During the cold winter months, it takes longer for your car to heat up to proper operating temperature. The warm-up time of your car should be increased from one to two minutes. Keep your car under 40 miles per hour for the first three miles to insure proper operating temperature. An automobile should never be raced in cold weather to force it to warm up more rapidly. A helpful hint to avoid prolonged warm-ups in winter is to change thermostats during the colder months. Automobile parts manufacturers make thermostats which allow a car to run colder or hotter as the climate dictates. For colder weather a hotter thermostat would be a fuel saver, while in the summer a cooler thermostat should be used.

14. Keep all fluid levels high: All the fluid levels in your car are directly related to the type of gas mileage you will get either on the open road, or just around town. The radiator water should be to the base of the cap stem to keep your car running cool. The oil level should be kept at full capacity to keep the crank case from getting hot and all of the moving parts in your engine from getting sluggish. The most infrequently checked fluids in the car are the transmission and brake fluids; however, both are just as important to good gas mileage as the oil and radiator water. A helpful hint for those cars using regular gasoline: using unleaded gasoline every third fill-up will clean up the spark-plugs keeping them firing hotter longer, enhancing gas mileage. When filling your gas tank on hot days, don't let the gas attendant fill it to the top. Leave some room for expansion so that gas doesn't spill out and ruin your paint job and mileage.

15. Shift into neutral in stop and go traffic: When you're stuck in stop-and-go traffic and there is no way out, the only thing you can do to improve gas mileage is to slip the car into neutral when stopped. This diminishes the flow of fuel into your carburetor, cutting down fuel consumption. Shifting into neutral in stop-and-go traffic also allows the engine to run cooler.

16. Purchase cars with high gas mileage ratings: The Environmental Protection Agency road tests cars at the beginning of each model year. The test results for 1990 car models are listed at the end of this chapter. For E.P.A. figures on vans, trucks, and sport vehicles, refer to **Edmund's Vans, Pickups, and Sport Utility Vehicles Buyer's Guide**.

The Not-So-Obvious

1. Keep your car clean: Dirt on the outside of the car creates drag, and harms gas mileage. A clean car gets up to 2 miles per gallon more than a dirty car.

2. Try to keep the windows shut: It's very easy to keep the windows in your car shut during the winter, but it becomes more difficult to keep them closed during the scorching summer months. Open windows create a draft inside the car which tends to "hold" the car back, especially during acceleration. Some experts feel that open windows at speeds of 55 miles per hour or more cut 10% off your miles per gallon.

3. A straight line is the shortest distance between two points: This law of geometry also applies to driving long distances, especially when you're trying to conserve gasoline. Gripping the wheel firmly and keeping your vehicle on a straight line enhances the gas mileage of your car. Change lanes as infrequently as possible to conserve gasoline. Keeping your car on a straight path to your destination can save up to 1 mile per gallon.

4. "The back roads will get me there faster:" But maybe not more economically. Many times motorists will opt for short cuts that cut travel time; however, many short cuts off the main roads are filled with stop and yield signs, railroad crossings and traffic lights. That's a lot of stop and go traffic that is murder on gas mileage. Continuous driving always is better than stop and go, so the next time you think of taking the short cut, think about your money per gallon.

5. Buy cars with a more economical standard transmission: Normally, a standard transmission can get up to 32% better gas mileage than a similarly equipped car with an automatic transmission. However, that savings can be cut in half by driving your standard transmission improperly. To realize the full economy of your standard transmission, shift into high gear as quickly as possible. A car in second gear uses 30% more gas to operate properly than it does in high gear. In first gear, the standard transmission uses almost 50% more gas than in high gear. When slowing down with your standard transmission, it is more economical to go from high gear directly into low gear without any intermediate stops. Shifting to slow down from fourth gear to third, to second is a 20% waste of gas according to the Environmental Protection Agency. You achieve better gas mileage by just applying the brake.

6. Pedularly shift your automatic transmission: It may not seem possible to manually shift an automatic transmission but it is—with your foot. Every car with an automatic transmission slips into the next gear automatically as the R.P.M.'s (Revolutions Per Minute) get faster and faster. You can feel it in your own car. The R.P.M.'s will get to a point, and then the automatic transmission will shift itself into a higher gear. It is tricky, but an automatic transmission can be shifted pedularly if you are aware of the ride and the feel of your car. The key to turning an automatic transmission into a pedular (standard) transmission is to momentarily ease your foot off the gas pedal as the car is about to shift into a higher gear. When you put your foot back on the accelerator, it will have shifted. Even though the gas savings is not as dramatic as with a manual transmission, you can save about 2 miles per gallon by making this a standard practice for your car.

7. Service the air filter regularly: A dirty air filter (which sits on top of the carburetor) can cause a decrease in power output by restricting the flow of air to the engine. Change the air filter at 12,000 or 24,000 mile intervals. More frequent servicing should be done if driving is done in sandy or extremely dusty conditions.

8. When going on a trip, pack evenly: When most people go on a long trip they just throw everything into the trunk. According to the Environmental Protection Agency, you can lose up to 22% of your gas mileage on the open road by doing this. When a trunk is loaded, the front of the car is raised up causing an unnatural wind resistance shield, so your once-sleek automobile becomes a wind plow and a gas guzzler. When going on a long trip, it is "gas-economically" wise to pack evenly throughout your car, sacrificing leg room for better gas economy.

9. Don't use the gas pedal as a brake: When driving a car with an automatic transmission and stopping on an incline, some drivers feed the car just enough gas to stay stationary on the hill without having to brake. This wastes gas at approximately four times the rate of normal idling, and is a certain way to burn up gallons of gas unnecessarily. Some people also do this with a manual transmission by riding the clutch, putting the car in first gear and depressing the accelerator just enough to prevent the car from rolling down the hill. This wastes gas and burns out clutches.

10. On extended trips, stop only to fill up: Gas mileage is improved on a long trip when the car is in continuous motion. You can calculate that each stop will rob you of at least 5% of your M.P.G. rating.

11. Being too slow is as bad as being too fast: Logically it would seem that the slower you travel below 55 miles per hour, the less gas you would use. That holds true to a point. The Environmental Protection Agency and the editors of Road and Track Magazine estimate that in 97% of the cases, optimum fuel burning for a car occurs at 35 miles per hour. Driving at 20 miles per hour with an automatic transmission burns up as much gas as if driving 70 miles per hour. Coincidentally, the E.P.A. ratings for highway driving are gathered by sending a car around a test track at 40 miles per hour. The fuel consumption difference from 40 to 55 miles per hour is about 18%. So, if the E.P.A. says that a car gets 30 M.P.G. on the highway, you can deduct 18% of that to get the total M.P.G. that you get on the highway traveling at 55 miles per hour.

12. Only run the rear defroster when necessary: Rear defrosters burn as much gasoline as a car air conditioner. Never use the rear defroster to thaw ice on the rear windows. Do not run the rear defroster after the fog on the window has disappeared. Running the front and the rear defroster simultaneously drops fuel efficiency by about 13%.

13. Proper turning increases fuel economy: Most turns and exits off highway exit ramps are negotiated improperly. Most drivers only slow down when they're in the turn instead of slowing down before it. By slowing down before the turn and then speeding up while in it, 20% of the gas normally used during this turning procedure is saved.

14. Get a running start up a hill: By increasing your speed 20% before entering the incline, and then easing off the gas pedal, you can actually save gas for the overall run. On inclines of 20 degrees or more, your car's engine works almost three times as hard. By increasing the speed on the flat surface 20%, you are saving a substantial amount of gas going up an incline.

15. Never turn on an air conditioner while idling: If you must use an automobile air conditioner which wastes fuel, you should never turn it on when you first start the car or if you're idling. The first surge of power from the auto air conditioner robs your engine of 25% more gas mileage than normal. An automobile engine can work up to four times as hard when a conventional auto air conditioner is at full blast.

16. Idling your car to save gas: Needless idling deteriorates gas mileage. However, it is recommended that a driver let his car idle for about a minute after the car has been through a long trip. This relieves some of the "hot spots" in an engine. Idling after a long trip also prevents vapor lock which might make it difficult or prohibit you from starting your car the next time you want to use it.

17. Service the manifold heat control valve: Make sure the manifold heat control valve is inspected and serviced at regular intervals. This valve, located in the exhaust system of some cars, allows exhaust gases to heat the intake manifold during cold engine operation. A valve stuck in the open position causes slow engine warm-up and poor cold engine performance. A valve stuck in the closed position will cause a loss of power and hard starting with a hot engine. Sticking in either position makes the engine less fuel efficient.

18. Sub-freezing starting economically: In sub-freezing or sub-zero conditions, a tremendous amount of gasoline is wasted while starting a car because the butterfly valve will stick closed not allowing any air to mix with the gasoline in the carburetor. The best way to start your car under these conditions is to lift the hood, remove the air filter cover from your carburetor, and stick an object through the butterfly valve to keep it wide open. Your car should start instantly, saving gasoline and preventing your car from flooding.

19. Garage your oldest car: Although most owners of more than one car keep their newest car in the garage to keep that new finish, for gas economy this is not best. The oldest car should go into the garage because historically they have more trouble starting than newer ones. A garage will raise the temperature of the overall environment of your engine, and this will help your car get started saving gas and starting time.

20. Using more than one car wisely: Many American families now own two cars—usually a small "around town" car and a larger family-size auto. The economical use of these can be a big gas-saver. For example, on short trips make a habit of using the car with better gas mileage. Also, try to use the car that was used last, as long as it hasn't been sitting for more than an hour or so. Use the larger, less fuel-efficient car sparingly.

21. Plan trips carefully: Combine those short trips and plan the route so that it is the shortest possible. This avoids unnecessary stopping and cuts gas mileage.

22. Be certain the parking brake is off: At times the brake warning light does not come on for a slightly depressed brake. Even if the brake is partially engaged, it can rob you of gas mileage. Besides saving energy, you will be saving wear and tear on your rear brake shoes.

23. Anticipate stop lights: Stopping and starting at every light is not only frustrating, it saps up a lot of gas. Plan ahead and try to time lights to avoid unnecessary stops. Write to your local Traffic Safety Council and encourage them to keep lights synchronized.

24. Lubricate wheel bearings: Unnecessary friction in the wheel bearings from poor lubrication can cause costly repairs and significantly reduce mileage. Rear wheel bearings normally are automatically lubricated; however, front wheel bearings require maintenance every 15-20,000 miles.

25. Replace worn shock absorbers: Worn shock absorbers allow the car to wander back and forth on the road wasting fuel and increasing tire wear.

Changing Your Gas Consuming Lifestyle Comfortably

There are some overall changes in driving habits that can be comfortably incorporated into your daily driving routine which will save a lot of gas and ultimately a lot of money. The editors of **Car Savvy** have assembled a list of changes that will help the average driver conserve gasoline. Most of the items in the following list are affordable as well as within reach and tolerance of a changing lifestyle. Even though most car drivers will look at these changes as a sacrifice, the alternatives could be even more distasteful. It's just a question of how frequently and how much you are willing to pay at the pumps.

1. **All future cars should have a standard transmission:** A well-driven standard transmission is one of the best ways to save gasoline. Even station wagons, one of the biggest group of gas-guzzling automobiles, are becoming equipped with standard transmissions. Even though E.P.A. gasoline consumption estimates vary from standard transmission to transmission, and from model to model, the editors of **Car Savvy** have estimated that two cars similarly equipped will show a difference of up to 32% in gas consumption with a standard transmission. However, to maximize savings, the standard transmission must be driven correctly. An interesting benefit of the standard transmission is an increase in driver control of the vehicle. Lower gears can slow down a car in an emergency, and a properly down-shifted car in the turns and banks of highway driving decrease the possibility of driving your car off the road. Also, many standard transmission cars come with a fifth gear or "overdrive" which considerably decreases the R.P.M.'s (Revolutions Per Minute) at high speeds saving gasoline and increasing engine economy. Another benefit of the standard transmission is that an automobile can get to highway speeds faster while using less gas.

2. **Decrease the overall size of your automobile:** Car size has a lot to do with the amount of gasoline used. A wide wheelbase, the overall length, and the total weight play an important part in your car's basic fuel economy. The size of the engine plays the most important role in fuel consumption. A V-8 burns gas more quickly than a 6- or 4-cylinder. The ultimate in fuel economy comes from a 4-cylinder engine. These engines are being made now for peak performance and low gas mileage. Scaling down the size of your car will enhance your gas mileage appreciably.

3. **Stay away from electrical convenience items:** Many car buyers purchase expensive electrically run options for their automobiles like air conditioners, power windows, power side-view mirrors, power radios and C.B. antennas, power disc brakes, additional lights on the inside of the car, electric gauges and clocks, power seats, electric door locks and electric sun roofs. All of these options in a car rob it of gas mileage. The Environmental Protection Agency estimates that 15-25% of all fuel economy is lost on electric options in an average automobile, and that if there were no air conditioners in automobiles, the savings in oil would average 10 million barrels per day.

4. Never buy exotic carburetors or exhaust systems: There are many cars on the road that use two-barrel carburetors and two exhaust systems that "turbo-charge" the engine by providing it with more power. However, this is a tremendous waste of gas with the gas feeding two sides or "barrels" of the carburetor at the same time. Stay away from dual exhaust systems. If there are two tail pipes, then the engine is too big for one, and guzzles the gas that necessitates both of them.

5. Use alternative means of getting there: The idea of car-pooling arrived when the gasoline shortage of 1974 hit the United States. Car-pooling to work or school was successful during and immediately after the 1974 gasoline shortage, but as the gas lines got shorter, more commuters returned to their cars to drive alone. Car-pooling is an effective way to save gas even if at times it may be inconvenient.

Suburban commuters working in a major metropolis also should start turning to mass transit whenever possible. Many major cities throughout the country are adding express bus and train service to the business districts, and commuters can drive to convenient, free parking lots and take public transportation.

M.P.G. Ratings

The editors of **Car Savvy** have simplified the task of figuring your M.P.G. rating by producing an M.P.G. Ratings Chart. It is simple to use, and can be used regardless of the vehicle you drive.

GALLONS USED ⟶

	1	2	3	4	5	6	7	8	9	10	11	12	13	14	15
50	25.0	16.7	12.5	10.0	8.3	7.1	6.3	5.6	5.0	4.5	4.2	3.8	3.5	3.3	
60	30.0	20.0	15.0	12.0	10.0	8.6	7.5	6.6	6.0	5.5	5.0	4.6	4.3	4.0	
70	35.0	23.3	17.5	14.0	11.7	10.0	8.8	7.8	7.0	6.4	5.8	5.4	5.0	4.6	
80	40.0	26.7	20.0	16.0	13.3	11.4	10.0	8.9	8.0	7.3	6.7	6.2	5.7	5.3	
90	45.0	30.0	22.5	18.0	15.0	12.9	11.3	10.0	9.0	8.2	7.5	6.9	6.4	6.0	
100	50.0	33.3	25.0	20.0	16.7	14.3	12.5	11.1	10.0	9.1	8.3	7.7	7.1	6.7	
110	55.0	36.7	27.5	22.0	18.3	15.7	13.8	12.2	11.0	10.0	9.2	8.5	7.9	7.3	
120	60.0	40.0	30.0	24.0	20.0	17.1	15.0	13.3	12.0	10.9	10.0	9.2	8.6	8.0	
130	65.0	43.3	32.5	26.0	21.7	18.6	16.3	14.4	13.0	11.8	10.8	10.0	9.3	8.7	
140	70.0	46.6	35.0	28.0	23.3	20.0	17.5	15.5	14.0	12.7	11.6	10.8	10.0	9.3	
150	75.0	50.0	37.5	30.0	25.0	21.4	18.8	16.7	15.0	13.6	12.5	11.5	10.7	10.0	
160	80.0	53.3	40.0	32.0	26.6	22.8	20.0	17.8	16.0	14.5	13.3	12.3	11.4	10.7	
170	85.0	56.7	42.5	34.0	28.3	24.2	21.3	18.9	17.0	15.5	14.2	13.1	12.1	11.3	
180	90.0	60.0	45.0	36.0	30.0	25.7	22.5	20.0	18.0	16.4	15.0	13.8	12.9	12.0	
190	95.0	63.3	47.5	38.0	31.7	27.1	23.8	21.1	19.0	17.3	15.8	14.6	13.6	12.7	
200	100.0	66.7	50.0	40.0	33.3	28.6	25.0	22.2	20.0	18.2	16.7	15.4	14.3	13.3	
210	105.0	70.0	52.5	42.0	35.0	30.0	26.3	23.3	21.0	19.1	17.5	16.2	15.0	14.0	
220	110.0	73.3	55.0	44.0	36.7	31.4	27.8	24.4	22.0	20.0	18.3	16.9	15.7	14.7	
230	115.0	76.7	57.5	46.0	38.3	32.9	28.8	25.6	23.0	20.1	19.2	17.7	16.4	15.3	
240	120.0	80.0	60.0	48.0	40.0	34.3	30.0	26.7	24.0	21.8	20.0	18.5	17.1	16.0	
250	125.0	83.3	62.5	50.0	41.7	35.7	31.3	27.8	25.0	22.7	20.8	19.2	17.9	16.7	
260	130.0	86.7	65.0	52.0	43.3	37.1	32.5	28.9	26.0	23.6	21.7	20.0	18.6	17.3	
270	135.0	90.0	67.5	54.0	45.0	38.6	33.8	30.0	27.0	24.5	22.5	20.8	19.3	18.0	
280	140.0	93.3	70.0	56.0	46.6	40.0	35.0	31.1	28.0	25.5	23.3	21.5	20.0	18.7	
290	145.0	96.7	72.5	58.0	48.3	41.4	36.3	32.2	29.0	26.4	24.2	22.3	20.7	19.3	
300	150.0	100.0	75.0	60.0	50.0	42.9	37.5	33.3	30.0	27.3	25.0	23.1	21.4	20.0	

MILES TRAVELED

The accuracy of your calculation depends upon filling up your car every time you get gasoline as well as keeping track of how many miles you have driven between fill-ups.

The bold numbers on the top of the chart indicate the amount of gallons pumped into your car at fill-up. The bold numbers down the left-hand side of the chart indicate the amount of miles driven between fill-ups. (Round the miles driven off to the nearest ten miles.) After you have noted how many miles you have driven between fill-ups and how many gallons you used, you should get an approximate miles per gallon rating for your car. For example, you just filled up your car with 18 gallons, and you have traveled 270 miles; you look at the column on top which says '18' and follow that column of numbers down to the '270' level showing an M.P.G. rating of 15.0.

GALLONS USED ⟶

	16	17	18	19	20	21	22	23	24	25	26	27	28	29	30
50	3.1	2.9	2.7	2.6	2.5	2.4	2.3	2.2	2.1	2.0	1.9	1.8	1.7	1.6	1.5
60	3.8	3.5	3.3	3.2	3.0	2.9	2.8	2.6	2.5	2.4	2.3	2.2	2.1	2.1	2.0
70	4.3	4.1	3.9	3.7	3.5	3.3	3.2	3.0	2.9	2.8	2.7	2.6	2.5	2.4	2.3
80	5.0	4.7	4.4	4.2	4.0	3.8	3.6	3.5	3.3	3.2	3.1	3.0	2.9	2.8	2.7
90	5.6	5.3	5.0	4.7	4.5	4.3	4.1	3.9	3.8	3.6	3.5	3.3	3.2	3.1	3.0
100	6.3	5.9	5.6	5.3	5.0	4.8	4.5	4.3	4.2	4.0	3.8	3.7	3.6	3.4	33
110	6.9	6.5	6.1	5.8	5.5	5.2	5.0	4.8	4.6	4.4	4.2	4.1	3.9	3.8	3.7
120	7.5	7.0	6.7	6.3	6.0	5.7	5.5	5.2	5.0	4.8	4.6	4.4	4.3	4.1	4.0
130	8.1	7.6	7.2	6.8	6.5	6.2	5.9	5.7	5.4	5.2	5.0	4.8	4.6	4.5	4.3
140	8.8	8.2	7.7	7.4	7.0	6.7	6.4	6.1	5.8	5.6	5.4	5.2	5.0	4.8	4.6
150	9.4	8.8	8.3	7.9	7.5	7.1	6.8	6.5	6.3	6.0	5.8	5.6	5.4	5.2	5.0
160	10.0	9.4	8.9	8.4	8.0	7.6	7.3	7.0	6.7	6.4	6.2	5.9	5.7	5.5	5.3
170	10.6	10.0	9.4	8.9	8.5	8.1	7.7	7.4	7.1	6.8	6.5	6.3	6.1	5.9	5.7
180	11.3	10.6	10.0	9.5	9.0	8.6	8.2	7.8	7.5	7.2	6.9	6.7	6.4	6.2	6.0
190	11.9	11.2	10.5	10.0	9.5	9.0	8.6	8.3	7.9	7.6	7.3	7.0	6.8	6.6	6.3
200	12.5	11.8	11.1	10.5	10.0	9.5	9.1	8.7	8.3	8.0	7.7	7.4	7.1	6.9	6.7
210	13.1	12.4	11.7	11.1	10.5	10.0	9.5	9.1	8.8	8.4	8.1	7.8	7.5	7.2	7.0
220	13.8	12.9	12.2	11.6	11.0	10.5	10.0	9.6	9.2	8.8	8.5	8.1	7.9	7.6	7.3
230	14.4	13.5	12.8	12.1	11.5	11.0	10.5	10.0	9.6	9.2	8.8	8.5	8.2	7.9	7.7
240	15.0	14.1	13.3	12.6	12.0	11.4	10.9	10.4	10.0	9.6	9.2	8.8	8.6	8.3	8.0
250	15.6	14.7	13.9	13.2	12.5	11.9	11.4	10.9	10.4	10.0	9.6	9.3	8.9	8.6	8.3
260	16.3	15.3	14.4	13.7	13.0	12.4	11.8	11.3	10.8	10.4	10.0	9.6	9.3	9.0	8.7
270	16.9	15.9	15.0	14.2	13.5	12.9	12.3	11.7	11.3	10.9	10.4	10.0	9.6	9.3	9.0
280	17.5	16.5	15.6	14.7	14.0	13.3	12.7	12.2	11.7	11.2	10.8	10.4	10.0	9.7	9.3
290	18.1	17.1	16.1	15.3	14.5	13.8	13.2	12.6	12.1	11.6	11.2	10.7	10.4	10.0	9.7
300	18.8	17.6	16.7	15.8	15.0	14.3	13.6	13.0	12.5	12.0	11.5	11.1	10.7	10.3	10.0

↑ MILES TRAVELED

TOP MILEAGE PERFORMERS BY CAR CLASS
BASED ON E.P.A. MILEAGE FIGURES

| Manufacturer/Make | Estimated MPG | | | Engine Descr. | Trans. | Fuel Sys. |
	City	Hwy	Cmb	CID / Cyl (Type)		
TWO SEATERS						
Honda Civic CRX HF	49	52	50	91 (1.5L) / 4	M5	FI
Mazda MX-5 Miata	25	30	27	98 (1.6L) / 4	M5	FI
Alfa Romeo Spider	23	30	26	120 (2.0L) / 4	M5	FI
MINI-COMPACT CARS						
Volkswagen Cabriolet	25	32	28	109 (1.8L) / 4	M5	FI
Nissan 240 SX	20	27	23	146 (2.4L) / 4	M5	FI
Porsche 944 S2	17	26	20	183 (3.0L) / 4	M5	FI
SUB-COMPACT CARS						
Geo Metro XFI	53	58	55	61 (1.0L) / 3	M5	FI
Chevrolet Sprint	46	50	47	61 (1.0L) / 3	M5	FI
Suzuki Swift	46	50	47	61 (1.0L) / 3	M5	FI
COMPACT CARS						
Volkswagen Jetta	37	43	40	97 (1.6L) / 4 D	M5	FI
Ford Escort	32	42	36	113 (1.9L) / 4	A3	FI
Pontiac Le Mans	31	40	35	98 (1.6L) / 4	M5	FI
MID-SIZE CARS						
Chevrolet Corsica	24	34	28	134 (2.2L) / 4	M5	FI
Plymouth Acclaim	24	32	27	152 (2.5L) / 4	M5	FI
Mazda 626/MX-6	24	31	27	133 (2.2L) / 4	M5	FI
Volkswagen Passat	21	30	24	121 (2.0L) / 4	M5	FI
LARGE CARS						
Volvo 740	21	28	24	141 (2.3L) / 4	M5	FI
Saab 9000	21	28	24	121 (2.0L) / 4	M5	FI
Buick Electra/Park Avenue	18	27	22	231 (3.8L) / 6	L4	FI
Buick Le Sabre	18	27	22	231 (3.8L) / 6	L4	FI
Chevrolet Caprice	19	27	22	262 (4.3L) / 6	L4	FI
SMALL STATION WAGONS						
Honda Civic Wagon	31	34	33	91 (1.5L) / 4	M5	FI
Colt Wagon	31	34	33	91 (1.5L) / 4	M5	FI
Ford Escort Wagon	27	36	31	113 (1.9L) / 4	M5	FI
Nissan Sentra Wagon	27	36	31	98 (1.6L) / 4	M5	FI
MID-SIZE STATION WAGONS						
Chevrolet Celebrity Wagon	23	31	26	151 (2.5L) / 4	L3	FI
Volvo 740 Wagon	21	28	24	141 (2.3L) / 4	M5	FI
Volvo 240 Wagon	21	27	23	141 (2.3L) / 4	M5	FI
Buick Century Wagon	21	27	23	151 (2.5L) / 4	L3	FI
Oldsmobile Cutlass Cruiser	21	27	23	151 (2.5L) / 4	L3	FI
Pontiac 6000 Wagon	21	27	23	191 (3.1L) / 6	L4	FI
Lincoln-Mercury Sable Wagon	20	29	23	182 (3.0L) / 6	L4	FI
Volkswagen Passat Wagon	20	29	23	121 (2.0L) / 4	L4	FI
LARGE STATION WAGONS						
Buick Le Sabre/Electra Wagon	17	24	20	307 (5.0L) / 8	L4	4
Chevrolet Caprice Wagon	17	24	20	307 (5.0L) / 8	L4	4
Ford LTD Crown Victoria Wagon	17	24	20	302 (5.0L) / 8	L4	FI
Lincoln-Mercury Grand Marq. Wgn	17	24	20	302 (5.0L) / 8	L4	FI
Oldsmobile Custom Cruiser	17	24	20	307 (5.0L) / 8	L4	4

## Chapter 13

Understanding Car Systems

Engine power: A car engine functions by burning a mixture of air and fuel. The heat or thermal energy thrown off by this process is converted into the mechanical energy which moves the car.

In most cars this is accomplished in four cycles or strokes of the pistons in the cylinders. After the fuel is mixed with air in the carburetor and the engine starts, the piston moves down, pulling the fuel/air mixture into the cylinder (induction stroke). Next, the piston creates pressure by moving up and the spark plug ignites the fuel/air (compression stroke). Heat becomes energy through burning of the fuel/air, thus moving the car. The expanding gas from the combustion forces the piston down once again (power stroke). In the fourth cycle, burned fuel is released in the form of exhaust gases (exhaust stroke).

The pistons in your car do not all move up or down at the same time. Depending on the cylinder arrangement, they will move either successively or in an overlapping pattern. As they move, they push the connecting rod, pushing the crankshaft which turns and sends power to your wheels. This power is also used by the many components that fill the car's body.

The first element in the driveline affected by the engine's power is the transmission (gearbox). This collection of gears transmits power to the driving wheels. The gears have notched wheels of different sizes which engage and disengage, rendering power to the car. The need for power depends on the road incline and whether the car is traveling forward or in reverse. An automatic transmission still requires the driver's selection of four gears: park, reverse, neutral or drive.

After the transmission, the power travels down the driveshaft (propeller shaft). It runs the length of the car ending in the differential which continues the rotation speed of each of the rear wheels. The differential transmits the power to the rear axle. The rear wheels are attached to this axle.

There are six more systems to consider in understanding a car's mechanics. They are the brake, fuel, lubrication, cooling, and electrical systems, and the tires.

Brakes: There are two kinds of brakes: conventional and disc.

Conventional: Pressure from the foot on the brake releases hydraulic fluid which travels down the brake line and reaches the wheel cylinders. At the end of the cylinders there are shoes which apply pressure to the brake drum. This stops the car. When they get wet they drag or fail.

Disc brakes: Instead of brake shoes and a brake drum, discs have brake pads and brake discs on the front wheels. The system basically functions in the same way as the conventional one. Generally, disc brakes are considered safer because they create more even braking, and are less affected by water.

Power brakes: The most important thing to remember about power brakes is that they do not stop a car more quickly—only more easily.

Both power steering and power brakes utilize a fluid to create pressure on the steering/brake system. Because they require less physical strength to operate, most full-size cars today are equipped with power steering and/or brakes.

Fuel: Fuel is stored in the gasoline tank which is in the rear of most cars. A gauge on the dashboard indicates how much fuel is left in the tank. Generally, there is a gallon of gas left in the tank even after the gauge registers "E" for "empty." It is best not to count on that extra fuel since a slight inaccuracy of the gauge could leave you stranded. When the car is in operation, gas travels from the tank to the carburetor through the fuel line. Gas is propelled by the fuel pump in the front of the car and is freed of foreign matter by a fuel filter before it reaches the carburetor.

Oil: Because so many parts in a car rub against each other, all engine parts must be well oiled, otherwise they will wear out or freeze up. The crankshaft is supported by the crankcase and is a reservoir for oil. The crankcase also supports the oil pump and filter. Below it lies the oil pan. Oil is carried to all moving parts of the engine by the oil pump and strained of impurities by the oil filter. Some cars have a gauge on the dashboard that indicates the amount of oil left in the car.

Coolant: American cars are almost always water-cooled. Coolant, or water with antifreeze, lowers the temperature of the car. It is pumped into the radiator by way of openings in the engine and washes around the cylinders. The air that enters through the radiator is propelled by a fan (which also drives the water pump) and helps cool the engine. Engine temperature is indicated on the dashboard. A bright red light indicates a shortage of coolant or lack of water.

Electrical: The three parts of the car that make up the electrical system are: the battery, generator (alternator), and voltage regulator.

The initial power given the car comes from the battery. It charges the electrical motor which turns the engine crankshaft. The battery also stores electricity to start the car while the generator is building electricity for the engine and other mechanisms. Some of the other electrical parts requiring this energy are the headlights, cigarette lighter, clock and radio.

Connected to the generator and the battery is the voltage regulator. It feeds energy to different parts of the car such as the distributor and headlights. It also returns electricity to the battery. In stop-and-go traffic it monitors the car's electricity needs, sending electrical power to the battery whenever needed.

An ammeter or indicator light on the dashboard indicates the working order of your electrical system. When the key turns in the ignition (before the car starts), a light goes on; after the engine starts, if the car is charging properly, this light goes out. This indicates the generator is producing power.

Tires: *Tire valves:* These are made of rubber and are exposed to extreme temperature, road chemicals and natural deterioration. Their life expectancy is similar to that of a tire. When they deteriorate, air seepage may occur resulting in a loss of air pressure and rapid tire wear. Generally they are changed when the tires are changed.

Wheel balance: A wheel assembly and tire in an out-of-balance condition can cause excessive tire wear—as much as 50% over normal wear. It also can cause annoying vibrations and bounce. Wheel balance should be checked periodically as a matter of good tire maintenance, more often when excessive wear becomes evident.

Tire rotation: The front and rear tires of a car wear differently under normal driving conditions primarily because they perform different functions. The front tires steer and absorb the shock of cornering forces while the rear tires deliver the drive force. An uneven distribution of weight can cause tires on one side of the car to wear differently from tires on the other side. Periodic rotation of tires helps to equalize this uneven distribution and will result in greater tire life (see page 60 for rotation method). Tire wear will be different on front wheel drive autos.

Front end alignment: The front wheels of a car always should point in the exact direction you are steering. Improper alignment may result from worn out steering and suspension parts or by wheels being knocked out of position by hitting the curb or a hole in the road.

Steering: A properly adjusted steering mechanism is necessary for safe control of your vehicle. This is even more important on wet or slippery surfaces. When operating correctly, steering should be smooth and easy. The car should hold to its course down a straight level road with little or no correction. If the vehicle pulls to one side or the front end vibrates excessively ("shimmy"), you should seek immediate servicing. The steering wheel should respond quickly to turning without excessive freedom of movement before the car responds.

Ignition and electrical systems: Beginning with chemical reactions in the storage battery, the electric current produced operates the starter to start the engine, produces high-voltage sparks at the engine spark plugs, operates various gauges, electric fuel pumps, auxiliary motors, heaters, radios, solenoids and an assortment of controls.

Ignition switch: This switch, located on the dashboard or steering column, turns on the starter. It requires no regular service. However, as the switch ages, resistance builds up sometimes preventing enough electricity from reaching the starter.

Battery: The electricity needed to start the car and operate all auxiliary power units is stored in the battery. When buying a battery, use the original equipment quality level as a guide, and carefully read guarantees. If kept clean, filled, and in a healthy state of charge, a good battery will last for three or more years depending on the climate. Most new batteries require no maintenance except for cable cleaning.

Battery cables: There are two cables on every battery. One delivers electric current to the starter, and the other is a ground completing the electrical circuit. These cables must be kept free of corrosion and excess dirt and must be connected securely to the battery. Otherwise your car may have difficulty starting and operating properly.

Starter solenoid switch: This switch connects the battery to the starter and carries the biggest load of any switch in the car. Poor connections and age reduce its ability to transmit sufficient current to turn the starter and start the car.

Starter: The starter is an electrical motor that moves a gear which cranks the car engine. Because of internal wear, the starter may eventually be unable to crank the engine fast enough or it may run down the battery. It then must be replaced.

Starter drive: This is the gear that connects the starter to the engine. If the starter whines but the engine doesn't turn over, the starter drive gear probably needs replacing.

Ignition coil: This mechanism is the heart of the ignition system. It boosts the 12 volts from the battery to as high as 30,000 volts and delivers the needed voltage to the spark plugs. At 30 M.P.H. this is done about 100 times a second. When the coil weakens, the entire electrical system is affected.

Distributor cap: This contains the terminals for each spark plug wire and ignition coil. The distributor cap is designed to insulate the terminals and keep dirt and moisture out. Eventually, moisture, dirt and high voltage corrode the connections and cause spark plug leakage or a short circuit. This results in hard starting and engine "miss." The distributor cap then must be replaced.

Rotor: This mechanism turns inside the distributor. It is connected to the coil wire and in one revolution touches the spark plug terminal connecting each spark plug with the coil. Replacement should be made while tuning-up the engine.

Contact set (points): This is a switch located in the distributor that turns the ignition coil on and off igniting the spark plugs in each cylinder. The points wear with use resulting in loss of efficiency. They should be replaced during a tune-up.

Condenser: The condenser absorbs the excess electrical surges caused by the rapid opening and closing of the points. It should be replaced with the points.

Spark plug wires: They connect the spark plugs to the distributor cap and carry up to 30,000 volts. Inspect these wires to assure that they are not corroded or defective in any way. Deteriorated wires can cause engine "miss."

Spark plugs: The plugs fire the ignition spark into the gasoline mixture in each cylinder. This provides the power which propels the car. The plug gap and the distances between the two electrodes should be properly adjusted to deliver the correct spark for your car. Improper gapping will cause a loss of power and gas economy. Plugs should be changed as often as the manufacturer suggests.

Alternator (generator): This produces electric power for everything except the starter and also recharges the battery.

Voltage regulator: This mechanism adjusts the voltage produced by the alternator in accordance with the demands of the electrical system needing power. Poor connections can alter or damage it. A defective regulator must be replaced.

Windshield wipers: Wipers should clean the windshield evenly leaving no streaks. Wiper arms should have the proper tension to hold the blades securely against the windshield during rainfall and when the vehicle is operating at high speeds. Failure of the wiper to operate may be due to a defective switch, short circuit, blown fuse, or a burned out wiper motor.

Windshield washer: Fill it with a solvent mixture that will clean and not freeze in winter. If not squirting fully, the washer may need new hoses or a pump. If the outlet is clogged, clear it by blowing compressed air through the lines.

Turn signals: You communicate your intentions to other drivers by means of directional signals. Therefore, it is most important that they are in operating condition. You can hear the ticking and see the flashing light on your instrument panel. If you cannot, this may be an indication that there is something wrong such as a defective steering column switch, burned out flasher unit, short circuit or burned out signal bulb.

Lights: a) Brake lights—These lights are important in communicating with other vehicles. They warn following motorists of your intention to slow or stop. Check to make sure they work when brakes are applied. If one of the lenses is broken, have it replaced as soon as possible because the glaring light from a broken brake light can blind a following driver. b) Headlights—Your headlights are of critical importance in night driving, in rainy weather and in fog. They must work properly and be correctly adjusted at all times. They should be kept clean because dust and dirt on the lenses reduce their effectiveness and create glare for others by distorting the beam. Dimming of lights is caused by a weak battery, alternator trouble, or a faulty voltage regulator.

Fuses and circuit breakers: These serve as safety valves, protecting lights and accessories from surges of excess electrical current. Most lighting circuits are protected by circuit breakers. The radio, heater, wiper motors and other accessories are protected by fuses. A blown fuse can be replaced easily, but the cause should be traced to prevent further, more severe damage, or even fire. Fuses often are located under the dashboard on the driver's side.

Horn: This is your warning signal. To drive a car without a working horn is dangerous. Always make certain it is operational.

The brake system: Brakes must operate so that they bring you to a smooth and rapid stop. Pulling to one side may be an indication of improperly adjusted brakes. Wet brakes also may pull unevenly until they dry out. This can be accomplished usually by depressing the brake pedal slightly which generates heat. Uneven pulling of brakes may cause loss of control.

Master cylinder: This is the brake fluid reservoir and pressure regulator. It is located under the hood for easy access and should be checked periodically for loss of fluid. Any appreciable loss is an indication of malfunction in the brake system and is a potentially dangerous problem. Internal friction and corrosion eventually will wear out the master cylinder resulting in a loss of braking action. The master cylinder usually is replaced as a unit.

Brake lines: These are the metal tubes and rubber hoses that carry the brake fluid from the master cylinder to the brake at each wheel. A loss of fluid will decrease the effectiveness of the brakes. Look for punctures, leakage and corrosion when your auto is serviced.

Wheel cylinders: The hydraulic wheel cylinder is located inside the brake assembly of each wheel. It acts on the brake lining, forcing it outward against the revolving drum to stop the car. Corrosion of the cylinder walls and leakage at the rubber seals will cause a loss of fluid and decrease braking power. They should be rebuilt or replaced whenever leaking occurs or brake linings are installed.

Brake linings: These are heat resistant frictional materials attached to a metal backing (the brake shoe). Their function is to come in contact with the rotating drum at high pressure in order to force the drum to stop. As the lining wears, the heat-resistant qualities diminish, making it more difficult to stop the car. Brake linings should be checked every 10,000 miles and replaced as needed.

Brake hardware: These include the self-adjusting parts, the hold-down parts, and return springs that activate the brake shoes. Heat, corrosion, and fatigue from stress cause these parts to wear out. These parts should be checked when inspecting brakes and replaced when needed.

Wheel bearings and grease seals: The wheel bearings support the weight of the car and allow the wheels to roll freely. They must be well-lubricated to function properly. The front wheel bearings should be greased every 15-20,000 miles and the grease seals replaced. They should be routinely replaced and new grease seals installed at the time of a brake job. Rear seals should be inspected for leakage.

Brake drums: They revolve with the wheels and should be resurfaced with each brake job to smooth out wear and restore braking efficiency. The drums must be replaced when worn beyond minimum safety specifications.

Disc brakes: The disc brake uses a flat plate secured to the wheel hub rather than a brake drum. The disc is gripped from both sides by the shoes and since the disc brake shoes are directly opposite each other and operate simultaneously, great pressure can be applied to the disc resulting in greater braking power.

The exhaust system: The function of this system which includes the exhaust pipe, muffler and tail pipe is twofold: to transfer exhaust gases from the engine and to reduce the noise of combustion in the engine. It is subject to both internal and external corrosion and must be inspected periodically to guard against escaping exhaust gases.

Exhaust pipe: This pipe transfers the exhaust gases from the engine to the muffler. When the pipe becomes heavily rusted due to internal corrosion or develops pinholes, it should be replaced.

Muffler: The muffler assembly contains a combination of chambers, baffle plates and tubes built to absorb the noise of the gasoline explosions blasting from the engine up to 15,000 times per minute. At the same time it handles accompanying gas vapors as hot as 1400°F. The greatest cause of muffler failure is inside corrosion due to "acid water" which condenses in the muffler. Backfiring and vibration may weaken the assembly and necessitate replacement. The muffler should be checked periodically for looseness, rust and pinholes. A leaking muffler is dangerous as it allows toxic carbon monoxide to escape into the car.

Tail pipe: The subdued gases and vapors are carried out of the muffler through the tail pipe. This pipe should be checked during inspection of the muffler, looking for the same tell-tale signs of wear. Replacement of the exhaust system varies from car to car.

The suspension system: The purpose of the suspension system is to support the weight of the vehicle. It must provide not only for the absorption of road shocks, but must allow the driver to steer the vehicle efficiently over a wide range of speed and load conditions.

The pitman arm: A steering wheel turn transmits movement through the steering column and gear box to the pitman arm. As the pitman arm moves, it pushes or pulls the center link to the left or right.

The idler arm: Mounted on the passenger side of the car, the idler arm is the companion to the pitman arm. It supports the other end of the center link and resists undesired movement.

Center link: It connects the two tie rod assemblies which are connected to the hub assembly by steering arms. The two steering arms, tie rods and center link combine to turn the front wheels in unison.

Shock absorbers: "Shocks" are hydraulic mechanisms that control spring action, reduce suspension vibrations, and restrict body roll. Most problems arise from loss of fluid, broken mountings, and worn inner parts. Worn, inefficient shocks are characterized by severe body sway, front end dip when braking, and a bouncing ride. A badly worn shock can cause irregular tire wear and lead to other mechanical problems, some affecting the steering and stability of the vehicle creating a safety hazard. Under normal conditions shock absorbers will need to be replaced every 25,000 miles.

Ball joints: There are two ball joints in each front wheel assembly. Their function is to provide stability through all pivoting and turning motions of the wheel. They are worn by continuous pounding, turning, and exposure to dirt and grit.

The fuel system and the engine: The fuel system supplies a combustible mixture of gasoline and air to the engine cylinders. It stores the gasoline in liquid form in a fuel tank, then converts this liquid into a vapor and mixes it with air. The mixture enters the engine cylinders, is compressed and ignited. In burning, the fuel-air mixture increases in temperature causing it to expand, producing a high pressure in the engine cylinders. This pressure forces the pistons downward.

Fuel tank: This tank stores the gasoline in liquid form.

Fuel lines: The fuel lines carry the gasoline in liquid form from the gas tank to other components in the fuel system.

Fuel gauge: This is a gauge which appears on the instrument panel signalling the amount of fuel in the fuel tank.

Fuel pump: The fuel pump is driven by the engine and pumps gasoline from the fuel tank to the carburetor. When there is low pressure leakage, it must be replaced.

Fuel filter: It filters dirt and water in the gasoline before entering the carburetor. Failure to replace a clogged filter can result in restricted flow of fuel to the carburetor. It should be replaced every 12,000 miles.

Carburetor: The carburetor supplies the proper mixture of vaporized gasoline and air to the engine cylinders. Wear from age or neglected cleaning may require replacement of internal parts or a new carburetor. It requires periodic adjustment and cleaning every 20,000 miles to assure the proper mixture.

Air filter: This filter keeps abrasive dust out of the carburetor and engine. The engine consumes 10,000 times as much air as gasoline. A dirty or clogged air filter will restrict air flow and reduce gas mileage. Replacement is suggested every 12,000 miles or sooner if the filter is punctured or clogged.

PCV valve: This mechanism recycles the unburned gases from the crank case back into the engine's combustion chambers where they are safely reburned. Residue will eventually clog the valve restricting its function, allowing polluting fumes to escape. It should be examined regularly and replaced every 12,000 miles.

Oil pump: This pump forces oil through the filter to lubricate all vital parts of the engine. Defects are noticed by low oil pressure, engine knock and a hot engine. Poor circulation of oil will result in excessive wear of moving parts or complete stoppage. When defective, the pump is usually replaced as a unit.

Oil filter: This filter increases the life of the engine by preventing sludge, metal particles or other foreign materials from reaching moving parts. Replacement periods should follow manufacturer suggestions. Generally, it is a good idea to change the oil filter with each oil change at least every 6,000 miles.

The cooling system: All internal combustion systems are equipped with some type of cooling system because of the high temperatures generated during combustion and operation. Excessive temperatures are necessary to produce the high gas pressures needed to act on the pistons. Without such temperature, power cannot be produced efficiently. It has been estimated that the temperature in the combustion chamber during the burning of fuel is roughly twice the temperature at which iron melts. Therefore, if nothing is done to cool the engine during operation, valves will burn and warp, lubricating oil will break down, pistons and bearings will overheat, and pistons will seize in the cylinders.

Fan: The fan circulates a large volume of air through the radiator core. In addition to removing the heat from the radiator, this flow of air also provides some direct air cooling of the engine.

Water pump: This pump forces the coolant through the engine and transmission and returns it to the radiator for recooling. A worn out seal or moving part will result in leakage or excessive noise. The pump is replaced when this occurs.

Fan belt: The fan belt is connected to the water pump, alternator and engine. As the engine turns over, the fan belt drives the water pump and alternator. If the belt is cracked or frayed, it should be replaced. Periodic inspection of the belt should be made to assure that it is tight enough. A loose belt causes overheating and battery discharge.

Heater hoses: The system of hoses in the engine compartment should be inspected periodically, especially each spring and fall, as they are subject to internal pressure as well as deterioration because of heat, oil, grease and harmful chemical agents.

Radiator pressure cap: The radiator pressure cap seals the proper amount of pressure and releases excess pressure in the radiator to allow the engine to operate safely at the designated temperature. A leaking cap allows coolant to escape resulting in overheating and potential engine damage.

Radiator: The radiator should be checked regularly to insure sufficient water in the cooling system. More careful attention to water levels should be given during warmer months.

Engine thermostat: The thermostat maintains proper temperature of the coolant. It should be checked each spring and fall. A defective thermostat could result in a slow warm-up, increased engine wear, overheating or engine failure.

## Chapter 14

How To Beat The Auto Mechanic Runaround

After the insurance premium and the cost of gasoline, the next most expensive proposition in owning a car is to keep it running. Preventive maintenance and repairs hold the dubious distinction of being a major facet of driving that most people know little or nothing about. Therefore, most of us have to take the mechanic's word for it. As in any skilled-trade industry, the auto mechanic field has some dishonest tradesmen, but many more are honest. When you find a good, reliable mechanic, stick with him.

Even if you don't know the mechanic you're using, getting your repair or preventive maintenance job done to your satisfaction at a fair price is possible. The editors of **Car Savvy** have devised a list of ten questions that a consumer should ask himself before deciding if an auto mechanic is giving him a fair shake.

1. Does your mechanic give you a written estimate before he starts work? More and more states have consumer protection laws that stipulate that an auto mechanic must give a consumer a written estimate if asked, and most mechanics comply with these laws. If your mechanic refuses to issue a written estimate when asked, refrain from using that mechanic. If you are shopping for the best price, make sure the jobs are comparable before accepting to the lowest quote. For instance a "brake job" can mean new brake shoes only ($35-$40), or rebuilt or new wheel cylinders with mechanized drums or discs ($175-$200). Be aware that some repair shops may be adding a surcharge for the removal of waste materials. The charge is fair, and must be itemized in the estimate.

2. Does a mechanic inform you if and why the job is going to take more time and money than quoted? Oftentimes while a mechanic is looking under your hood, he finds other things that could be trouble in the future. He should call to inform you of these additional problems, and shouldn't just go ahead and do the work. Ask the mechanic to be specific about the nature of the extra repairs. You should be able to allow or disallow any extra work not covered in the original estimate. There should be no surprises when it comes time to pay the bill.

3. Does your mechanic return the parts that he took out of your car? A good mechanic always will return the parts he took from your car if he is asked to do so. Most people don't bother to ask, but asking keeps the mechanic honest and keeps the consumer satisfied. Sometimes the returned parts may come in handy in an emergency situation.

4. Do you try to diagnose a problem in your car before you take it to your mechanic? If the answer is "No," you are opening yourself up to whopping repair bills. Never go into your auto mechanic without any idea of what is wrong with your car for two reasons. First, the mechanic will spend a lot of time test driving your car and trying to diagnose the problem himself, for which he will probably charge. Second, you will have to take his word for the magnitude of the repair work. However, you do have the right to decline all proposed repairs if you think they are unnecessary. If you successfully diagnose your problem or approximate its location, the mechanic has something to go on which will probably save you money.

5. For major parts, does your mechanic offer you the option of a new or rebuilt part? If the answer is "No," ask about rebuilt parts. Be aware that there are some parts that can't be rebuilt. For example, a carburetor can be rebuilt, but spark plugs, brakes, and points cannot be rebuilt. Some gasoline pumps can be rebuilt, but gas filters cannot be rebuilt. To familiarize yourself with parts of your car that can be rebuilt, go to any parts dealer and ask what rebuilt parts may be used in your make and model. It is the law in most states that when a mechanic has replaced a defective part, he must signify on the written estimate or invoice whether the parts used are original equipment, new non-original equipment, or used.

6. Does the mechanic let you provide your own replacement parts? He should; however, this may not be in your best interest in some cases. Most repair shops get a 15% to 30% discount on the parts they buy, so the mechanic pays less for the part than you. However, in calculating the retail price to you, the garage may add back more than their discount to increase their profit margin. If this is the case, you are better off buying your own replacement parts. If you discover that the garage is charging you the same amount of money that you would spend for the parts from a parts dealer, you are better off letting the garage get the parts that you need.

7. Does your mechanic guarantee his work? If he doesn't, then you should not be going to that mechanic for repairs. Most garages will guarantee repairs for a certain period of time. The normal guarantee period is 30 days, but better shops may guarantee a job from three to six months according to the type of repair made. Be sure to get your guarantee in writing.

8. Do you have a log of repairs, and will your mechanic sign it? Every time your car goes in for a repair job, it should be recorded (see log in Chapter 8) and signed by your mechanic with the guarantee noted. If the mechanic is confident that he did a good job, he will not hesitate to sign your repair log; if he refuses, you should discontinue doing business with him. Keeping a repair log has several benefits. First, if there is any dispute over how long it has been since a problem was fixed, you have the repair log to back you up. Second, a repair log is an organized record of all maintenance done on your car. Additionally, keeping the log for your vehicle enhances the resale value of your car; it shows prospective buyers that you have been a conscientious car owner.

9. Is your mechanic's shop well organized? Most good mechanics are so well organized that they can immediately find any tool needed. One way to spot an organized mechanic is to watch the way he removes parts from a car. A sign of a good and orderly mechanic is if he takes off parts and lines them up in the order in which he removed them. In most repair garages, each mechanic has his own work area. If the tools seem to be scattered throughout the garage and the mechanic doesn't have his tools in one location, chances are his repair job will be just as disorganized.

10. Is your car road-tested before and after work is completed? The prerequisite of any good auto mechanic is his ability to spot a problem; however, there are many times when this is difficult to do without road-testing the vehicle. A simple way to check if an auto mechanic has road-tested your car is to check the odometer reading before you leave the car at the shop. If the odometer has moved ¼ of a mile or so, then you can be assured that the car was road-tested. If you find that your mechanic has not road-tested the car, tell him that you would like to road-test the car with him in it before you pay the bill.

Additional helpful hints: If you have read this chapter carefully, you are probably well-fortified against any inflated repair cost evaluation. Even so, ask a lot of questions about the repair work to be done and be *very specific* in your questions. If the mechanic says he will have to look at the car first before getting back to you with an estimate, instruct him to do *no* repairs until you have the estimate. Then ask all your questions regarding labor and parts. Ask him how much each part will cost and how long it will take to install. Mechanics are a lot less likely to cheat you in the final bill if they know they are dealing with someone who is knowledgeable and who might check with another authority on the validity of the estimate. If you have any doubt about the trustworthiness of the repair shop or any of its employees, go somewhere else.

Before using any repair shop, find out if it is licensed by local government agencies. It should be; in most states mechanics are certified. Ask or notice if the mechanics have received diplomas of advanced or additional training. With more advanced technologies, methods of diagnosing a problem may be more difficult unless the mechanic has kept his skills current. Many mechanics completed their apprenticeships before the current trends of electronic fuel injection, anti-lock brakes, logic modules, and touch screen controls.

The increased demand for improved consumer automotive service has moved many dealers to upgrade their service departments. Auto manufacturers have also sought to improve the communication between themselves and the consumer. If you have a new car and there is something chronically wrong with it, you might try contacting the Consumer Relations Department of the manufacturer.

Until there is a rating system for auto repairs shops, you are largely guessing when you choose a shop to repair your car. Nonetheless, there are a few basics to look for in any repair shop. They certainly should have the right equipment on hand to do the job. As a minimum, look for the following:

Battery charger with ammeter: Check your old battery with this device before letting anyone sell you a new one.

Brake drum tester: This machine checks the brake drums.

Power tools: The hand tools should be electrically powered. They are used to remove lugs and bolts and to work with bent metal parts.

Compression gauge: This gauges the cylinder valves, insuring correct fuel/air mix and proper escapement of exhaust gas.

Lift(s): Every mechanic should have at least one lift. A lift is used to raise the car so the mechanic can see what is underneath.

Engine analyzer: Indicates how to tune up your engine and whether or not to replace the alternator or voltage regulator. It is a machine with lots of dials and rolls up to the car for use.

Which type of repair shop? If your car needs repair, there are a number of alternatives. You can go to your dealer's service department, the local gas station, a franchised repair shop or an independent repair shop. If your car is still under warranty or if it requires a complicated repair job, your dealer is probably the best place to go. If the repair is very small, we suggest a gas station; it will probably be less expensive and more prompt in doing the work. Develop a good relationship with your local gas station, and it will be the best place to take your car for an oil change, battery charge, cleaning or changing of spark plugs, brake adjustments and replacement of fan belts or fuses.

Franchised repair shops often are not a good solution to repair problems. According to the authors of one book, **The Great American Auto Repair Robbery,** these shops sometimes suffer from a poor contract arrangement with their franchiser. This means that most of the profits go into his pocket, and the shop hustles to make ends meet. For you, that often means poor service at a disproportionate price. Unfortunately, franchises often attract people who know very little about the kind of business they are buying. Thus, unless a repair shop has hired experienced, skillful mechanics, you will not benefit from the best possible service. Too often the franchisee was more attracted by the need to be in business for himself than by the particular line of work his franchise represents. It might have even been a toss-up between buying into McDonald's® and leasing an auto repair shop!

However, if you decide that a particular franchised shop looks good, talk to the owner before you enlist his services. Ask him about his experience in the business and check out the mechanic who will be working on your car. If your questions are resented, don't risk using the shop.

Independent repair shops are usually the best places to go, especially when they are run by car fanatics, as many of them are. But it still pays to ask a lot of questions, being very specific, and showing that you know something about your car. It is essential that there be good communication between you and the mechanic because he needs to know exactly how your car behaved when it broke down. The early symptoms are as important as the final collapse.

It might be beneficial to contact the *American Automobile Association* for their list of approved garages. Approximately 4,500 are approved across the United States, and their number represents only half that apply.

## Chapter 15

Tools And Safety Devices To Keep In Your Car

Through careful reading of **Car Savvy**, you now have a basic understanding of how your car operates. To utilize that knowledge, you should supply your car with some necessary tools. If you get stuck on the highway and you can isolate the problem and fix it, you could save an emergency call to a garage. Most towing charges average between $35 - $100, based on the time of day and where the breakdown occurs, and roadside repair services are even more costly. Properly equipped, chances are you could emerge from a breakdown dilemma with only a little time spent and no money. Here's what you should keep in your car:

Jack and lug wrench: These are essential for changing a tire. Check your car manual for instructions on how to jack up your car to change the tire. You must block the wheel diagonally across from the tire you are changing to prevent the car from slipping off the jack. Most roadside conditions warrant using a large rock or a piece of wood from a fallen tree. If those are not available, and the flat occurs in one of the rear tires, then turn the wheel in the same direction as the side of the flat. For example, if the flat occurs in the left rear tire, turn the wheel all the way to the left. If the flat occurs in a front tire, and there is no object to block the rear tires, the best thing to do is apply the emergency brake as far as it will go. Instructions for placement of the jack are in the owner's manual.

Wrenches and other small items: If your car doesn't come outfitted with a small tool assortment, put one together yourself. The expense is not great and you are likely to save a lot of money on towing and service charges, particularly if you are handy. Some of the most important tools to have are listed below.

Oil filter band wrench: For removing or tightening the oil filter.

Adjustable wrench: For tightening or loosening nuts and bolts; adjusts to all sizes. Usually called a crescent wrench.

Open end wrench: For nuts of different sizes. Usually comes in a set with different sizes.

Flat-blade screwdriver: For loosening or tightening screws.

Phillips screwdriver: For the screws with two crossed slots on the top. This is the only screwdriver that will turn these screws.

Pliers: Important for holding or bending wires; vise-grips are most useful.

Socket and drive set: For removing and inserting nuts and bolts; provides maximum torque for loosening and tightening.

Fuse puller: For removing burned out fuses and inserting new ones.

Tire pressure gauge: For testing air pressure in tires.

Spark plug socket: For removing burned out spark plugs and inserting new ones. It is a long, lined socket to protect the porcelain on a spark plug. This may come in your socket set.

Universal joint wrench: For the nuts you cannot get to with a standard wrench. Attach universal joint, allowing wrench to go in at proper angle for loosening of the nut.

NOTE: Before buying tools, check with your car dealer or mechanic regarding the exact sizes. Foreign cars usually require their own tools; the wrench that works on a Chevrolet may not fit the parts of a VW. Keep a few *spare parts* in your car trunk; extra fuses, spark plugs and drive belts are recommended. Rags and a grease-solvent hand cleaner are handy items to have with you; almost all parts of a car are very greasy.

Even though the manufacturers' manuals supplied with most cars are complicated, make sure you keep them in your glove compartment. What you don't understand may be useful for the mechanic handling the car in crisis. Also keep all other literature offered by the manufacturer or dealer. If you do not have a *Chassis Service Manual* or *Owner's Maintenance And Light Repair Manual,* write to the company's home office, being specific about your car's model and year. There is usually a small fee for these manuals.

Flares vs. reflectors: Recent studies have indicated that the use of highway flares at night during most simple repair operations may not be the best way to alert oncoming traffic that you are in trouble. Latest studies by the National Highway and Safety Administration indicate that the use of triangular highway reflectors which stand up on a tripod type stand are better for long range viewing than flares.

There are many reasons for this. The first is that triangular reflectors are more stable and are not prone to go out. They also have a larger reflective area than a flare. Another advantage of the triangle reflector is that it can be carried when walking down the highway to a set-up position. This signifies to everyone on the road that you are in trouble. On the other hand, flares have to be set-up before they are lit, so the driver who is stuck in the middle of the night would probably be doing this operation in relative darkness. If you cannot fix the problem yourself, and you must leave the scene to get help, there is a risk that your flare could go out, leaving your disabled car unmarked. If you fix your car quickly, flares which are not readily put out and can burn for up to three hours, would create an unnecessary hazard.

The only time a flare is preferable is when there is ground fog. A reflector does no good if the beams of car lights don't hit it, and a flare is especially designed to penetrate fog, whether it be light or dense. The optimum solution during either light or dense fog is to put a reflector between the flares, spacing them 10-15 feet apart. The light from the flares will bounce off the reflectors, and will give an excellent glow to the oncoming traffic.

Have both flares and reflective triangles in your car to keep you safe from oncoming traffic during simple repairs.

Lights: A large flashlight in your glove compartment or trunk is a must for night driving. If you should get stuck, you may need the flashlight to get equipment and tools out of the back of your car. Also, you could use it to warn oncoming traffic that you are in trouble.

The best flashlight to buy is one with a removable yellow filter on the front. This type also comes with a flashing red beacon which can be extended from the top. The yellow filter is for penetrating fog, and the red flasher indicates trouble on the road. Make sure to use nothing but alkaline long-life batteries in your flashlight. They last up to five times as long as normal batteries. Also, if your car is disabled, but the electrical system is fine, turn on your emergency flashers. All new cars are required by law to have them.

## Chapter 16

Breaking Down On The Road: What To Do

You are driving down the highway and suddenly your car sputters and you lose power. Don't panic. Steer carefully to the right side of the road, if possible. You may find yourself in a situation where you are unable to move out of the lane in which you are driving. Move carefully to the closest shoulder. Then engage the emergency warning flasher, usually found on the steering column. Be sure to check the traffic before leaving the car. Next, raise the hood to signal an emergency and then set warning flares or reflectors 20 feet behind your car, then 300 feet farther back, and one 50 feet in front of the car. If you have a white cloth, tie it to your door or antenna as a signal for help.

If you are in an unfamiliar neighborhood, it is best to remain with your car, safely locked inside, until help arrives. If you go to call, make sure you note where you are first so you can explain it to the person you call. If the tow truck comes, or the police have to call the tow truck, identify your problem as a relatively inexpensive problem because that is what they will tell the garage. Otherwise, if it's a minor job but the garage thinks you expect it to be a major repair, you may wind up getting a larger bill than necessary. If you are towed to a strange garage, try to stay with the car while the repairs are done. Ask for old parts after the repair and make sure you get an estimate. If it turns out to be a large repair, tell the mechanic you want the minimum to get home and then have your mechanic finish the job. There are some things you can check yourself *before* the tow truck comes.

1. Although it may seem obvious, check your gas gauge. On long trips it is easy to lose track of gas levels.
2. Raise the hood and check for the obvious: loose wires, especially the wire from the distributor to the coil, and the wires from the spark plugs to the distributor (see Chapter 13). Breakdowns frequently involve the car's electrical system. See the trouble-shooting chart at the end of this chapter.
3. Some problems may only be temporary such as a faulty fuel pump or corroded starter switch. Be sure to try to start the engine again as it may well turn over and allow you to get to that next service station.
4. Suppose your car just won't start. There are a few things that you can do. If the car is turning over but won't catch, there could be a problem with the intake manifold in the carburetor. That's the steel flap covering the throat of your carburetor. You can take off the air filter cover by unscrewing the bolt at the top, and pry the intake manifold open with a pen or other long object. This will keep the air flowing into your carburetor so you will insure against flooding the car. If it still won't start, turn on your lights. If the

lights go dim while starting, you probably have a loose or corroded battery connection. Take the cables off the terminals, (ground side first) and clean them with a knife or wire brush. Replace them and turn the screws on them tightly. If the lights are still dim when you turn on the ignition, your battery is probably too weak to start the car.

5. Attempting to start a disabled car numerous times uses up the power in the battery causing ignition problems. You may need a jump start to get going. Of course you will need another car to assist you. Steps in jump starting a car with a dead battery are:

   a) Position the cars so they are facing one another, close enough to connect the cables, but **not** touching.

   b) Turn off all power in both cars and set the parking brakes.

   c) Make certain the voltages on both batteries are identical and that their fluid levels are in the normal range.

   d) Connect the **red** cable to the **positive** poles on each battery.

   e) Connect one end of the black cable to the good battery and the other end to a bare metal part bolted to the frame on the car with the dead battery. Be careful the black and red clamps do not touch.

   f) Try to start the car with the dead battery. If it won't turn over, start the booster car and wait a few minutes before attempting to start the dead car.

   g) Remove the clamps in the exact reverse order. (*Warning:* The sudden voltage surge that results from jump-starts can damage the car's computer system. To draw electricity away, turn on the lights and heater before connecting the jumper cables.)

6. Perhaps the most common roadside emergency is changing a flat tire. You should always make sure your trunk contains a useable spare tire, jack, lug wrench and screw driver before going out on the road, and you also should be familiar with the operation of that jack and where to place it under the car's frame. Most owner manuals have very explicit instructions. Check below for a step by step method to change a tire.

To Change A Tire:

1. When pulling off the road, pull as far to the right as possible, preferably onto a level surface.

2. Put the car in park and set the emergency brake. Turn on warning flashers.

3. Get everyone out of the car, and away from the car. If the jack slips, no one will be unnecessarily injured.

4. Place a rock or board under the wheel on the opposite corner to avoid rolling.

5. Remove the jack, lug wrench (often a part of the jack handle), screw driver, and spare tire from the trunk.

6. Remove the wheel cover with the screw driver. This will expose five lug nuts.

7. Loosen each nut about one turn. This may take a lot of strength. If they are stuck, it is handy to have a commercial spray which helps loosen tight bolts and nuts.
8. Place the jack on solid and level ground and raise the car so that the wheel is about one inch from the ground.
9. Remove the lug nuts placing them in the wheel cover so they won't get lost.
10. Put the new wheel on and hand tighten the lug nuts exercising care not to knock the car off the jack.
11. Begin tightening the lug nuts. Tighten evenly from **side to opposite side**.
12. Lower the jack and finish tightening the lug nuts.
13. Leave the wheel cover off as a reminder to fix your flat.

Following is a list of materials you should keep in your car for emergency road-side repairs:

Jumper cables	Tire inflater	Spare fan belt
Flash light	Plastic water bag	2 quarts oil
Siphon pump	Screw drivers	Emery board or
Bolt solvent loosener	maps	sand paper
Distress flag	Adjustable pliers	Phillips head
First aid kit	Ice scraper	screw driver
Flares	Hose clamps	Rags
Duct tape	2 sizes of hose	Wire brush
(for hose leaks)	(which fit your car)	Fuses
Wire	Empty gasoline can	Fire extinguisher

Trouble-Shooting
The Electrical System

Symptoms (Causes →)	Battery discharged	Loose or broken cables	Faulty starter or solenoid	Faulty ignition switch	Faulty distributor points	Faulty neutral switch	Spark plugs fouled	Improper spark plug gap	Faulty coil	Faulty condenser	Damaged dist cap or rotor	Damaged ignition cables	Incorrect spark timing	Alternator belt slipping	Faulty voltage regulator	Low regulator setting	Faulty alternator	Battery worn out
Starter won't operate	●	●	●	●		●												
Starter turns, engine won't start				●	●		●	●	●	●	●	●	●					
Engine stalls					●		●	●			●							
Engine misfires					●		●	●	●	●	●							
Engine cuts out at high speed					●		●	●	●	●	●							
Engine knocks, or 'pings'													●					
Engine lacks power					●		●	●	●	●	●	●						
Engine idles roughly					●		●	●			●							
Battery frequently discharged														●	●	●	●	●
Alternator does not charge														●	●		●	

## Chapter 17

Special Driving Situations

Most of the time, we drive under optimum conditions—dry roads, good visibility, good traffic conditions. Listed in this chapter are some special driving conditions that you may not have encountered before. While experience is the best teacher, you should be familiar with what you can expect to minimize the trouble which may confront you.

Winter driving: When pavements are slippery, reduce speed and increase distance from the car in front. Avoid quick or sudden changes in speed and direction to avoid skidding. When starting, accelerate slowly to avoid spinning your wheels. If the car doesn't move, rock it back and forth by shifting from forward to reverse gear and back again until the car rolls free. Signal well in advance of any change in direction. If you start to skid, do not brake or decelerate abruptly. Steer gently into the skid until you recover control. Then gently straighten the wheels. Slow down at intersections, downgrades and unbanked curves.

Winter equipment: The best way to stay one step ahead of Ol' Man Winter is with an ounce of prevention (see Chapter 8). Make sure to attend to the following basics:

Get a tune up: Fresh points and plugs help to insure good engine starting in cold weather.

Check the battery: A strong battery is needed for cold starts. Batteries may need replacing as often as every three years.

Change the oil: Most mechanics recommend that the oil be changed every 3,000 miles during winter driving.

Maintain the cooling/heating system: Put in fresh antifreeze and check all cooling/heating hoses for cracks. Stiff hoses upon squeezing signal replacement time is close. Run the air conditioning unit at least ten minutes each week to keep the system lubricated and in good working order.

Maintain proper tire pressure: Cold temperatures can reduce air pressure in tires by as much as eight to ten pounds. Underinflated tires do not improve traction on winter snow or ice.

Keep the gas tank full: This helps eliminate any condensation in your tank which may interfere with your car's driving performance.

Adjust brakes and alignment: Proper stopping power is crucial on slick winter surfaces.

Before you leave on a winter trip, plan your itinerary depending on road and weather conditions. Make sure someone else knows your route so that they can notify emergency personnel as to your whereabouts if need be. If possible, travel with one or two passengers as their assistance in a winter emergency may be crucial to survival. Make sure you are carrying a good set of chains and that your snow tires have adequate tread. If you have been driving in freezing slush, it is best not to set your emergency brake after parking as the cable may freeze. Instead, just use the "Park" position on automatic transmissions or a low gear on a standard transmission. When parking, try to keep the nose facing toward the front of the driveway or parking stall. This makes it easier to reach the engine compartment if battery cables are needed.

For people who must do a lot of winter driving in high density snow zones, **Car Savvy** recommends the following equipment for safety:

Special Winter Driving Equipment

1. Warm boots
2. Shovel
3. Broom
4. Good sunglasses
5. Antifreeze
6. Warm gloves and hat
7. Plastic ground cloth
8. Candles
9. C.B. radio
10. Extra clothing
11. Windshield washer fluid
12. High calorie, non-perishable food
13. Sleeping bag and blankets
14. Matches
15. Metal coffee can
16. Booster cables
17. Small bag of sand
18. Horn, sounding device
19. Transistor radio

Night driving: Drive at a lower rate of speed than during the day and in the range of your headlights. That's about 1,000 feet and you should be able to stop within that distance. Headlights must be put on one-half hour after sunset to one-half hour before sunrise. Parking lights cannot be substituted for headlights during these hours. Low beams must be used when you are within 500 feet of an approaching vehicle, or 200 feet of a vehicle you are following. Keep headlights clean to avoid distortion and glare for oncoming drivers. Keep the windshield clean inside and out. Dirt on glass causes glare which interferes with your vision. Keep dash and other interior lights low so that your vision is not impaired. Remember that every 13 years the light one needs for good night vision doubles; at age 46 you need four times as much light to see well at night as you did at age 20. Some states are so concerned about the hazards of driving at night, that there are legalized restrictions against it for teenagers.

Operating in the vicinity of a fire: You must not follow within 300 feet of a fire apparatus traveling on the roadway. You must not drive your vehicle over a hose unless told to do so by a fireman. You must not park your vehicle within fire lines set up by the Fire Department. Always pull safely to the right of the roadway and stop as fire vehicles approach.

Driving under adverse weather conditions: Adjust your speed; slow down on wet, snowy or icy roads. Test your brakes occasionally to get the feel of road conditions. Keep windshield and windows clean for maximum visibility; remove ice and frost. Make sure windshield wipers, headlights and defrosters are all in working condition. Use snow tires or chains to improve the stopping distance, starting and driving ability. Pump brakes when slowing or stopping—sudden heavy braking may cause skidding. Follow at a safe distance allowing more than the normal distance between cars to stop on ice and snow.

Steep downgrades: Brakes should be used off and on to control speed. Use a lower gear so that the engine works as a brake and allows better control. Monitor speed closely so that the car is in complete control.

Passing a school bus: When approaching from either direction, you must stop when a school bus turns on its flashing lights. School buses are clearly identified; they are colored bright yellow with large black markings. The only time you may pass such a bus is when waved on by an official who is directing traffic near it.

Right-of-way (automobile): It is important to know when your car has the right-of-way. Here are several general rules to observe: 1) When there is no traffic control device at an intersection, the car on your right has the privilege of going first. However, a car already in the intersection has the right-of-way over a car preparing to enter. A car traveling straight ahead has the right-of-way over a vehicle turning left; 2) Emergency vehicles such as fire engines, police cars and ambulances have the right-of-way over all traffic; such vehicles will generally display a light or sound a horn or siren. Move to the right side of the road and come to a complete stop allowing passage of such emergency vehicles; 3) Pedestrians in crosswalks have the right-of-way over all vehicles; 4) A vehicle entering a main road from a private road must yield to all traffic on the main road; 5) Vehicles in a traffic circle have the right-of-way over those entering.

High Speed Driving Situations

Entering a highway: Highway driving is high speed driving and the motorist should be prepared to react more quickly in this special driving environment. If there is an acceleration lane onto the highway, turn on your directional signal and accelerate to cruising speed while in this lane, making sure that you will blend easily with the moving traffic. If you do not see a gap in the traffic, proceed slowly at the beginning of the acceleration lane, speeding up when you observe a large gap in traffic permitting easy blending. If there is no acceleration lane or the lane is short, remain at the entrance until you see a gap large enough to permit you to reach cruising speed without interfering with oncoming vehicles. Signal your intention to enter the traffic lane, making sure that you turn off your signal once you enter the highway.

Leaving a highway: Move into the traffic lane for your exit well in advance of the exit. Start signalling your intention to leave the highway. If there is a deceleration lane, maintain cruising speed until you reach this lane, then decelerate to a lower speed. If there is no deceleration lane, begin to slow down before you approach the exit. When the exit is reached, decelerate further to the exit speed. Continue to observe legal speed limits off the highway.

Passing: The expert driver does not wait until coming up to a slow-moving vehicle to start a passing maneuver but prepares for this move well ahead of time. This allows for maximum safety and easy maneuvering. Before passing the car ahead of you, make sure that the passing lane into which you are planning to move is clear. Use your rear view and side mirrors to make sure there is no car approaching. Signal your intention to move onto the passing lane well behind the car you are overtaking. Accelerate and pass quickly. Passing a car safely takes about three-quarters of a mile. Once past make sure you are a sufficient distance in front of the passing car—at least two car lengths—before signalling your intention to return to the driving lane. Move into the driving lane making sure you have turned off your passing signal. Continue your slightly higher speed so as not to annoy the driver you have just passed, but do not disobey the posted limits. Remember it is not safe to pass when the road has a high crown, when the road surface is bumpy or under construction, or when you cannot see a clear road for more than three-quarters of a mile.

Tailgating: Rear end collisions account for many of the motor vehicle accidents on streets and highways. Most of these accidents are caused by tailgating—allowing too little space from the vehicle ahead. Make certain that you leave a sufficient amount of space between your car and the one in front—at least one car length for each 10 miles of speed. However, when traveling at super highway speed—55 miles per hour or over, it is wise to increase the distance to two car lengths for every 10 miles per hour. This distance should be extended still further during inclement weather.

Parking on a highway: Never park your car where it could be a hazard to traffic. On a highway try to exit your car through the right door. If you must get out on the traffic side, check first for oncoming vehicles before opening the door. To prevent car theft, turn off the motor and remove the keys. In cars with ignition locks, lock the ignition before leaving the vehicle. Lock the car doors for further protection. Set reflectors if appropriate. If you need assistance, tie a handkerchief to the antenna and put the hood up.

Speeding: Speeding is the single most significant cause of auto deaths and highway accidents. You should always observe posted limits. When poor weather or poor road conditions prevail, speed should be reduced accordingly. An important point to remember is that you do not have to drive as fast as the allowable limits permit. Drive at the speed that makes you most comfortable and enables you to completely control your car remembering that too low a speed also can also be a hazard on surface roads and superhighways.

## Chapter 18

Emergency Driving Situations

While all good drivers try to practice safe driving habits, there are certain unforseen events that can occur that are not predictable and are not always the fault of the driver. However, if they occur they can cause serious complications to the driver and the car. In most cases they can be avoided if the driver remains calm and performs the necessary maneuvers described in this chapter.

Blowouts/flat tires: When a flat or blowout occurs, immediately slow your speed by taking your foot off the accelerator. Expect the steering wheel to vibrate heavily and the car to quickly pull toward the side of the blowout. Under no circumstances should you apply the brakes. Survey your immediate locale to assess the situation. Look in front for a wide shoulder to take you out of the traffic lane. Check behind to make sure the approaching drivers will have time to ascertain the situation. After safely maneuvering your car to the best available stopping place, put reflectors and flares at least 300 feet behind you, especially if you are stopped in a traffic lane. Do not try to fix the tire if you are in such a lane; this could be dangerous.

Collision course: If you see another car coming toward you, keep your wits. Your quick thinking can help avert a serious accident. The first thing to do is to brake hard as you move to the right. Every mile you take off your speed reduces the impact force. If there is time, use your horn and lights to attract attention. If the car continues toward you, take the ditch or any open ground to the right that is free of obstructions. Even risking a roll-over gives you a better chance than a head-on collision. Whatever you do, do not turn into the oncoming lane because the other driver may correct his course at the last minute and return to the proper lane.

Stalling on railroad tracks: If your car stalls on railroad tracks and you have a manual transmission, you may be able to move it by running the starter while the car is in low or second gear. If the transmission is automatic, you will have to push it off the tracks. If you cannot get the car off the tracks and a train is approaching, get out and walk away from it in the direction of the oncoming train to avoid being struck by debris after impact.

Brake failure: If your brake pedal does not respond, pump it several times to try to build up pressure. If pumping action does not bring up the pressure, apply your emergency or parking brake gently so that you do not lock the brakes and throw your car into a skid. If you can shift into a lower gear, the engine will provide some braking force. You also can turn the ignition off; however, you will lose power steering assistance, so grip the wheel firmly. As a last resort, try to sideswipe something like a guardrail or curb in order to slow down the vehicle. Use your horn or lights to warn other drivers and pedestrians that your car is out of control. Brake failure usually is preceded by a spongy brake pedal which gradually sinks to the floor. If you notice this in your car, be sure to have it checked immediately.

Wet brakes: Step lightly on the brake pedal as you drive and the heat will soon dry your brakes out. Usually brakes become wet in heavy rain after going through standing water.

Steering failure: If you suddenly lose control of your steering and the wheel does not respond to turning movements, ease up on the accelerator but do not brake. Application of the brake when still moving fast may throw the vehicle off balance and out of control. Brake very gently only after the car has slowed sufficiently to bring it to a stop.

Hydroplaning: This occurs on wet road surfaces when the speed of the vehicle exceeds 35 miles per hour. The wheels, rather than "wiping" the road, begin to ride up on a film of water just like water skis. Hydroplaning increases with speed until about 55 miles per hour when the tires may be totally up on the water losing all contact with the road. To avoid losing control of your car when hydroplaning, take your foot off the accelerator and let the car slow down. If you brake hard or turn while your car is hydroplaning, your car may skid, but you should be able to regain control by correcting for the type of skid that occurs. However, if you're car has no contact with the road, there is not very much you can do except release the accelerator and ride out the skid. Good tires with deep treads aid in overcoming this phenomenon except when the depth of water exceeds the depth of the treads. To avoid losing control of your car because of hydroplaning, reduce your speed to less than 35 miles per hour whenever you are traveling on wet surfaces.

Immersion: If your car plunges into deep water but does not sink immediately, escape through a window. Most cars with the windows and doors closed before entering the water will float from three to ten minutes. Attempting to open the door is difficult and, in any case, will permit water to enter more quickly. If the car sinks beneath the surface before you can escape, the engine weight will push one end of the car down first, creating an air pocket on the opposite end of the car. Move to the area of air, breathe deeply and, after the car has settled, escape through a window.

If escape through a window is impossible, opening the door may be easier as the car fills with water. Remember, the door is always the second-best way out of your sinking automobile. Above all, don't panic; three minutes is a long time and should allow you to remove yourself safely from this dangerous situation.

After your car is on dry land, don't try to start it immediately until you check the oil level and color. If the level is unusually high or the color light, suspect that water has entered the engine. If you attempt to start the car, irreparable damage could be done to the pistons and rods. If the oil appears normal, starting cars with computer-generated engines may be attempted. If the computer is wet, the car will not start.

Excessive engine temperature: Overheating usually occurs when you are stuck in stop-and-go traffic. If your temperature warning light appears or steam is coming from under the hood, pull over immediately. Before attempting to do anything, wait until the engine cools, (about 30 minutes under normal conditions). Check under the hood. If the fluid level in the radiator is low and there are no obvious leaks in the hose, add water and continue driving. If there is an obvious leak in the hose, tape it up and fill the radiator with water before driving again. If there are no obvious leaks and your radiator is full, check the fan belt; it may be either loose or broken. If nothing appears to be wrong, there may be a blockage in your radiator; your mechanic must pressure test it to be sure. After the engine cools down, you may resume driving, but only until the warning light comes on again. If the temperature gauge keeps rising, there are no leaks, and nothing is apparently wrong under the hood, turn on the heater or defroster to divert some of the excess heat in the radiator, and rev the engine in neutral when stopped to speed up the fan and circulating water pump. This may reduce the engine temperature enough to enable you to limp to a service station, and is a good preventive to overheating in the first place.

Fire: If there is actual fire and no chemical fire extinguisher is available, use dirt or sand to smother it; do not use water as burning gasoline can be spread by water. When opening the hood, use rags and turn your face away.

Most car fires are caused by a short circuit in the electrical system. It's almost impossible to disconnect the battery terminals in such an emergency. Instead, get the jack handle and rip loose any burning wires. If the fire is in the rear, stand clear of your car.

Headlight failure: If your headlights suddenly fail, try your parking lights and directional signals—they may give you enough light to leave the road. If failure occurs on a busy or lighted highway, you will probably have enough light to guide you off the road. If all lights fail on a dark highway, slow down and slowly guide yourself to the shoulder. Once stopped, set out reflectors and flares to warn oncoming traffic. If all electrical systems are dead, the problem is probably the battery cables. Check the terminals at both ends (see Chapter 14). If only the headlamps are out, the circuit breaker has opened. Since it is heat activated, it should open and close intermittently while the engine is running, giving you enough light to get safely off the road to assistance.

Windshield wiper failure: If the wipers suddenly fail in a heavy storm, slow down, roll down your window and put your head out so that you can see in front of you. Slowly move your car onto the shoulder. Do not try to continue driving.

Hood opening: Always be sure your hood is secured properly and you won't have to worry about this one. If your hood should suddenly spring open blinding you, slow down, roll down the driver's window and put your head out for navigation. Turn on your warning flashers. Slow down and gradually guide your car to the shoulder. If you have a passenger, ask for his/her guidance on your right. On some model cars, you can see between the hood and the bottom of the windshield. Find out if this works in your car before this driving emergency occurs!

Stuck accelerator pedal: Having the accelerator stick creates instant panic, but it can be easily handled if you keep cool. The easiest way to free it is to hook your toe under it and pull up. Don't reach down with your hand or do anything that will take your eyes from the road. If there is no time to do this, turn the engine off but do not lock it. Shift into neutral and brake to a stop. Remember, this will compromise the power brakes and steering so be prepared to grip the wheel and hold on. If you don't have time to turn off the engine, shift to neutral and brake hard. When stopped, turn off your engine immediately as a racing motor with no load will tear itself apart.

Rain and fog: Wet pavements can be just as hazardous as icy roads. Reduce speed to compensate. Allow for greater than usual distance between your car and the one in front; you may need the extra distance for stopping. Rain and fog cut vision as well. Put your headlights on low beam. Do not use the high beams because the light will be reflected back into your eyes. You may want to flick your high beams up at intervals just to alert oncoming motorists of your whereabouts. Turn on the windshield wipers and defroster for best visibility. Signal all turns and brake well in advance of a stop so that vehicles behind you will have ample warning of your intentions.

Skidding: If your car begins to skid, take your foot off the gas pedal right away. Steer in the direction of the skid in order to get the wheels rolling, rather than skidding. Pump the brake, being careful not to push the brake pedal all the way to the floor. Use an easy pressure in an up and down motion of braking. Under *no* circumstances should you try to counter-steer (steer in the opposite direction), or slam your foot down on the brake, even though both of these reactions frequently occur instinctively.

Engine swamping: Heavy showers can leave deep puddles on the road, especially in areas with poor drainage. Driving through these puddles can become particularly hazardous because the high water can stall your engine in midstream. If the water is above your wheel rims, do not attempt to go through at normal speeds as this tends to throw water up into the engine. Instead, shift into a low gear and move through slowly. If the car stalls, attempt to coast to the side of the road. Wait at least 45 minutes for the engine to dry and then attempt to start it. If you are familiar with the car's ignition system (see Chapter 13), take a dry cloth and wipe off the spark plugs, wires, and other parts around the distributor. For those who drive diesel cars, never go through water more than eight inches high as this could cause permanent engine damage.

Failure of power steering: If the wheel suddenly becomes difficult to turn, do not panic into thinking you have lost all steering control of the car. You will still be able to steer to the side of the road. Get help rather than trying to cope with the unfamiliar feel of the steering mechanism. Inspect for adequate power steering fluid.

Brake failure: Most people experience terror when their brakes fail. Keep a cool head. Whether you drive a standard or an automatic transmission, immediately shift to a lower gear and then apply the emergency brake slowly. The car will stop gradually.

Oil pressure deficiency: If your oil light comes on, pull off the road immediately. Check your oil dipstick. If the stick is dry, or it reads very low, don't drive until you've added engine oil.

Alternator failure: If the alternator light comes on, it indicates that the alternator is not charging the battery. You don't have to stop immediately, but it should be checked as soon as possible.

Getting stuck: Should you get stuck in snow, mud, sand, or anything else, try to give the wheels something to grip. Attempt putting something under both the front and rear wheels. Branches, boards, leaves—anything may do the trick. If you drive frequently in places where one might get stuck, it is best to have a shovel in the trunk. Use the shovel to dig under the wheels to provide better traction.

Trapped by a blizzard: If you have the unfortunate experience of being trapped in your car by one of Nature's worst, don't panic. Follow these steps:

Stay in the vehicle: Do not attempt to walk in a blizzard. Disorientation comes quickly in blowing and drifting snow. Being lost in open country during a blizzard is extremely dangerous. You are more likely to be found in your car and will at least be sheltered there.

Avoid overexertion and exposure: Exertion from attempting to push your car, shoveling heavy drifts, and performing other difficult chores during strong winds, blinding snow, and bitter cold of a blizzard may cause a heart attack—even for persons in good physical condition.

Keep a down-wind window slightly open for fresh air: Freezing rain, wet snow and wind-driven snow can completely seal the passenger compartment.

Beware of carbon monoxide: Run the engine, heater, or catalytic heater sparingly, and only with a down-wind window open for ventilation. Make sure that snow has not blocked the exhaust pipe. Warnings that carbon monoxide is entering the car include unusual drowsiness or headaches.

Exercise: Keep yourself warm by clapping hands and moving arms and legs vigorously from time to time, and do not stay in one position for too long. Exercise warms you but it also increases body heat loss, so don't overdo it.

Take turns keeping watch: If more than one person is in the car, don't all sleep at the same time. If alone, stay awake as long as possible.

Turn on the dome light at night: This will make your car more visible.

Tie a warning handkerchief on the antenna: If possible, use a handkerchief or rag that is colored, not white, for better visibility.

Spinning wheels: Rocking the car back and forth is the best way to move it past a slippery surface. There are two ways to do this: manually, by pushing the car forward then letting it roll back; and by shifting from reverse to low or first gear and back again, keeping your foot lightly on the gas while doing so. Do not rock the car in this way more than a couple of minutes as it is very hard on the transmission.

Loss of a wheel: Similar to a blowout, you are warned by a thumping noise and sometimes a pull to one side. Hold the steering wheel tightly, steer straight ahead, and ease up on the accelerator.Brake only when the vehicle has slowed to the point where it is under control.

Use of alcohol: Mixing alcohol and driving is the number one cause of fatal accidents in the U.S. today. As little as 2 oz. of alcohol in your bloodstream will impair your reflexes, coordination, judgment, and visual acuity. You are not as cautious and it is difficult to concentrate. You are not acting rationally and are not aware of it. No two people react the same way to alcohol. Such factors as the alcohol strength, time elapsed between drinking and driving, body weight, and quantity and kind of food in the stomach can all contribute to the effect on the central nervous system. Foods that are high in protein and water if taken while drinking, can slow up alcohol absorption and delay its effects. Old antidotes such as coffee, cold showers, fresh air, and exercise have no curative power. The best cure is to not drive after drinking.

Narcotics: Both the illegal kind as well as some prescription and over-the-counter drugs affect ability to handle an automobile. Antibiotics and antihistamines affect vision and coordination and may cause drowsiness. You are not in your most alert state of mind when under the influence of a drug. Most drugs which make driving hazardous carry warnings marked on their bottles.

Fatigue: This is a common problem particularly in extended highway driving. Plan your trip so that you can rest every few hours. If you feel yourself becoming drowsy, open the window for fresh air. Stop to have a cup of coffee to wake yourself up.

Sensory impairments: If you are required to wear glasses behind the wheel, do so. High speed driving puts an even greater strain on vision and you will not be able to accumulate all the visual knowledge necessary to make proper driving decisions unless you are able to see well. People with significant hearing deficits must be able to compensate as important information, especially from emergency vehicles, comes from sounds. People who suspect that either visual or hearing defects interfere with their driving should consult a physician before continuing to drive.

Mental attitudes: Driving a vehicle under adverse psychological conditions such as extreme stress, anger or severe depression is considered unsafe. Approximately 11% of all traffic accidents are related directly to motorists who are unable to control their emotions, losing all sense of good judgment.

## Chapter 19

Consolidating Your Driving Records And Expenses

Because of the new tax law enacted in 1987, people who use their cars for business purposes must be more careful than ever in recording and documenting that use. The Internal Revenue Service requires substantiation of all auto expenses in order for a taxpayer to claim a deduction on his taxes.

Your records should include the following data to satisfy I.R.S. rules: total miles driven during the tax year; if the vehicle was available for personal use and if there was another vehicle available for such use; the percentage of total miles driven for personal use and the number of miles driven for commutation purposes. Naturally, all data should be backed up by written documentation.

If your employer provides you with a vehicle and operating costs of that vehicle which you may use for personal purposes, the expenses are treated as compensation and are subject to income tax, social security tax, and withholding tax. To figure the amount your employer will have to include in your W-2 form at year end, multiply the percentage of personal use by the cost you would incur to lease and operate that car. You can obtain the leasing cost by calling a leasing company or by calling the I.R.S. to determine the "annual value of use" figure based on the fair market value of the car.

If the car you use for business purposes is owned or leased by your employer and kept on his premises, with minimal use by you for personal reasons, no detailed records by you are required by the I.R.S., and there is no compensation included in your income for business use of the car. However, your employer will undoubtedly require detailed records to substantiate the company's deduction of the auto for tax purposes.

To help you keep the records you will need, complete the table on the next page, making an entry for each trip. Also included at the end of this chapter is a handy mileage chart that is useful in providing you with approximations of the cost of a trip based on the known distance.

Keeping good records of your expenses will save money and headaches when completing your tax return. Be sure to keep your receipts and other documentation in an orderly fashion should you be required to produce them during an audit. Remember, you can't take any deductions if you don't have a record of your expenses.

TRIP AND EXPENSE RECORDS

Date	Destination	Mileage	Tolls	Gas	Meals	Lodging	Misc	TOTAL
Date	Destination	Mileage	Tolls	Gas	Meals	Lodging	Misc	TOTAL

Cross Country

	ANCHORAGE, ALASKA	ATLANTA, GA.	BOSTON, MASS.	CHICAGO, ILL.	DALLAS, TEXAS	DENVER, COLO.	DETROIT, MICH.	LOS ANGELES, CAL.	MIAMI, FLA.
Albany, N.Y.	4664	1058	178	795	1703	1840	538	2883	1496
Atlanta, Ga.	4618		1087	714	830	520	740	2254	661
Atlantic City, N.J.	4716	844	350	811	1590	1824	643	2881	1283
Baltimore, Md.	4597	678	406	697	1427	1626	525	2776	1147
Birmingham, Ala.	4573	159	1252	686	658	1365	756	2090	785
Bismarck, N. Dak.	3036	1567	1851	874	1293	712	1147	1722	2234
Boston, Mass.	4843	1086		993	1870	2010	708	3128	1550
Buffalo, N.Y.	4379	964	465	542	1416	1559	264	2677	1481
Chicago, Ill.	3901	714	990		957	1047	273	2191	1387
Cincinnati, Ohio	4203	480	878	300	988	1246	250	2294	1145
Cleveland, Ohio	4239	725	645	337	1228	1375	172	2485	1368
Colorado Sprs., Col.	3544	1452	2071	1112	732	68	1375	1189	2115
Dallas, Texas	4285	828	1868	958		807	1196	1433	1396
Davenport, Iowa	3807	782	1136	170	861	874	432	2019	1446
Denver, Colo.	3479	1522	2010	1045	807		1303	1190	2127
Detroit, Mich.	4147	743	705	272	1196	1303		2450	1397
Dubuque, Iowa	3733	858	1160	181	908	889	456	2035	1522
El Paso, Texas	4186	1452	2426	1521	633	655	1757	808	2069
Erie, Pa.	4335	817	541	435	1328	1476	268	2586	1394
Glacier Natl. Park	2390	2375	2620	1638	1844	953	914	1372	3042
Gr. Canyon Natl. Park	3727	1886	2721	1810	1070	800	2046	541	2517
Houston, Texas	4524	872	1965	1115	241	1047	1328	1566	1309
Indianapolis, Ind.	4093	551	949	192	919	1066	274	2183	1220
Jackson Miss.	4566	413	1499	781	418	1303	969	1875	978
Jacksonville, Fla.	4934	319	1202	1034	1100	1791	1056	2540	342
Kansas City, Mo.	3883	879	1440	506	500	616	754	1630	1484
Los Angeles, Cal.	3672	2256	3128	2194	1432	1191	2449		2886
Louisville, Ky.	4213	434	987	310	881	1170	362	2215	1104
Miami, Fla.	5277	663	1544	1384	1396	2128	1397	2889	
Minn. St. Paul, Minn.	3485	135	1403	421	982	857	690	2031	1788
Montreal, Quebec	4463	1297	326	856	1777	1881	586	3028	1730
Nashville, Tenn.	4356	261	1169	458	691	1203	551	3000	920
New Orleans, La.	4764	517	1627	975	510	1316	1144	1950	883
New York, N.Y.	4744	865	222	842	1652	1854	633	2912	1322
Omaha, Nebr.	3672	1090	1450	487	694	541	747	1705	1688
Philadelphia, Pa.	4667	778	310	763	1565	1772	590	2831	1230
Phoenix, Ariz	4054	1896	2751	1840	1071	906	2071	394	2494
Pittsburgh, Pa.	4365	740	596	467	1280	1422	296	2547	1265
Portland, Maine	4726	1240	110	1055	1944	2083	782	3207	1675
Portland, Oregon	2660	2874	3230	2253	2147	1349	2525	1014	3435
Providence, R.I.	4965	1031	47	959	1754	1945	797	2959	1506
Raleigh, N.C.	4726	424	730	829	1251	1776	691	2671	836
Richmond, Va.	4693	550	551	784	1352	1761	618	2743	997
St. Louis, Mo.	4138	581	1187	293	658	897	515	1940	1236
Salt Lk. City, Utah	3338	1958	2434	1469	1288	516	1728	743	2624
San Francisco, Cal.	3351	2556	3200	2235	1790	1268	2493	402	3239
Santa Fe, N. Mex.	3865	1460	2298	1375	647	386	1620	891	2095
Seattle, Wash.	2657	2952	3164	2186	2224	1428	2460	1195	3472
Sioux City, Iowa	3569	1128	1484	503	798	591	774	1738	1795
Spokane, Wash.	2602	2503	2859	1881	1961	1146	2153	1257	3166
Tampa-St. Pete, Fla.	5082	465	1431	1218	1188	1931	1225	2628	264
Toronto, Ont.	4275	966	586	504	1425	1535	230	2675	1596
Tulsa, Okla.	4076	854	1634	722	282	735	951	1477	1515
Washington, D.C.	4596	643	441	697	1416	1706	527	2756	1098
Wilmington, N.C.	4878	439	830	977	1259	1836	851	2716	767
Yellowstone Nat. Pk.	2776	1957	2423	1401	1380	538	1616	1068	2613

Mileage Chart

	Nashville, Tenn.	New Orleans, La.	New York, N.Y.	Philadelphia, Pa.	Portland, Me.	St. Louis, Mo.	Salt Lk. City, Utah	San Francisco, Cal.	Seattle, Wash.	Washington, D.C.
Albany, N.Y.	1020	1557	151	240	248	1025	2250	3015	2937	392
Atlanta, Ga.	264	520	865	778	1240	580	1961	2558	2956	643
Atlantic City, N.J.	887	1341	123	62	461	943	2248	3015	2998	178
Baltimore, Md.	752	1205	185	103	528	803	2121	2900	2796	39
Birmingham, Ala.	219	366	992	891	1360	526	1856	2395	2709	761
Bismarck, N. Dak.	1315	1724	1714	1635	1800	1008	1003	1769	1316	1569
Boston, Mass.	1170	1624	221	309	110	1190	2432	3200	3165	442
Buffalo, N.Y.	730	1320	384	367	531	736	1978	2746	2706	380
Chicago, Ill.	457	975	840	769	1055	292	1467	2235	2188	698
Cincinnati, Ohio	291	845	648	579	956	345	1684	2451	2488	491
Cleveland, Ohio	543	1135	501	422	719	548	1798	2568	2535	359
Colorado Sprs., Col.	1193	1245	1850	1768	2144	886	584	1327	1497	1693
Dallas, Texas	694	511	1651	1560	1943	655	1288	1797	2226	1416
Davenport, Iowa	526	967	987	907	1213	245	1296	2065	2095	841
Denver, Colo.	1208	1316	1853	1772	2085	894	517	1268	1430	1709
Detroit, Mich	557	1141	633	589	782	516	1727	2496	2460	526
Dubuque, Iowa	600	1042	1021	950	1237	308	1310	2077	2023	880
El Paso, Texas	1350	1133	2210	2130	2504	1243	882	1213	1826	2056
Erie, Pa.	641	1232	438	391	618	648	1895	2668	2637	365
Glacier Natl. Park	2120	2351	2482	2396	2535	1811	693	1220	583	2338
Gr. Canyon Natl. Park	1686	1578	2500	2418	2789	1532	391	834	1312	2342
Houston, Texas	813	390	1741	1650	2072	819	1506	1987	2446	1503
Indianapolis, Ind.	300	847	730	649	1025	239	1576	2356	2377	576
Jackson, Miss.	435	195	1280	1186	1608	523	1791	2208	2671	1040
Jacksonville, Fla.	587	570	984	890	1340	907	2286	2896	3130	758
Kansas City, Mo.	568	886	1225	1145	1518	260	1138	1904	1986	1068
Los Angeles, Cal.	2100	1950	2909	2830	3206	1945	746	408	1195	2759
Louisville, Ky.	182	735	769	690	1071	274	1665	2436	2494	612
Miami, Fla.	920	883	1327	1230	1675	1235	2623	3241	3470	1098
Minn.-St. Paul, Minn.	867	1282	1263	1180	1474	557	1314	2079	1694	1117
Montreal, Quebec	1124	1715	381	472	269	1098	2308	3079	2850	620
Nashville, Tenn.		551	950	856	1262	308	1702	2405	2551	705
New Orleans, La.	550		1408	1313	1735	726	1795	2300	2735	1169
New York, N.Y.	951	1408		89	329	972	2274	3085	3028	241
Omaha, Nebr.	768	1100	1296	1215	1524	456	978	1745	1826	1154
Philadelphia, Pa.	859	1315	89		420	888	2195	2963	2946	144
Phoenix, Ariz.	1716	1554	2528	2447	2825	1542	718	808	1595	2372
Pittsburgh, Pa.	581	1175	378	309	697	600	1930	2712	2651	230
Portland, Maine	1260	1735	328	420		1264	2506	3276	3117	566
Portland, Oregon	2519	2654	3091	3008	3183	2206	841	684	177	2948
Providence, R.I.	1094	1501	186	271	3093	1118	2393	3146	3019	476
Raleigh, N.C.	569	960	514	419	841	880	2227	2977	3012	273
Richmond, Va.	641	1100	350	260	680	869	2208	2976	2970	105
St. Louis, Mo.	308	721	970	888	1265		1392	2159	2240	810
Salt Lk, City, Utah	1703	1796	2276	2194	2508	1394		756	925	2132
San Francisco, Cal.	2411	2302	3084	2962	3274	2160	755		863	2896
Sante Fe, N. Mex.	1266	1157	2078	1998	2372	1109	625	1202	1634	1922
Seattle, Wash.	2549	2733	3027	2945	3116	2240	925	868		2882
Sioux City, Iowa	872	1194	1346	1265	1560	562	1015	1784	1740	1196
Spokane, Wash.	2244	2475	2721	2638	2809	1935	730	931	289	2576
Tampa-St. Pete, Fla.	748	640	1207	1116	1537	1065	2426	2980	3278	969
Toronto, Ont.	785	1372	494	483	596	745	1958	2724	2690	495
Tulsa, Okla.	657	761	1410	1328	1703	422	1228	1818	2165	1250
Washington, D.C.	709	1168	241	146	570	810	2134	2895	2877	
Wilmington, N.C.	628	951	607	517	935	938	2330	3050	3163	370
Yellowstone Nat. Pk.	1695	1892	2268	2185	2462	1345	322	976	780	2122

## Chapter 20

What To Do In Case Of An Accident

The inevitable accident. Will you be prepared? Most of us panic, forgetting what we have learned. It is natural to be upset and nervous. Utilization of this chapter may help you through it all.

It is important that if you are involved in, or think you may be involved in an accident, you remain at the scene. If your parked car created an accident, you are involved.

When approaching an accident, it is recommended that you do not stop behind the wreck or on the opposite side of the road, as both positions create more danger. Instead, pull ahead of the accident and engage your warning lights. Check to see if you can assist the victims and then call or have someone else call for help. You may want to direct traffic around the accident until help arrives.

Every good driver carries an emergency first aid kit and should be familiar with some basic emergency medical techniques, especially cardio-pulmonary resuscitation (CPR).

Following is a check list of things to do in case you get into an accident:

1. Check to see if anyone is hurt. Don't leave the scene under any circumstances.
2. Exchange all proper paperwork; license, registration, insurance card, and the names of the occupants in the car.
3. Fill out all the information on the **Car Savvy** accident report form (end of this chapter). You later can transfer the information from the **Car Savvy** accident form to the form supplied by your insurance company.
4. Be sure to get the names and addresses of all witnesses to the accident.
5. Do not say anything. Phrases like, "I didn't see you coming," or "I didn't see the stop sign," are some of the worst things you can say at the scene of an accident, especially within earshot of a witness.
6. Do not admit any guilt. Say only what you have to say. Remember, if there is a question of personal liability, the courts and insurance companies will decide where to place the liability.
7. If you suspect that you or any member of your party is hurt, you may administer some basic first aid.
8. If someone is injured seriously, or even if you suspect someone is seriously injured, call an ambulance immediately.
9. If your car is damaged, call a tow truck. Do not attempt to drive the car away.

Car First Aid Kit

1. Blankets
2. Old sheets which may be used as bandages or slings
3. Magazines which can be used to make splints
4. Gauze bandages
5. Multiple rolls of 3 inch elastic bandages
6. Heavy duty diapers or feminine napkins for use as pressure bandages for severe bleeding
7. Adhesive tape—paper tape is easier to work with
8. Scissors
9. Safety pins
10. Distilled water for cooling burns
11. Ammonia inhalants to revive a fainting victim
12. Steps involved in CPR printed on a card (find them at the end of this chapter).

Emergency First Aid*

Generally, medical assistance should be given only by a properly trained person. However, you may find yourself in a situation where immediate assistance is unavailable and you may have to help the injured victims. Minutes are critical particularly on highways distant from professional medical facilities. You can help if you know what to do.

There are some basic steps you must take in order to effectively administer aid to the victim:

1. Protect and reassure the injured.
2. Stop the bleeding.
3. Provide for breathing.
4. Keep victim in the same position as you found him unless there is imminent danger of fire or further injury. If the victim must be moved, be as gentle as possible. Then keep the victim lying down, and make him as comfortable as possible.
5. Maintain the victim's body temperature.
6. Immobilize broken bones.
7. Prevent contamination of wounds and burns.

When you encounter an accident, park your car safely in front of the accident. Immediately provide warning to oncoming cars, having someone redirect traffic if possible. Quickly size up the situation. How many injured? Who of those are in need of the most immediate attention? Bleeding and breathing difficulties require first attention. Unless the victim is endangered by fire or is exposed to traffic on the road, do not move him. Better to redirect traffic around the victim than attempt movement as this can be dangerous and may add to his injury. But if he must be moved, pull him in the direction of the long axis of his body, keeping the body in a straight line. Notify, or have a passing motorist notify police giving them information on the number of victims requiring ambulances. Stay with the victims until the police arrive at the scene.

Bleeding: Follow the steps below when bleeding occurs:

1. Keep the injured person lying down to prevent shock.
2. Apply direct pressure to the wound with a sterile dressing if available. If not, use any clean cloth. If none is immediately

available. If not, use any clean cloth. If none is immediately available use your bare hand until material can be found. Do not remove material if it becomes saturated; simply supply more. Be careful not to apply too much pressure as this can cause increased bleeding by restricting the blood flow of other vessels. If an extremity is involved, elevate it to further reduce the pressure, but only if those parts are not fractured.

3. Indirect pressure can also be applied to arm and leg pressure points to diminish bleeding, for instance, under the armpit or in the groin area.

4. A tourniquet is rarely needed. However, in the case of severed arteries, partial or complete severance of an extremity, or when bleeding cannot be controlled by direct or indirect pressure, the tourniquet should be used:

   a. Place flat material (don't use rope or wire) just above wound and wrap it around the limb and tie a half knot.

   b. Place a short stick or other strong handy object on the half knot and tie a full knot.

   c. Twist the stick until the blood flow stops.

   d. Secure the stick in place with another strip of cloth.

   e. Make note of the time the tourniquet was applied and record it, leaving it with the victim. Do not release the tourniquet. This should be done by a doctor only.

Shock: To help prevent and care for shock the following procedures should be followed:

1. Keep victim lying down so that blood circulates easily to the chest and head.

2. Elevate the lower part of the body 8-10 inches as an added measure. However, do not raise legs when there is a head injury, difficulty in breathing, or the victim complains of discomfort or chest pains when this is attempted.

3. Prevent loss of body heat by covering him on top and underneath. The amount of protective covering will depend on prevailing temperature. Do not cause the victim to sweat.

Breathing difficulties: Seconds are important when a victim has difficulty breathing or has stopped breathing. Aid must be administered immediately— within two to four minutes to avoid serious brain damage and death.

First you must create an air passage. To do this, tilt the head back gently, as far as possible, lifting with one hand under the neck, pushing down with the other hand on the forehead.

The chin is now elevated and the base of the tongue moved forward. Keep the head in this position and spontaneous breathing may resume. If there is visible material in the mouth, use your fingers to clear it. If breathing starts, turn the victim on his side with head tilted to allow fluids to drain freely and keep the tongue clear.

If the above procedure does not produce respiration, you must inflate the lungs. Pinch the nose to prevent air leakage, take a deep breath, hold your mouth tightly to victim's mouth and blow until you see his chest rise. Raise your mouth and let him exhale. Continue this procedure about every five seconds for thirty seconds. If there is no air getting into his lungs, possibly some object is blocking the air passage. Roll him on his side, keeping his head and body in line. Strike him between the shoulder blades to help dislodge foreign materials. Clear the mouth and begin CPR. (See Steps in CPR at the end of this chapter.)

When the victim is breathing well by himself, turn him on his side to allow fluids to drain freely.

Burns: Do not apply ointments to a serious burn; simply cover the burned area immediately with a large, dry cloth—the cleaner the better. Add more layers of cloth to cut off exposure to air and to help reduce pain. If the victim's face is burned, do not block mouth or nose with protective dressing. If burns involve a large area of the body, wrap the victim in towels, sheets or blankets. Be sure no smouldering cloth remains in contact with the victim's body, but do not remove clothing as it may be stuck to the skin. If breathing difficulties and shock are also in evidence, treat for those problems as outlined previously.

Broken bones: Fractured or broken bones should be suspected when an area of the victim's body is painful, swollen, discolored or misshapen. Broken bones in the neck or vertebra are most serious and are many times accompanied by loss of feeling or tingling in the arms or legs. Do not move victims with this type of injury unless absolutely necessary to prevent additional injuries. Damage to the spinal cord with resultant paralysis or death is a very real possibility.

In the event of arm or leg fractures, the broken bone should be immobilized by keeping the bone ends and the joints above and below the break from moving. Splints should be applied only if you plan to transport the victim. Otherwise, protect him by placing blankets, pillows, or clothing alongside the limb or body to prevent movement. A leg fracture can be immobilized by placing a tightly rolled blanket between the legs and tying them together above and below the break. In the case of a broken arm, bind the arm to the chest in the position most comfortable for the injured person.

***Courtesy of the Red Cross**

CPR Steps

1. **If the victim is not breathing on his own after a few short exhalations into his lungs, begin CPR.**
2. **Place the heel of both hands on the breast bone and push down with 15 consecutive quick strokes.**
3. **Pinch off the nose and provide 2 ventilations to the lungs through the victim's mouth. Then provide 15 more compressions on the breastbone.**
4. **Continue this pattern (15-2) until medical help arrives or until the victim regains consciousness.**
5. **If two rescuers are present, one should provide 5 compression strokes while the other provides 1 ventilation. Repeat this sequence until medical assistance arrives. Check for a pulse on the side of the neck during the procedure.**
6. **The strength of the ventilations and compressions should be reduced in treating children and infants.**

Typical Accident Form

Accident occurred:

Date _________________________________ Time _________________________________

Location ____

Conditions: Road _____________________________ Weather _____________________________

Speed—Your car _____________________________ Other car _____________________________

Location of impact—Your car _____________________ Other car _____________________

Diagram: Sketch scene of accident in diagram, indicate north direction, name of streets, signal lights, center lines, location of each vehicle before and after accident. Number of vehicles involved 1, 2, etc.

Brief description of accident ____

____

____

____

____

____

____

Witnesses:

Name ____

Address ____

____

Name ____

Address ____

____

Statement made by witnesses:

____

____

____

____

Policemen on the scene:

Name _____________________________ Badge No. _______________

Name _____________________________ Badge No. _______________

Other Drivers:

Name ____

Address ____

____

Name ____

Address ____

____

Statement made by them:

____

____

____

____

Other Cars:

Year _____________________________ Make____________________

Body Type _________________________ Color___________________

License No. ________________________ State ___________________

Year _____________________________ Make____________________

Year _____________________________ Make____________________

Body Type _________________________ Color___________________

License No. ________________________ State ___________________

## Chapter 21

Preparing For The Driver's Examination

Recognizing the fact that some traffic rules and regulations change from state to state, we have attempted to assemble some questions that reflect the law in the majority of states. Each state publishes its own driving manual, some of which have test questions. After studying the manual thoroughly you are ready to take the written examination. All examinations are in the multiple choice format; you have to choose the answer that best completes the statement or question posed by the examiners. We asked the state examiners in New York for suggestions on how people should take their written test in order to minimize the errors they make. Here are the pointers we came up with:

1. Read the manual completely and more than once before coming to take the test; many answers come exactly out of the manual.
2. Relax, many people put too much effort into each question.
3. Read each question carefully before making your choice.
4. Eliminate answers that are obviously incorrect before you make a choice; usually the choice is between two answers.
5. If you do not know an answer, move on to the next question; getting overly nervous because of one question can interfere with your thinking on subsequent questions.
6. After finishing, recheck all of your answers; chances are you will find at least one obvious error.
7. Most of the time your first decision is the best one; changing many choices at the end is usually counterproductive.

Now that you have these handy tips in mind, take a crack at our test. Circle the letter of the answer you think is right. The correct answers appear at the end of this chapter. Good luck!

1. A rectangular-shaped sign is a
   a. speed limit sign.
   b. railroad crossing sign.
   c. school crossing sign.
   d. stop sign.
2. If your brake pedal suddenly sinks to the floor, you should first
   a. try to pump it to build up the pressure.
   b. try to raise it by hooking your toe under it.
   c. shift into neutral and shut the engine off.
   d. apply the parking brake hard to stop the car.
3. Seat belts can be most effective as injury preventive devices when they are worn by
   a. passengers when they are on a long drive.
   b. the person driving the car.

c. all occupants of a car being driven on an expressway.
d. passengers and the driver whenever they are in the car.

4. You are making a left turn from a two-way street into a one-way street. When you have completed the turn your car should be
a. in the left lane of the street.
b. in the center of the street.
c. in the lane with the least traffic.
d. in the right lane of the street.

5. You are driving in the middle lane on a three lane expressway. A car begins to pass you on the right. The actions of that driver are
a. OK if no signs forbid passing on the right.
b. OK as long as he does it on a limited access highway.
c. wrong because "pass to the left" is a firm rule.
d. wrong because he's passing you in your "blind spot."

6. When you get ready to leave an expressway, you should begin to use your turn signal
a. before you reach the exit lane.
b. once you are in the exit lane.
c. just as you get to the exit lane.
d. when you see cars behind you in the exit lane.

7. Your car starts to skid on a slippery road. You should
a. steer away from the direction of the skid.
b. lock your brakes until you come to a full stop.
c. steer gently into the direction of the skid.
d. brake quickly and keep the wheel straight.

8. You are waiting in the intersection to complete a left turn. You should
a. drive around the rear of a car if it blocks you.
b. flash your headlights so the driver will let you get through.
c. signal and keep your wheels turned to the left.
d. signal and keep your wheels straight.

9. Which of the following is used on some highways to direct drivers into the proper lanes for turns?
a. white lines on the side of the road.
b. flashing yellow lights.
c. flashing red lights.
d. white arrows in the middle of the lanes.

10. The driver's left arm and hand are extended downward. This hand signal means that the driver plans to
a. stop.
b. start up.
c. turn right.
d. turn left.

11. As you near an intersection, the traffic light changes from green to yellow. Your best action would be to
a. be prepared to stop before the intersection.
b. be prepared to stop in the center of the intersection.
c. apply the brakes sharply to stop.
d. speed up to beat the red light.

12. When you drive in heavy fog during daylight hours you should drive with your
    a. headlights on high beam.
    b. headlights off.
    c. headlights on low beam.
    d. parking lights on.
13. Why is driving on an expressway different from driving on an ordinary street?
    a. You must think faster and handle your vehicle more effectively.
    b. There is more of a tendency to "tailgate."
    c. Trucks have to go slower on the expressways.
    d. There is more of a tendency to exceed the speed limit.
14. What does it mean when a school bus is stopped and its red lights are flashing?
    a. You may not pass while the red lights are flashing.
    b. You may pass if no children are on the road.
    c. You may pass if it is on the other side of a divided highway.
    d. You may pass if you are facing the front of the bus.
15. If you drive past your exit on an expressway, you should
    a. drive to the next exit and leave the expressway.
    b. make a u-turn at the next service area.
    c. make a u-turn at the nearest emergency turn area.
    d. pull onto the shoulder, then back up to the exit.
16. The car behind you wants to pass. You should
    a. slow down slightly and stay in your lane.
    b. blow your horn to allow him to pass.
    c. maintain your speed so traffic will flow smoothly.
    d. pull to the right and stop so he can pass.
17. You come to an intersection which has a flashing red light. You should
    a. stop only if cars are already in the intersection.
    b. come to a full stop, then go when safe to do so.
    c. go through the intersection slowly.
    d. stop only if cars are approaching the intersection.
18. If there is no curb on the side of the road and you are parking downhill, turn your wheels
    a. straight ahead and set the brake firmly.
    b. to the right.
    c. to the left.
    d. to the left and leave the car in neutral.
19. A triangular, fluorescent orange sign means
    a. yield.
    b. emergency stopping only.
    c. slow-moving vehicle.
    d. construction zone.
20. When travelling behind other drivers
    a. allow a minimum of 40 feet.
    b. allow one car length for each 5 miles of speed.

c. allow one car length for each 10 miles of speed.
d. slow down if you can easily visualize their bumper.

21. The maximum highway speed in the U.S. is:
a. 60 M.P.H.
b. 70 M.P.H.
c. 55 M.P.H.
d. 65 M.P.H.

22. When approaching a car from the front you must dim your high beams within:
a. 100 feet.
b. 200 feet.
c. 400 feet.
d. 500 feet.

23. When leaving a parking space from which you have parallel parked, it is **best** to:
a. Use a hand signal.
b. Sound your horn.
c. Use your directional light.
d. Check behind the car.

24. You must signal your turn at least:
a. 50 feet from the intersection.
b. 100 feet from the intersection.
c. 125 feet from the intersection.
d. 200 feet from the intersection.

25. The triangular red sign pointing down is a:
a. yield sign.
b. stop sign.
c. caution sign.
d. astrological sign.

26. A no stopping zone means:
a. No stopping for any purpose.
b. You may stop there if a policeman directs you to.
c. You can unload packages.
d. **a.** and **b.**

27. You cannot park within:
a. 10 feet of a crosswalk.
b. 15 feet of a crosswalk.
c. 20 feet of a crosswalk.
d. 25 feet of a crosswalk.

28. You may not park within:
a. 15 feet of a yield sign.
b. 20 feet of a yield sign.
c. 30 feet of a yield sign.
d. 35 feet of a yield sign.

29. When parking facing downhill with a curb you should
a. turn your wheels straight.
b. turn your wheels left.
c. turn your wheels right.
d. should not park there.

30. When parking facing uphill without a curb
    a. turn your wheels right.
    b. put it in "park."
    c. turn your wheels left.
    d. keep wheels perfectly straight.
31. Before backing up, the best thing to do is:
    a. visually inspect behind your car.
    b. beep the horn.
    c. check the mirrors.
    d. go slightly forward, then back-up.
32. Bicyclists must:
    a. stay to the left.
    b. face traffic.
    c. follow the same rules as cars.
    d. use their front brakes.
33. Always first obey the:
    a. yield sign.
    b. flashing red.
    c. policeman.
    d. stop sign.
34. When you approach a driver from the rear you must dim your beams at:
    a. 100 feet.
    b. 200 feet.
    c. 300 feet.
    d. 500 feet.
35. You should check your tire pressure:
    a. frequently in winter.
    b. when you get gas.
    c. after 10 minutes of driving.
    d. after 5 minutes of driving.
36. When exiting an expressway:
    a. move right and speed up slightly.
    b. signal right, slow up, then speed up.
    c. signal right and brake abruptly.
    d. signal right and reduce speed.
37. For most highway driving conditions you should:
    a. make the best time possible.
    b. pass on the left.
    c. maintain a speed consistent with road conditions.
    d. b. and **c.**
38. Night driving is more difficult because:
    a. lights are bright.
    b. it is easy to get sleepy.
    c. it is harder to see.
    d. people speed more.
39. To put out an engine fire use:
    a. a blanket.
    b. water.

c. dirt or sand.

d. soapy water.

40. If you have a blowout:

a. gently pump your brakes.

b. don't brake, steer straight.

c. move right while braking.

d. gently accelerate and move right.

41. Who has the right-of-way?

a. a car turning left.

b. a car passing on the left.

c. a car in the intersection.

d. a car approaching the intersection.

42. Diamond shaped signs indicate:

a. stop.

b. yield.

c. warning.

d. merging traffic left.

43. A flashing yellow means:

a. slow up and proceed with caution.

b. stop and proceed with caution.

c. stop, then go.

d. slow up and stop, then go.

44. You may not pass on the left when there is:

a. dotted line on your side.

b. a free lane of traffic.

c. a two lane highway.

d. a double white line closest to you.

45. A "No Standing" sign means:

a. you cannot stop there.

b. you cannot park there.

c. you can unload packages.

d. you can unload passengers.

46. You must not park within how many feet of a fire station:

a. 10 feet.

b. 20 feet.

c. 30 feet.

d. 50 feet.

47. You must not park within how many feet of a railroad crossing:

a. 10 feet.

b. 20 feet.

c. 50 feet.

d. 75 feet.

48. You must park within how many inches of the curb:

a. 15 inches.

b. 14 inches.

c. 12 inches.

d. 10 inches.

49. How much tread must a tire have to be legal; at least:

a. 1/4 inch.

    b. 1/8 inch.
    c. 2/32 inch.
    d. 3/16 inch.
50. The best thing to do when it rains is:
    a. clean your windshield.
    b. have a tune-up.
    c. reduce your speed.
    d. don't drive at all.

Now, that wasn't too difficult, was it? You can check your answers at the end of this chapter. Before we let you off the hook, we compiled some additional questions about and driving safety that you may find interesting and helpful. Some information might appear on your state's driving examination. Circle either T (True) or F (False).

1. Many personalities undergo a change as soon as they get behind a steering wheel.	T F
2. The most dangerous drivers are youngsters between 16 and 17 who haven't been driving very long and get a big thrill out of being behind the wheel.	T F
3. Motorists tend to be jealous and resentful of people in brand-new cars and you'll receive more courtesy and consideration from other drivers if you are driving an old car.	T F
4. Women show less consideration for other drivers than men do.	T F
5. Drivers who use seat belts are better educated than those who don't.	T F
6. Children of extremely rich or extremely poor parents make the worst drivers.	T F
7. The most intelligent people drive best.	T F
If head-on collision threatens:	
8. Swerve left and avoid him.	T F
9. Swerve right, into the ditch.	T F
10. Step on the brake.	T F
11. Blow horn.	T F
12. Speed up to slip past him.	T F
If headlights go out or hood flies up:	
13. Brake quickly, then pull off the road.	T F
14. Steer straight ahead and let car coast.	T F
If a tire blows out:	
15. Slam on the brakes.	T F
16. Brake smoothly.	T F
17. Coast to a stop.	T F
If the accelerator sticks:	
18. Reach down and pick it up.	T F
19. With power steering, turn off ignition.	T F
20. Shift to neutral and brake to a stop.	T F
If your brakes fail on grade:	
21. Pump brake pedal.	T F

22. Shift to low gear.   T   F
23. Sideswipe wall.   T   F
24. Blow horn.   T   F
    If you start to skid:
25. Turn in direction of skid.   T   F
26. Steer away from skid.   T   F
27. Pump brakes.   T   F

   The next group of questions are taken from the *Good Morning America* TV show in cooperation with the American Automobile Association:

28. Stopping a car on wet pavement requires about twice the distance it takes to stop a car on dry pavement.   T   F
29. Drivers notice most signs posted along the roadway.   T   F
30. The best way to discourage a tailgater is to tap your brakes lightly.   T   F
31. You are about to enter an expressway. The best method is to come to a complete stop, find a gap and then accelerate into traffic.   T   F
32. When stopping at a traffic light or stop sign, you have allowed enough space if you can still see the bumper of the car in front of you.   T   F
33. If you smoke, eat or drink non-alcoholic beverages while driving, the chances of being involved in an accident are significantly greater.   T   F
34. Proper adjustment of the rear- and side-view mirrors, plus your normal side vision, will eliminate all blind spots.   T   F
35. A collision occurs in the immediate path ahead. To avoid becoming involved, the best action to take is to slam on your brakes.   T   F
36. If you can't avoid a collision with an object in front of you, the best thing to do is cross your arms on the steering wheel, drop your head and rest it on your arms.   T   F
37. When riding in a vehicle, a child is safe as long as the child is being held by an adult.   T   F
38. When you're too impaired by alcohol to drive you know it.   T   F
39. Beer and wine generally contain less alcohol per serving than most mixed drinks do.   T   F
40. If you think the person ahead of you is a drunk driver, the best thing to do is pass the car.   T   F

ANSWERS FOR THE DRIVING TEST 1-50

1. a	11. a	21. c	31. a	41. c
2. a	12. c	22. d	32. c	42. c
3. d	13. a	23. a	33. c	43. a
4. a	14. a	24. b	34. b	44. d
5. a	15. a	25. a	35. a	45. d
6. a	16. a	26. d	36. d	46. b
7. c	17. b	27. c	37. d	47. c
8. d	18. b	28. c	38. c	48. c
9. d	19. c	29. c	39. c	49. c
10. a	20. c	30. a	40. b	50. c

ANSWERS FOR DRIVING SAFETY QUIZ 1-40

1. T	9. T	17. F	25. T	33. T
2. F	10. T	18. F	26. F	34. F
3. F	11. T	19. F	27. T	35. F
4. F	12. F	20. T	28. T	36. T
5. T	13. T	21. T	29. F	37. F
6. T	14. F	22. T	30. F	38. F
7. F	15. F	23. T	31. F	39. F
8. F	16. T	24. T	32. F	40. F

How Well Did You Fare?

NUMBER WRONG

 0- 6 Excellent
 7-12 Good
13-18 Fair
19-23 Needs Improvement
24 and above Poor

** These grading criteria are not necessarily consistent with your local Motor Vehicle Department's standards. They are for the purposes of this test only.*

Edmund's
UNITED STATES
COIN PRICES

An indispensable tool used by coin dealers and collectors, Edmund's United States Coin Prices gives comprehensive information on all U.S Coins, circulated as well as commemorative. Included are complete grading information, mints and mintmark location, metallic compositions and weights, and first mint issues. Over 350 illustrative photographs are also included.

You can order a single copy or subscribe to this invaluable series of books (4 per year) by completing and returning the coupon below.

Edmund Publications Corp.,
Dept. CS-91
515 Hempstead Tpke., W. Hempstead, NY 11552

My order for Edmund's **COIN BOOK** as follows:

☐ I enclose **$16.85** for a **FULL subscription** (includes 4 books released - Jan., April, July, and Oct.).
  U.S. add $3.00 per subscription (bulk mail).
  Other countries add **$10.00** per sub. (via air mail).

☐ I enclose **$4.95** for a **SINGLE copy** (current edition).
  U.S. & Canada add **$1.00** per book (1st class).
  Other Countries add **$2.50** per book (via air mail).

Other Countries: pay through American bank or with American currency.

Name ____

Address____

City _____________________ State _________ Zip _________

Introducing...

Edmund's
1991 UNITED STATES COIN PRICES
Annual Investment Guide

Edmund Publications is proud to announce the initial release of an annual paperback investment guide which gives comprehensive price breakdowns of all U.S. coins, circulated as well as commemorative.

Some U.S. coin investments have well exceeded those in stocks, bonds, or real property, and indications are this trend will continue. Identify good opportunities and strategies for profit in this often overlooked investment area.

An overview of the coin market and specific investor tips begin each section with Key Dates and Best Bets for each class of coin identified, making it easy to build a diversified portfolio.

Each issue also includes bullion values, metallic composition and weights, grading information and standards, mints and mintmark locations, proof and mint set listings, and suggested reading materials.

Order this invaluable guide by sending in the handy coupon below.

Edmund Publications Corp.
Dept. CS-91
515 Hempstead Turnpike
West Hempstead, NY 11552

☐ I enclose $5.95 for each single copy   _____ × $5.95 = _________
   U.S. and Canada add $1.00 per copy (First Class)   _____ × $1.00 = _________
   Other countries add $2.50 per copy (Via Air)   _____ × $2.50 = _________

TOTAL ENCLOSED _________

Name ____

Address ____

City _______________________________ State _________ Zip _________

NATIONWIDE
Auto Brokers, Inc.

17517 West 10 Mile Road, Southfield, Michigan 48075

(313) 559-6661   Mon-Fri — 9-5 pm Eastern Standard Time

SAVE $1,000 Or More

On Your Next NEW

✓ Car ✓ Van ✓ Truck

We, at NATIONWIDE, have developed a simplified "COST ANALYSIS" plan and buying service designed to save our Clients money and assure Dollar-For-Dollar value. YOU WILL NOT PAY MORE than $50 — $125 over Dealer's Invoice! Simply tell us what car or truck you are interested in by either calling our toll-free number or using the coupon section of this ad at the right. Payment *must* accompany your request for your personalized "Cost Analysis".

When we receive your request, with payment, we will send your "Cost Analysis" for the vehicle you are interested in. The form lists all of the available equipment/options. Check off the options you desire and total the sheet to find your vehicle price. If you prefer, send the white copy of your "Cost Analysis" back to us and receive, by return mail, an itemized purchase order at no additional charge.

Your purchase will be made in the comfort of your own home. Your car, truck or van will be shipped to the destination of your choice.

Why Should I Buy From NATIONWIDE?

You will not pay retail prices! Our service is personalized. Delivery, if you choose, is to your doorstep and selection is enhanced by providing you with all available options.

Selecting Options Is Confusing, Does NATIONWIDE Make It Easier?

NATIONWIDE shows you exactly what options are available on the vehicle you are buying. You may eliminate those options you don't desire and customize the vehicle to *your* needs and wants. We tell you *exactly* what each option will cost you.

Does NATIONWIDE Finance Vehicles?

YES! Financing is available to qualified buyers through either GMAC or Ford Credit.

Car Salesmen Give The Impression Of Not Telling Me Everything. Why Would NATIONWIDE Be Any Different?

We have no reason to keep things from you. Our 20 plus year approach has been to be straightforward in working with our clients. The printout you receive clearly reveals our "hand".

I Don't Live In Michigan, How Will I Get My New Vehicle?

You have three options —

1) You may designate a local dealership as your pick up point. (Please provide us with a choice of three.)
2) We will deliver your vehicle to your home via a licensed ICC driveaway service.
3) Your vehicle may be picked up at our headquarters in Southfield, MI.

When I Buy From NATIONWIDE, Is The Vehicle Under Warranty?

All cars and trucks sold by NATIONWIDE Auto Brokers, Inc. are fully factory warranted and all authorized dealerships throughout the United States and Canada will honor the warranty.

MASTERCARD/VISA CUSTOMERS ONLY! 1-800-521-7257

Monday-Friday — 9 am to 8 pm; Saturday — 9 am to 1 pm Eastern Standard Time
Please have your credit card number and expiration date ready for our operators

---

Nationwide Auto Brokers, Inc.

17517 West Ten Mile Road • Southfield, Michigan 48075

ED
CS-91

Name ____

Address ____

City ________________ State ______________ Zip ___________

☐ MC/Visa ☐ Check ☐ Money Order

MC/Visa Card No. ____________________________________

Exp. Date ________________ Signature ___________________

MAKE	MODEL/DESCRIPTION	BODY TYPE (Check all that apply)	PRICE EACH
		☐ 2-door ☐ 4-door ☐ station wagon ☐ diesel ☐ turbo ☐ automatic ☐ manual ☐ hatchback ☐ notchback	$11.95
		☐ 2-door ☐ 4-door ☐ station wagon ☐ diesel ☐ turbo ☐ automatic ☐ manual ☐ hatchback ☐ notchback	$11.95
		☐ 2-wheel drive ☐ 4-wheel drive ☐ diesel ☐ turbo mfg's code _________ wheel base _______	$11.95

NOTE: Attach sheet with additional body type specs only if neccessary (do NOT list options).

Each Quote $11.95   TOTAL ____________

PLEASE NOTE: Some specialty imports and limited production models and vehicles may not be available for delivery to your area or through our pricing service. A message on your printout will advise you of this eventuality. You will still be able to use the printout in negotiating the best deal with the dealer of your choice. New car pricing and purchasing services void where prohibited by law. Some limited vehicles are higher.

8-90

car/puter INTERNATIONAL CORP.

The New Car Pricing & Referral Service

ED CS-91

Pricing Request Form

MAIL TO: CAR/PUTER
1603 Bushwick Avenue
Brooklyn, NY 11207-1897

YES! I want to save up to $1000 or more on my next new car. Send my Car/Puter printout package for each vehicle I have listed.

☐ I am enclosing my check or money order for $20 for each car selection listed. (Plus $1 postage & handling for each printout.)

☐ Please charge $20 for each car selection listed to my credit card as indicated. (Plus $1 postage & handling for each printout.) eg. FORD TAURUS LX

Name ______________________________

Address ____________________________

City_______________ State _______ Zip ______

Phone - Home (________) __________________

Phone - Business (________) _______________

Largest city nearest you: _________________

  ☐ MasterCard   ☐ VISA   ☐ Amer. Express   ☐ Diners Club

Expiration Date: _________________________

Credit Card Account No. ___________________

Signature _______________________________
    (Must be signed to be processed)

	Make	Model/Description	Body Type (Check all that apply)
Car 1			☐ 2-door ☐ 4-door ☐ station wagon ☐ diesel ☐ automatic ☐ manual ☐ hatchback ☐ notchback
Car 2			☐ 2-door ☐ 4-door ☐ station wagon ☐ diesel ☐ automatic ☐ manual ☐ hatchback ☐ notchback
Van/ Truck			☐ 2-wheel drive ☐ 4-wheel drive ☐ diesel mfr's code ____________ wheel base __________

Note: Attach sheet with additional body type specs only if necessary (do not list options).

Please note: Some specialty import and limited production models and vehicles may not always be available for delivery to your area or through our pricing service. In this case, a message will appear on your printout and you may use the printout to help negotiate the best deal you can with the dealer of your choice. New car pricing and purchasing services void where prohibited by law.

Edmund's car price guides

"An absolute must for the car buyer, seller and dealer."

In handy soft cover pocket size for quick reference. ONLY $4.95 each*

***PLUS** postage & handling charges:
U.S. & Canada - add **$1.00** per book (First Class)
Other Countries - add **$2.50** per book (Via Air Mail)

FOR SUBSCRIPTION OPTIONS AND ORDER FORM, SEE PAGES 3 AND 4

NEW CAR PRICES is the most complete, comprehensive and economical buying tool available anywhere. Absolutely indispensable to any thoughtful new car buyer, it includes the complete retail and dealer invoice prices of all new GM, FORD, and CHRYSLER cars and their factory installed optional equipment.

USED CAR PRICES. If you are buying or selling a used car, this book is an "absolute must!" A complete listing of all AMERICAN and popular FOREIGN makes for the past 10 years plus an 8 year listing for lightweight trucks, vans and offroad vehicles. Includes the original price of each and their current wholesale and retail evaluations. ALSO, details and listings of "RECALLED" vehicles are included. Utilized by dealers, libraries, and leading banks.

IMPORT CAR PRICES. Unique and indispensable—27 foreign makes are covered (over 200 models). Complete retail prices and confidential dealer costs on most models. Optional equipment AND full specification sheets. Warranty details and U.S. importers' names, addresses and phone numbers as well as photos of each model are also included. (Formerly published as **Foreign Car Prices**.)

VAN, PICKUP, SPORT UTILITY BUYER'S GUIDE. Over 65 popular models are listed. Included are factory installed options, dealer cost and suggested retail prices, specifications, gas mileage figures and dramatic photos. A must for the van, pickup or sport utility vehicle driver.

ECONOMY CAR BUYING GUIDE. Listings of popular AMERICAN CARS and FOREIGN CARS whose EPA estimated mileage exceeds 25 miles per gallon. Includes retail and dealer invoice prices of each model and their popular options, specifications and photos. **(Annual Publication**: release date: March 1.)

CAR SAVVY. Included in the 1991 revised and expanded edition are: *How to Buy a New or Used Car, How to Return Your Lemon, Insurance Tips, How to Save Money on Repairs, Breakdowns: What to Do, a Handy Maintenance Log and Accident Report Form,* PLUS *the EPA Mileage Ratings for all models* and much more. **(Annual Publication**: release date: Dec. 1.)